ALAN CARTER

Light in the Darkness

THE TRUTH ABOUT MAL, KENNY & ME

COVER PICTURES

Front (clockwise):
Alan Carter in action at Pembrey in 1991 (pic: Clive Challinor).
Alan with the 250cc French GP winner's trophy in 1983.
Kenny Carter riding for the Halifax Dukes at The Shay (pic: Ken Carpenter).
Kenny Carter, Mal Carter and Alan Carter at Kenny's wedding to
Pam Lund in 1981.

Back:
Alan Carter racing at Mallory Park in 1992 (pic: Clive Challinor).
Kenny Carter after retaining the British championship at Coventry in 1985.

ALAN CARTER

Light in the Darkness

THE TRUTH ABOUT MAL, KENNY & ME

First published in England in 2011
Reprinted 2016

© Copyright Alan Carter and Giles Waite

All rights reserved.
Without limiting the rights under copyright reserved above, no part of this publication may be reproduced, stored in or introduced into a retrieval system, or, transmitted, in any form or by any means (electronic, mechanical, photocopying, recording or otherwise) without the prior written permission of the copyright owners of this book.

Printed in Great Britain by Henry Ling Limited, at the
Dorset Press, Dorchester, DT1 1HD

Distributed by Giles Waite (Watches of Distinction) and Alan Carter

ISBN 978-0-9559340-6-3

I would like to dedicate this book to the following:

To the fantastic memories of my loving and inspirational grandparents,
Gladys and Willie Hanner.
I love you both and miss you dearly.
Alan
x

To my daughter Charlie, my little angel.
I love you.
Dad
x

Special thank yous to

Kenny – for showing me how to ride a motorbike and giving me the will and determination to be better than you. You were the best I ever saw, pure magic to watch.
You're always in my heart.
Love Alan
x

Mal – for giving me the chance to become a world champion.
You gave it all you had and so did I.
Thank you, Dad, and God bless.
Love Alan
x

ACKNOWLEDGEMENTS

Cathy, my future wife. I love you and thank you. We have laughed and cried together.
My sons, Louie, Jay and Joey. I love you and will always be here for you. Dad x.
Tony and Susie at Retro Speedway for taking on this project when no-one else would. Your vision is truly amazing and thanks for being so understanding.
Derek, my lifelong friend, it's been a long, hard road for both of us. You're a star, Del.
Bozzy for inspiring me to write this book, and making me ride my heart out to beat you. You were truly world class.
Mike Duffield. You showed me love and compassion like no other. I will be forever grateful, Mike.
Eggis, my best mate, who has stood right by me all my life. No words can say what I would like to say. Thank you, Paul.
Chris and Joanna Knight. Thank you for everything. What can I say, you have been amazing. xxx
James Whitham, a great racer who I loved to watch. You have a heart of gold. Cheers, bud.
Malky, my mate, we have had so much fun over the years. Keep pushing on, kid, you're a winner.
Kwai for always reminding Cathy what a great man I am, and how lucky she is! Cheers, Kwai.
Phil, my mate who calms me down and makes me laugh.
Mark and Mandy, my great friends who are always there for me no matter what.
I love you both.
My doctors. Thank you, because without you it would have been impossible to get back to some kind of normality.
Chris Spender for looking after me in his own special way. Cheers, Chris.
Doug for being my mate and building me the best engine I ever had, in 1982.
David Halliday for supporting me and helping me get back on the road.
Giles Waite and Ian Coles of www.watchesofdistinction.com. Thank you for giving me the opportunity to race again in 2011.
Wintersett Motors. Cheers, Jamie, for getting me back on the road - the car's amazing.

Thank you all for being there at one time or another, you are all always in my heart.
Alan xxxxxxxxxxxxxxx

My publishers and I would also like to acknowledge and thank the following for their hard work and assistance:
Martin Neal, Richard Clark, Derek Rhodes, James Whitham, Victoria O'Neill, Speedway Star.

For kindly allowing us to reproduce their photographs:
Jim Blanchard (www.jbsportsimages.co.uk), Doug Booth, Ken Carpenter, Bjorn & Sasha, Clive Challinor, Gordon Day, Hero Drent, Richard Johnson/Richard Naulls (J&N Racing Photos), Gerard Kampen (www. barrysheene.nl), Chris Knight, Keith Martin, Peter Preissler, Annie Richmond, Derek Rhodes, Mike Patrick (courtesy of The John Somerville Collection), Paul Soulby, Neil Ward, Gary Wilson.

With apologies to anybody who may have been inadvertently overlooked.

CONTENTS

Foreword by James Whitham	9	27 Why?	179
Introduction by Alan Carter	13	28 Kelly-Marie and Malcolm	187
		29 Down but not out	191
1 Day that changed everything	15	30 Like a black sheep	193
2 The family	23	31 The American dream	197
3 Growing up	31	32 Feeling the heat in Memphis	201
4 Let's go racing	43	33 Loving it in the States	205
5 Local hero	49	34 Focused on Kocinski	207
6 Losing Mum	55	35 Fading dreams	213
7 Farm life	59	36 Frozen out	219
8 The Haslams	61	37 Homecoming	229
9 Wembley	71	38 Envy of the paddock	233
10 The money machine	77	39 Pipped at the post	239
11 The art of speedway	81	40 Final countdown	247
12 Kenny and Bruce	89	41 Bad dreams	255
13 Overnight sensation	95	42 Nowhere to go	259
14 Wrong choice	97	43 Doing the business	265
15 Glory in France	103	44 Flower power	267
16 Shattered confidence	107	45 Devastated	271
17 Gold for Kenny	115	46 Dark days	275
18 Invite from Kenny Roberts	121	47 Gran's goodbye	281
19 Change in Kenny	125	48 Going downhill	285
20 British Champ with a broken leg	131	49 Fighting demons	289
21 Special treatment	139	50 Meeting my match and saviour	295
22 Broken dreams	143	51 Mal's last words	301
23 My biggest mistake	147	52 Under arrest	305
24 Will to win	157	53 Reflections	307
25 Beginning of the end	167		
26 Nurburgring nightmare	175	Index	317

FOREWORD

By James Whitham
Former road-racing star and current Eurosport TV commentator

I HAVE known Alan and the Carter family since we were both little kids growing up in West Yorkshire. My Dad was an MOT testing station and garage owner while Alan's father Mal had a string of garages. I was only about six or seven-years old – there are only two years between Alan and I – when Dad would tell me stories about the Carters, who were well known in our area as a scary family.

Mal was a monster – big, loud, in your face and with lots of money behind him - and people were frightened of him.

His two sons, Kenny and Alan, were very driven from a very young age. And because Kenny was an overnight sensation when he began riding speedway at Halifax in 1978, so lots and lots of pressure was piled on Alan to be an instant big success when he started in road-racing a couple of years later. Those expectations didn't come from supporters, they came from within his own family.

But it was clear right away that he was going to be very good, a natural talent with the heart of a lion, and he soon proved himself a winner.

Winning the 250cc French Grand Prix in 1983 was the highlight of Alan's career and it was an incredible achievement for an 18-year-old so early on in his first season of World Championship GP racing, especially as the bike he rode then wasn't particularly competitive.

What impressed me about him, though, was that just a week after covering himself in glory at Le Mans, where he'd virtually made it as a rider, he honoured an agreement to turn out in a low key pro-am meeting at Donington, riding a 350LT bike with rubbish road tyres. You couldn't have had a bigger contrast in machinery to what he'd ridden in France but he got on with it and, as usual, gave it everything he'd got.

He was clearly the fastest rider at Donington that day but got caught up in a bit of traffic, managed to stay on his bike after a huge slide coming out of the Old Hairpin, with both legs off the peg and arms everywhere, and ended up finishing third. His performance demonstrated how good he was at adapting to different bikes – he could ride just about everything very well.

Alan was a breath of fresh air to motorcycling when he burst onto the scene in the early 80s, a timely antidote to all things American. The Yanks, notably Kenny Roberts and Freddie Spencer, dominated the road-racing scene in those days and then you had Evel Knievel, the famous stunt rider, who was also big on both sides of the Atlantic.

Big, flash American cars were seen as cool things and our front rooms were invaded by US soaps and other TV programmes imported from Hollywood. Musically, American bands were also having a large influence here, so it wasn't surprising that most of us Brits developed an inferiority complex, as if we were still living in a black and white era and were brought up to believe that we were poor at just about everything compared to the colourful, flamboyant Americans.

But Alan and Kenny had been raised to believe that Yorkshire was the capital of the world, better than anywhere else, and they always remained dead proud of and true to their roots.

Like their father, they both had a cocky arrogance and huge self-belief about them. It could be a bit difficult for some people to take at times but when you look back on it now you realise it was a good thing. It's much easier today to share in their pride and understand and appreciate their burning desire to succeed for Britain, as much as for themselves. It was quite refreshing.

We'd had the charismatic Barry Sheene to fly the flag with great success in the 70s but there was little else in road-racing to get too excited about until Alan came along – he was the best we had for a few years. It's fair to say he was one of the most naturally talented riders we've ever had in Britain.

Mal was a notorious figure around the race paddocks and could easily start a fight. Then again, there were times when he'd be walking through the pits, see some lesser rider with knackered tyres on his bike, and think nothing of buying this complete stranger a new set so the bloke could race. He could be very generous like that. With Mal, you either loved him or hated him. When he died there were hundreds at his funeral who wouldn't have a bad word said against him.

Although only a little lad, Alan was not slow in coming forward either at times. I remember one ferocious on-track battle he had with his younger rival, Nigel Bosworth, at Brands Hatch. Alan didn't really like him, the two had banged fairings and ended up running each other off the track, costing either of them the chance of the win. When they got back to the pits after the race, Alan went to remonstrate with him and Boz just punched him in the face.

I was at Brands myself that day, racing a 750, and although I didn't see the actual incident, I was told that Alan just picked himself up and instead of continuing the fight, he simply said to Boz: "Fair play to you" – and walked away. Alan respected him for his reaction and recognised that he would have thumped Boz if the boot had been on the other foot. Those kind of things don't happen in road-racing anymore, it was more of a black and white world back then, but I was impressed by Alan's reaction.

He didn't have Mal's natural aggression and, as I've discovered after I got to know Alan well, he's a genuine nice guy and a softie at heart.

He'd rather make love than war and he was definitely one for the girls. When he started in the GPs he used to come to our family's airfield, near Huddersfield, for his av-gas. Whenever my dad, David, knew that Alan was about to pay a visit, he'd tell my three sisters to keep out of the way and stay inside the house!

Alan had so much natural ability that I think he found it difficult to define why or how he'd had so much success – and for that reason, when fortunes went against him, he perhaps struggled to pinpoint what the problems were.

The remarkable thing about him is that he did so well in racing despite the most awful personal problems that blighted his teenage years. I knew that his youngest brother had been killed in a car accident and that his mother was paralysed in the same crash, and that later she took her own life. And then there was the shock of what happened with Kenny when he died in 1986.

But I didn't know the full extent of this succession of terrible family tragedies and everything Alan had to cope with at such a young age, and also in later life, until after he'd retired from racing in the 90s. I got to know the real Alan Carter and I like him a lot.

About three years ago he came with me to a meeting I was riding in at Spa, Belgium and I sensed that after so long away from the racing scene, he felt a bit uncomfortable being back in the paddock.

That's why I hope that writing this book will do a lot to rebuild his self-confidence and allow him to exorcise the demons he has had to live with for too many years.

He deserves some long overdue good luck and happiness in his life. Having said that I now know him very well, there is still a bit of an enigma surrounding Alan and the legendary Carter family, so I can't wait to read the book. I'm sure it's a compelling story.

Huddersfield, West Yorkshire
June 2011

ALAN CARTER

INTRODUCTION

By Alan Carter

IT'S been heart-breaking writing this book but hopefully it will have helped me to finally overcome the bad things that have happened to me and the Carter family and, at the same time, inspire others to carry on through difficult periods.

To say that most of my life has been a rollercoaster ride is a massive understatement. Nothing will ever compare to the magnificent high I felt when I became the youngest ever winner of a 250cc motorcycling grand prix in April 1983, aged 18, but the great days like that one at Le Mans – and those my brother Kenny had with his back-to-back British speedway title wins in 1984 and '85 – have been overshadowed by a succession of off-track tragedies.

You'll see from the start of chapter one just how quickly things went horribly wrong while Kenny and me were both still at a very young, vulnerable and impressionable age.

Our domineering father, Big Mal Carter, played his part – both good and bad – in our destinies and I'll tell you all about him, too, over the next 300-plus pages.

In being totally honest and speaking from the depths of my soul, some may feel I have been overly critical of Dad and Kenny at times, but I don't think I've done so unfairly. I hope readers will agree that I have always attempted to balance any criticisms with praise for what they both achieved in life and shown gratitude for the positive things they gave me. I loved them both for different reasons.

Believe me, in re-living the first 46 years of my life, I've been equally critical of myself. It still pains me now to look back at some of the monumental mistakes I made, especially involving decisions that affected my racing career.

I figure everyone reading the book will already know the horrific way our Kenny's life ended, but what I've tried to do here is consider how and why his mind would have been unbalanced at the time and somehow try to make sense of what happened just over 25 years ago. I'm not going to make excuses for him – I wouldn't even begin to attempt to do that because there simply is no excuse for what he did and hardly a day goes by when the awful events of May '86 don't flash through my mind.

A lot of people have had their say about Kenny, so I suppose it's about time I had mine. Let's face it, no-one knew him better than me for the 25 years he lived.

But no matter what any of us say or believe about Kenny, none of us will ever know the full truth about why he killed his wife Pam and then himself.

I read Tony McDonald's book about Kenny, called *Tragedy*, which his company Retro Speedway published in 2007 and I told him when we first spoke last year that it was 99.9 per cent accurate. I couldn't get involved in that book at the time – Dad told all the family not to – but it made me think and that's why when I felt the time was right to tell my story, I decided to contact Retro Speedway. I also contacted a few road-racing journalists who have collaborated on books to sound them out about helping me to write mine but they showed little interest, so I hope the book is a big success for the sake of the people who have put their faith in me.

I know Tony and Susie at RS were a bit hesitant at first, mainly because we're in the midst of a recession, they have no experience of the road-racing book market and my story would obviously take them into unchartered territory. After our initial chat on the phone, Tony also needed to convince himself that I would be true to my word in providing an honest, heartfelt account of what being me has really been like, so he asked me to write down – or rather type out – everything that has been locked inside my head for years and let it all come flooding out.

I must have done a decent job of convincing him because here we are some 120,000-plus words later with the finished article and two badly worn typing fingers.

The writing process has been far from easy for me – in fact, it's been very difficult at times and, yes, tears have been shed along the way. There are a number of things that have affected me which I still struggle to come to terms with and probably never will. Of course, the accident to Mum and the day I was told she had taken her own life will stay with me forever.

I continue to have the occasional darker days when I'm feeling low but I'm pleased to say these are becoming less frequent and my state of mind is definitely getting better. I hope purging my soul across the pages of *Light in the Darkness* will also have a positive effect on my future. With the help of some kind and caring people around me, I've come through a lot and having made it this far, I hope to be around to enjoy life and my young family and friends for many years to come.

Oh shit! I almost forgot to say: I hope you won't be offended by the amount of swearing in this book. Like most true Yorkshiremen, I'm afraid, I speak as I find and I write as I speak, but at least my publishers have put their asterisk key to good use before it went to press!

Despite all the black moments at different stages of the story, I've also tried to inject some much needed humour and I hope this comes across, too. It's important to try and look on the bright side of life.

If only one person can find inspiration from my story and drag themselves out of the dark place where they are now and find the light, as I have done, then it will all have been worthwhile.

Wakefield, West Yorkshire
June 2011

1 DAY THAT CHANGED EVERYTHING

Car crash kills baby Malcolm and leaves Mum paralysed . . . Dad's heartless words before he leaves . . . hospital visits . . . cleaning up after Mum . . . Dave moves in.

OCTOBER 24, 1970, the day my family's world was turned upside down for the first time. Mum was in the process of decorating the whole house where we lived at 15 Brickfield Lane but she had to make an unplanned journey into town after Dad had bought the wrong coloured paint.

On that fateful Saturday morning she'd been shouting: "Where's Kenny and Alan?" Kenny was aged nine-and-a-half at the time and I'd not long had my sixth birthday. We must have been messing around in the garage or something and she couldn't find us. So, accompanied by a professional decorator and my four-year-old brother Malcolm, she dived in Dad's car and drove into town to swap the paint.

Dad very rarely arrived home before Mum but he had done on this particular Friday night because she was out playing bingo with friends. Mal pulled onto the drive with a nail embedded in the rear tyre of his car – a Ford Cortina, I believe – and it was to prove fatal.

It had been lodged in the tyre for ages but in those days slow punctures tended to be ignored. People would simply pump more air in, as and when necessary, rather than throw the faulty tyre away and buy a new one. But instead of attending to his damaged tyre, Dad left early the next morning in Mum's car, which is the reason why she had to use his Cortina to take little Malcolm and our decorator into town.

Talk about fate. She had only driven half-a-mile and was taking a bend in Shay Lane, Ovenden when the tyre burst, causing her to lose control of the car. It swerved violently before hitting a stationary vehicle and another car, a shooting brake, head-on. Mum went through the windscreen, breaking just about every upper bone in her body. Worst of all, she broke her neck and back and was left paralysed from the waist down.

Little did she know at the time of the accident that her youngest son, our little brother, had sustained a split liver and was bleeding internally.

The decorator, Robert Eliot, was fortunate to escape with cuts and bruising, although I'm sure he was scarred for a very long time due to this horrific accident, one of the worst ever recorded in Yorkshire.

According to the local newspaper report which I still have, at the inquest Eliot told the coroner he had been holding young Malcolm on his knees in the front passenger seat when the crash happened. He was quoted as saying that he dropped to the floor with the boy in his arms to get clear of the windscreen before the two cars collided.

A police vehicle examiner, Constable E. Jackson, told the court that he found the

ALAN CARTER

Mum as a young schoolgirl and (top left) with her mother, Gladys Hanner.

Light in the Darkness

rear offside tyre of the car had been punctured by a nail and was deflated. He said it contained 10lb of air pressure per square inch, compared with the recommended pressure of 24lb. "At this pressure, it would seriously affect the driver's control of the vehicle," he confirmed.

When Dad first got the call saying Mum had been involved in a serious accident, he just shrugged it off, saying: "The daft cow will be OK, she's always driving like a t**t." It was only after getting to the hospital that the severity of the crash hit him.

Years later he told me how he sat with my baby brother on his knee and that young Malcolm hardly had a mark on him. Dad was holding him in his arms at the Halifax Royal Infirmary when doctors told him that there was nothing more they could do. Despite carrying out an emergency operation the boy's internal injuries were so severe that he literally bled to death in Dad's arms two days after the crash. As the life drained out of his dying son, Mal placed a sixpence in his tiny hand.

Mum kept asking after their youngest son and saying how much she wanted to see him. He kept up the pretence for a few days but then broke down and had to admit the terrible truth when she said knowingly: "He's dead, isn't he?"

I can't remember Dad ever talking about Malcolm's funeral, so to this day I have no idea what happened or who attended the service. All I can think of is the deep pain my father must have taken with him to his own grave. Even a cold, hard man like Mal Carter must have broken down with guilt at times. God only knows how he kept going after Mum and little Malcolm's tragic crash.

On what would have been Malcolm's fifth birthday in March 1971, my grandparents placed a very touching poem in the local paper. I still have the cutting, which reads:

CARTER. – Loving birthday memories of a very dear grandson, Malcolm, who would have been five on March 7.
Although we smile and make no fuss,
No-one misses you more than us,
And when old times we oft recall,
Then we miss you most of all.
From Nana and Granddad Hanner and Granny Moss.

Mum spent nearly two years in the specialist spinal unit at Wakefield's Pinderfields Hospital. She was a beautiful woman, only 25-years-old, but now she would be wheelchair-bound for the rest of her life. She had to live with the awful guilt that she had effectively killed her youngest child when the car she was driving crashed.

But her pain and suffering certainly didn't end there.

She was quickly abandoned by her husband, who suddenly left her for another woman. I remember Dad talking to me in later years about Mum and her desperate situation, and he said: "You can't live with the dead or the dying."

When he uttered those heartless words, all I wanted to do was knock him out and inflict some pain upon him. What an evil bastard he was to talk about Mum in such a cold and callous way.

ALAN CARTER

Above: Mum with her film star looks in a foreign city.

Right: Mum with baby Kenny.

Below left: Malcolm, my youngest brother who died when he was four-years-old.

Below right: Kenny holding Malcolm at our house in Brickfield Lane.

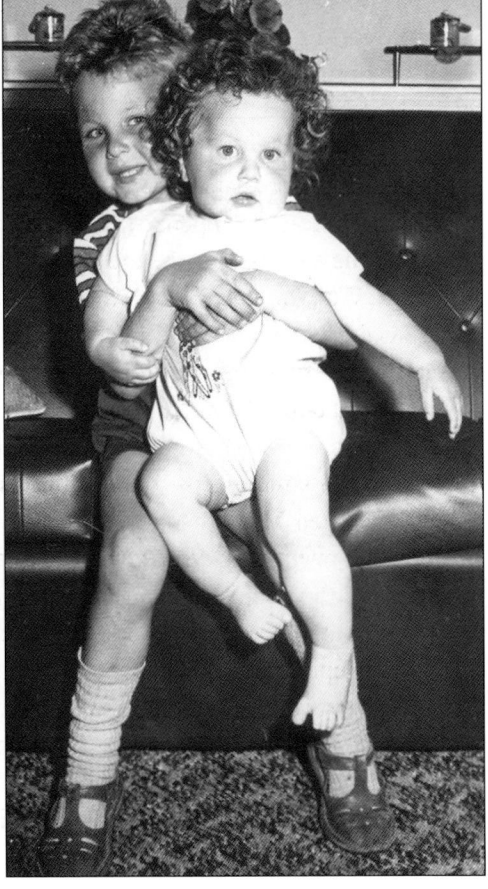

Light in the Darkness

Within days of the double tragedy, he'd left our home at Brickfield Lane and moved in with Janet – who would later become his second wife – at her small terraced house in Mixenden. Whether he would still have left Mum had the crash not happened, I don't know. All I can say is, people make choices in life and while some of us make good decisions, others have regrets and are full of remorse for their actions. He never mentioned anything to me about having any regrets, though. Mal was never a remorseful person. All he ever said about Mum was that she was the hardest woman he'd ever met – she was as tough as nails, according to him.

During the couple of years Mum spent in hospital Kenny and I were farmed out. We spent most of the time being looked after by her parents, Gran and Granddad Gladys and Willie Hanner, who were fantastic, loving, absolute salt of the earth people. They took us to visit Mum at Pinderfields most weekends, although it obviously wasn't nice seeing her in traction with screws through her skull and weights hanging over the bed to try and pull her spine back in line.

I'd sit on the bed with her and could see the agony written all over her face. She clearly looked very ill and in a lot of pain. The fact that her injuries also meant she had to have her head completely shaved must have been very hard to bear for this beautiful young woman with lovely long hair.

On the way to hospital Kenny and I would play a game to see who could name all the cars we passed and also guess what colour the next car would be. We had fun on these trips. I remember Granddad pulling in a lay-by next to a fruit stall and Kenny and me getting out with Grandma telling us "pick yourselves an apple, boys". Kenny being Kenny, he'd go for the giant one. To young kids like us, it looked as if he had the biggest apple in the world. I'd pick a normal looking one, valuing colour and shape over size. One day after we'd got back inside the car, our Kenny took a bite out of his apple and discovered to his horror that it was full of maggots. I had a little snigger at his expense that day.

Despite the sadness attached to our hospital visits, we tried to make the best of the situation. We'd regularly stop off at the Bon Bon coffee house in Dewsbury, where Gran would treat me and Kenny to a bottle of pop each and a beef sandwich to share. Those are the good things I remember from that otherwise sad period.

Mum spent a lot of time in rehab at Stoke Mandeville Hospital, where she became a great swimmer and, despite being confined to a wheelchair, also very good at table-tennis. I still have the tracksuit top she wore to play in – it's going with me in my coffin when I die.

When she eventually came out of hospital her parents took her to Morocco for a holiday and the people there looked after her like a princess – she even managed to ride a camel. How sweet. By contrast, the mean local British people mostly treated her like a leper simply because she was in a wheelchair and able to do little for herself. They were too ignorant to know that despite her accident, she was still the same Christine Carter. One of my sayings is, 'treat everyone with respect, because you never know what's around the corner' . . .

After a few home visits and lots of modifications to the house, Mum was allowed home. Fair play to Mal, he paid for the building of a ground floor extension on the rear of the house, which became Mum's new bedroom. But despite talk from him that some of the many people he knew around Halifax would come over to help with housework and chores, very little of it materialised. As they say, 'you're on your own'. I've figured it out that 50 per cent of the world is glad you're in the shit and the other 50 per cent don't give a shit.

Having said that, a lady called Mrs Beedon, who lived about six doors up the street from us, kindly came over to our house to clean, do the washing and ironing and generally help out. Carol, the eldest of Mrs Beedon's three kids, was a stunner and for a while I felt sure Kenny was going to end up with her. Then there was Tony, a nice quiet kid, and Susan, the youngest. Mrs Beedon always did everything she could for Mum and I would now like to take this opportunity to thank her for being there at such a difficult time.

Although Dad moved out of the family home, we did continue to see him. He gave me and Kenny 25 quid a week pocket money in a brown envelope every Thursday. It was quite a bit of cash at the time but it just about covered Mum's fag and whiskey bill – and the cost of re-treading my shoes. Come rain, snow or sunshine, I had to leg it two miles on foot, to one of his garages, to collect my money from him. Only in later life did I think 'what a c***'. He could easily have just popped it through our letter box.

He never visited us and I can honestly say that throughout my whole life, right up to his death, he never, ever rang me to see if I was OK or said the three words every child wants to hear from their parents: 'I love you'.

Most nights Mum would either piss or shit the bed, because she had no control over her bottom half. Imagine how humiliating this must have been for her. Kenny and me were on regular shit patrol and were awoken in the early hours of most mornings by Mum screaming our names over and over. It still makes me cry and go cold thinking about it.

I'm sure if Kenny was alive today we'd both laugh and cry about the many times we got shit on our fingers and over ourselves while caring for Mum's most basic needs. The one thing I could never get right was her piss-bag. I was a dumb f***** in them days – still am a dizzy t**t, to be honest – and I'd pull the wrong tube from her catheter or something and find myself soaked in piss, all much to Kenny's amusement.

Another nightmare job was dealing with Mum's periods, having to remove her Tampax because she couldn't do it herself.

As you can imagine, these were not my fondest childhood memories but, as always, we did what we had to do.

Mum was surviving on a diet of painkillers and Valium, plus sleeping pills. The other things she used to further dull the pain were whiskey and fags – in large amounts.

Our local pub was The Shant and I was round there most nights getting her supplies. But Kenny and me could be bad little buggers at times. We'd often see a certain truck driver we knew sat down having a pint before setting off on a long journey, and when his back was turned we'd let his live chickens out of their baskets

Light in the Darkness

and they would run all over the place. The poor truck driver would come rushing out of the pub but we'd just run off. They were brill times.

Apart from the help Mum received from neighbours, a nurse visited her once a week and Gran popped round a few days a week. Kenny and me doubled up as home help, doctors and fire fighters.

You see the trouble with Mum drinking and smoking was that, once a week, she'd fall asleep and set the bed alight. I can still see me now, slamming wet towels onto the smouldering sheets before the flames erupted. It was a bit scary at times and I tell you, we had more new sheets than Soft Mick.

Although Mum enjoyed a fag, she hated the idea of her sons smoking. Once she caught me trying my hand at smoking and was not impressed. I'd managed to buy a packet of 10 from a vending machine but when she found out she made me stand in front of her and eat all my cigarettes. I was crying my eyes out by the end and, thanks to that awful experience, never smoked another fag in my life.

Dad was right when he said she was a hard woman and not one to mess with.

He got Mum a Mini Traveller in purple with handicap controls which, to our great amazement, she drove fantastically well . . . when she was sober. Her problem was that she started to hang out at a pub called the Thorn Tree, near Queens Road, in a suburb of Halifax, where she'd sit in her wheelchair and get tanked up before driving home as pissed as a fart. On entering the driveway she'd occasionally wipe out the gates and the side of the car. How she even managed to get that far, I don't know. It got so bad, Kenny used to drive her home from the pub even though he was well under-age at the time.

She was a very popular, attractive woman and it was while socialising in the Thorn Tree that she met my future stepdad, Dave Wood, who worked in a foundry at the local Hartley & Sugden engineering factory. Dave was a grafter, an amazing guy who fell in love with Mum and married her when she was in her wheelchair. They would cuddle up together on the sofa and he couldn't do enough for her. He did all the cooking and he worshipped our Mum. I never heard a cross word between them.

I feel embarrassed to say this, but I don't think I could marry someone in her position. Dave should have got the Nobel prize for his amazing commitment to Mum, Kenny and me.

Before Dave came to live with us I'd eaten about as many tinned carrots, peas and potatoes any boy or man could take. We ate so many boil-in-the-bag dinners we must have had shares in Findus and Birds Eye. Things did get a lot better though, after Dave moved in – at least we went shopping once a week even if the food wasn't brilliant.

Every Thursday night Dave, Kenny and me would walk about two miles to Morrisons and trudge all the way back home weighed down with loads of carrier bags that were splitting and the shopping was going all over the place. After once complaining about how heavy the bags were, Dave gave me one of those old granny shopping trolleys. I thought, 'I'm not pulling that f****** thing'. But, all in all, we were happy.

I can't be sure of this but Dave must have met Dad from time to time or at least

Mal would have known that Mum had a new husband, although I never saw them together. They were chalk and cheese but surely Dad would have had a bit of respect for Dave.

He was a quiet, family man who loved his music – Elvis, Buddy Holly and Neil Diamond were his favourites. He was just a lovely guy who put some happiness back into Mum's life. Dave was all the things you could ever want from a father – calm, kind and easy-going. He took Kenny and me to the pictures, spent time with us and did all the things my father never did. I've always been a bit of a card shark and this is all thanks to Dave, who taught me as a kid how to play most card games.

Bearing in mind what happened later, I think Kenny, being the eldest, was more badly affected by what happened to Mum and our young brother than even I was.

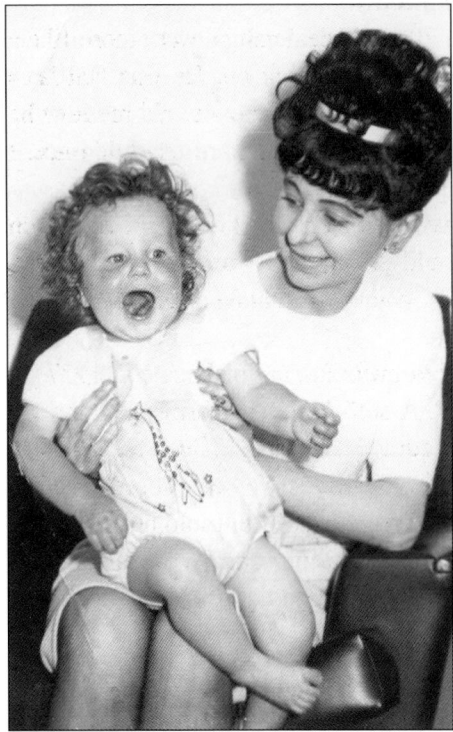

Left: Proud Mum with baby Malcolm.

Above: Now in a wheelchair following her car accident, Mum wearing a blonde wig to hide her shaven head on a night out with Dad.

Below: The local newspaper reports the tragedy.

Nail led to death of boy, aged 4

A FOUR-YEAR-OLD boy died after the car in which he was travelling crashed when a nail became embedded in a tyre, a Halifax quest was told today.

The coroner, Mr B. W. Little, OBE, recorded a misadventure verdict on Malcolm Carter, of 15, Brickfield Lane, Holmfield, who died on October 26 — two days after the car in which he was travelling hit a stationary car in Shay Lane, Ovenden, Halifax.

A passenger, Mr Robert Eliot, of 16, Moorside Gardens, Ovenden, said he was holding Malcolm on his knee in the front seat. The accident happened as the car, driven by the boy's mother, Mrs Christine Carter, rounded a left-hand bend in a...

ing brake coming in the opposite direction. From what he could remember of the accident, in which he was badly cut and bruised, he dropped to the floor with the boy in his arms to get clear of the windscreen before the cars collided.

The driver of the shooting brake, Mr Thomas Hallas, of 151, Cousin Lane, Ovenden, said he had stopped when the impact occurred.

He, Mr Eliot and Mrs Carter had to receive hospital attention, and Mrs Carter was still detained with serious multiple injuries...

E. Jackson, said the rear offside tyre of Mrs Carter's car had been punctured by a nail and had been deflated, contained 10lb of air pressure per square inch, compared with the recommended pressure of 24lb.

"At this pressure, it would seriously affect the driver's control of the vehicle. This was more likely to occur when the vehicle was negotiating a left hand bend, because of the increased load on the tyre due to weight transfer," said...

2 THE FAMILY

*Dad's rough upbringing on bread and milk was the making of him . . .
abuse and humiliation . . . change of identity . . . young man's suicide . . . Mum's a rebel.*

BEFORE we go any further, I should first introduce you to the rest of the characters known to me in the Carter family.

Dad was Mister Big in the car trade in the 70s. His dealerships were more like a Guy Richie film set with all sorts of crazy bollocks going on. He was Halifax's number one Del Boy and could sell snow to the Eskimos. He once told me how he nearly got eaten alive by some pigs when he was a kid. If I heard that tale once, I heard it a thousand times.

Our father would say to us: "You f****** have had a charmed life. I had to live on sugar bread and drip bread and anything I could get my hands on."

As a young lad, Dad had a big paper round in Wainstalls that he did while wearing a pair of wooden clogs.

I have a copy of an interview he gave to *Motorcycle Racing* magazine in 1977. In it, he was described as a "legend of Halifax". A self-confessed former delinquent, Dad revealed his tough upbringing and was quoted as saying: "I've broken every law in the book, even been done for assaulting the police. I've been in every cell in Halifax and Bradford for fighting. But all this was before I went into business.

"Between leaving school and the age of 19, I had 25 jobs and I was out of work more than I was in because I was always brawling and getting drunk.

"I was a scrapping man because I had a rough upbringing. I supped out of jam-jars as a kid and we never had carpets. My mother brought five kids up and we lived two miles from the nearest bus stop. I didn't see electric lights or a wet toilet 'till I was 14.

"We weren't brought up, we were dragged up. We lived on bread and jam, bread and dripping, bread and sugar, bread and sauce and we used to fry chips on a Tilley lamp mantle.

"It was that bloody pathetic, I don't know anybody who has had a worse upbringing than me," he told interviewer Ian Beacham.

The article went on to say how, when he was 19, Dad slept with his dog on a hay-loft. He was given a job with the Yorkshire Electricity Board, walking four miles in a blizzard to work on the first day without an overcoat. 'But this was the making of him,' said *Motorcycle Racing*.

Dad described how he toiled twice as hard as the others that first day, stole two chicken's eggs to boil up in an old bean can for his lunch and the next day was given two pairs of warm socks, a pair of Wellingtons and a YEB donkey-jacket.

Above: Dad's parents, Lionel and Mary Carter.
Below: Mal (left) at work with the lads.

Light in the Darkness

Above left: Uncle Alan and Dad.
Above right: Dad's mate Richard Dunn, who fought Cassius Clay for the world heavyweight title in 1976.
Left: Mum strikes another glamourous pose.
Below: Mum and Dad with Uncle David and Auntie Margaret socialising at Butlins holiday camp.

ALAN CARTER

Borough of Brighou[se]

ON LEAV[E]

Dear Willie,

You are now completing your last term at School and t[he] sensible person realises that education does not finish at the d[ay] school; only the foundation has been laid.

Join one of the Municipal Evening Institutes or Technical a[nd] Commercial Schools **AT ONCE** before you have time to forget wh[at] you have already learned. Your Head Teacher, or the officials [at] the Education Office and Evening Schools will only be too please[d] to give you any information or advice.

Great issues depend on this period of your life. Choice[s] are being made now by which the course of your life for goo[d] or ill, for success or failure, is determined. Here is a message [of] friendly counsel and good cheer.

YOUR LIFE WORK.—Very soon you must choose a Trad[e] or Profession. Let your choice be a wise and intelligent on[e]. Do not allow yourself to drift haphazard into any sort of blin[d] alley work. Consult your parents, your headmaster, your teache[r]; none know you better; no one can help you more. Serious[ly] conscientiously, take stock of your gifts, your preference, yo[ur] possibilities. Your life work should be the sphere in which y[ou] can do the best, not for yourself only, but for your home, f[or] your country, for mankind. There are lives in which the call [of] duty runs counter to capacity and desire, and that call mu[st] always be obeyed.

THE GREAT CHOICE.—The greatest of all choices is th[at] between good and evil; whatever else you may be or do, stri[ve] to be good. Speak the truth always, whatever it cost you. [Be] courteous to everybody; to honour another is to honour yourse[lf]. Keep your temper. There is no harm in **having** a temper; t[he] harm lies in **losing** it. Above all, endeavour to discover yo[ur] duty.

YOUR CHARACTER.—Your most precious possession [is] a pure character. Guard it closely. It is easily lost; it [is] terribly hard to regain.

E. J. Arnold & Son, Ltd., Leeds, Glasgow & Belfast.

Top left: Gladys Milton, my Gran on Mum's side, who married my Granddad Willie Hanner. They would both have such a big influence on my life.

Above: This was given to Granddad on leaving school in 1933. If only subsequent generations and today's kids lived by the same moral code that was expected of young people back in Willie's day.

Left: Willie and Gladys on what looks like one of their first dates.

Light in the Darkness

Education Committee.

SCHOOL.

NEVER BET OR GAMBLE.—Gambling is an unhealthy triving to gain something without giving a proper return for it. t robs work of its zest and interest. It is a great evil, destructive f character, disastrous in its consequences.

SAVING.—When you begin to earn wages, you should save part. Start by saving a small amount each week, and increase his amount as your wages increase. By the time you reach 1anhood or womanhood you will have saved a considerable sum.

YOUR BODY.—By fresh air, by cleanliness, by recreation, y regular habits, keep your body fit. Be temperate in all things. Beware of strong drink. Athletes in training abstain from alcohol, nd surely it is our duty to be always at our fittest.

YOUR MIND.—Keep your mind clean and well-informed. Good ooks are "Kings' Treasuries." Read only the best. The best f all books is the Bible. Read it daily; get to know it horoughly. The reading of a few verses every morning or evening s the best of all tonics for mind and soul.

YOUR CHURCH.—We would earnestly advise you, if you are ot already connected with one, to link yourself up with some Christian Church. Make the link real. Take your part in its vorship, in its activities—Boys' Brigade, Boy Scouts, Girl Guides, nd so on—and in its friendships.

Straight, clean, believing, devout, a good soldier of Jesus Christ; vith God's help your life will be a success, a blessing to home nd country, a source of happiness to yourself and to your riends.

We wish you all that is best.

Yours very sincerely,

Moore

19 Oct 1933.

Top: Granddad Willie in his days as a Boy Scout.

Above: Gran and Granddad dancing in 1969.

Left: Willie was a top angler – unlike me.

ALAN CARTER

He went from a navvy to top linesman with the YEB, working with Richard Dunn, his boxing pal and future British heavyweight champion. "I used to be able to pick my own team of navvies and we could put a line up in half the time as the other gangs. When I got promoted to being a live linesman, I began to dabble in a few cars," Mal said.

Mal Carter was the middle son of Lionel and Mary Carter. Lionel was a miserable, stone-faced old bastard who never had any time for us, while his wife Mary could be a very stern woman herself at the best of times.

Dad's parents split at some point and as I was growing up a bird called Katie became Lionel's partner – she was Dad's car cleaner, along with father's second wife Janet.

Dad used to tell me that Lionel behaved badly towards him. Lionel would cook lovely roast dinners for his fancy bit and leave his son sleeping on a hay-loft with a dog blanket, and Dad basically lived on pobs – bread in milk.

Having told me how much he hated and resented his father, I remember in later life that Dad purchased two houses and allowed Lionel to live in one of them, so if he did that I struggle to see how he could have hated his father as much as he told me he did.

I can't ever remember going to visit Lionel and Mary, or Katie after she moved in with him. They hardly ever spoke to us and we never even received a birthday card from them. I don't remember Dad giving us birthday cards either.

Dad was a bugger for the girls in his day and spent more time with his pants down than up. His first child was our Lynn, my half-sister, who had a very difficult childhood. Her mother became a hooker, so Lynn spent time in care homes and often got into trouble. Dad never really bothered much with Lynn as a kid. He'd abuse and humiliate her by calling her 'the ugly daughter' in front of others. But I'm glad to say that today Lynn Flaws is married to a great guy called Peter and they live a happy life in Halifax.

Dad had two brothers – David, the eldest, and Alan. Uncle David married Auntie Margaret and they lived on a farm on the outskirts of Halifax. They had three children – Gail, the eldest, followed by Paul and Samantha, the rebel of their family.

David and Margaret always invited us over to their house on bonfire night. We'd all eat like kings and enjoy a fun evening playing around on their farm. This was about the only time our family ever got together and I have very happy memories of those great nights.

Uncle Alan married Auntie Pat and they had two sons, Wayne and Lee. Alan was a great guy who would do anything for me. He treated me much better than my own Dad did.

Both Wayne and Lee love motorbike racing. Wayne, who is six years younger than me, became a very good and popular speedway rider for a number of years after making his debut for Wolverhampton in 1989, while Lee was very handy at motocross.

Dad had a twin sister, Mary, a lovely woman who was married to Uncle Bernard. But she paid the price for smoking too much and died of lung cancer at a relatively

Light in the Darkness

young age.

Mary and Bernard had three children – Elaine, Andrew and Steven. Elaine got polio as a child and needed callipers on her legs to walk. It was a very hard time for her but she is a lovely woman.

Cousin Elaine married local hard man Mick Briggs. I liked Mick and he seemed to like me. Although I never had any trouble with the notorious Briggs personally, he would make Elaine's life a living hell, beating her to a pulp many times and putting her in hospital.

Eventually the police took her away from him and gave her a new identity. She changed her name to 'Fran' and moved to a very remote part of the British Isles. She kept having to be moved around, though, because Mick was hot on her trail many times and used a private investigator to track her down.

He was eventually gunned down being involved in a drug-related incident at the infamous Regales pub on the outskirts of Halifax.

Our Elaine – or Fran, as she is now known – lives on Scotland's Isle of Arran, where she runs the island's best pub in the south-east coastal village of Lamlash called the Pierhead Tavern. It has attracted some very high profile customers, including Billy Connolly and Chris Evans.

Elaine's eldest brother, Andrew, was a local government councillor who got embroiled in a situation in which I believe he was falsely accused of 'kiddie fiddling'. Due to the immense stress brought on by the case, he took his own life at a young age.

As I said, Dad moved in with Janet soon after Mum became paralysed. Janet already had a daughter, Tina (Jackson), from her previous marriage, so she became my half-sister. Tina was a lovely kid, never a minute's trouble, and she went on to become very successful in business with her partner Edward. They have two teenage children, Scott and Luke.

Janet had two daughters with Dad – first Lindy and then Lucy. Lindy was a great kid who grew into a lovely woman. She lives with Paul, a real character in his own right.

Then came the rebel of the family, Lucy, who was born in 1980. Boy, can she party! A nice girl who, like her late father, is not to be messed with.

Lucy has a son, Lewis, whose father just happens to be the former speedway rider Garry Stead. He began his league racing career with Stoke in 1990 but was left paralysed from the waist down following a freak accident at Somerset in May 2007. Despite his disability, Garry has a great sense of humour and he's a clever man, too.

Well, if this side of the family seems like a bunch of crazy nutters, thank God for Mum's side.

She was the only child of Gladys and Willie Hanner, who tried to give her a strict upbringing. They wanted the perfect daughter. So what did she do? She rebelled.

One day Granddad found his bathroom sink blocked up. No problem, he could fix anything, but what does he find? Mum had been ramming fag-ends down the plug hole, so now she's in for it. But Gran and Granddad got nowhere by talking to her.

You know what it's like being a parent. Your kids think you're a nobody and that you know absolutely nothing. God, if my kids talked to my Dad like they have to me at times, he would have killed them. But it's amazing how times have changed. Parents, teachers and even the police have little control over children, which in turn means the kids show little respect for adults. Now I'm quite chilled out about what my kids do, because if I tried to stop them having a drink or doing certain other things, they would only go and stand on street corners and do it behind my back anyway.

Mum was a hairdresser in her short, young life and I must say a stunning lady.

Her parents were the most loving, kindest and compassionate people on earth. I have no idea how I would have turned out if it wasn't for them instilling into me some great family values and beliefs. Once I'd grown up, Gran used to tell me that Dad never had any time for me as a kid, and that one day he would live to regret it.

She'd take me shopping most Saturdays and we'd always go to the same coffee shop, The Merry England, where I'd drink orange squash and eat apple pie and cream. I still go there sometimes. I sit in the same chair I sat as a kid and, with tears in my eyes, think back on the happy memories the place still holds for me.

Gran's mum, my great grandma Emilia Moss, was a fiery little character. She was as hard as nails and worked well into her seventies. Many times as a young kid I would go strawberry-picking with my great friends Eggis and Welsey and it always ended in a strawberry fight. It amazed me why the guy who owned the field never gave us a beating because whenever we came to pay him we were always splattered with red juice. We'd leave the field and go to Granny Moss's for a drink and some home-made cake.

Granny Moss suffered two big falls. The first time she broke her hip when slipping on some dog poo. Then on another occasion she fell down her staircase at home. Sadly, she never really recovered and passed away shortly afterwards. I miss her fiery character and see a lot of myself in her.

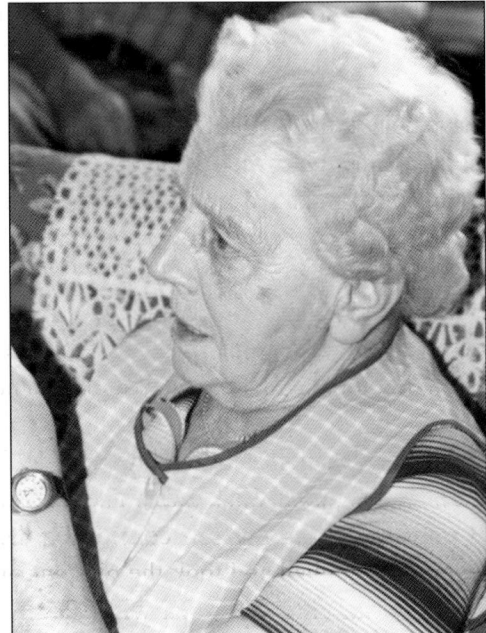

Above: Gran and Granddad Hanner.
Right: Granny Moss.

3 GROWING UP

Why Gran detested Mal . . . Kenny outsmarts me at school . . . a can of baked beans to the head . . . shot at by my brother . . . stealing from Woolies . . . Sheene, Hunt and other heroes . . . how a boy's wig saved me from a beating.

KENNY was born in Halifax General Hospital on March 28, 1961. Not only was he Christine and Mal Carter's first child, he also got the VIP treatment – i.e. he was born with a silver spoon up his arse. I followed Kenny almost three-and-a-half years later, born at the same place as my eldest brother (well, as far as I know that's where I came into the world) on August 19, 1964.

Mum and Dad met in one of the pubs in Halifax she frequented while still under-age. Their relationship was doomed from day one because Mal only ever had two things on his mind – shagging anything and making money – so they seemed to fight a lot in the early days. Dad would say "I'm off out" and Mum would reply: "No yer f****** not."

He'd lock her inside the house but she'd climb out of the window and shout all sorts of abuse at him at the top of her voice. Many times he was so embarrassed he just came back in. That's how it was.

Gran and Granddad begged Mum not to marry Mal on the morning of the wedding but she wouldn't listen. They didn't like him because they saw him as a bit of a rogue and a womaniser and I believe they thought he knocked their daughter around. I'm certain he did too. To be honest, in those days lots of men behaved that way towards their women. It was the norm back then but in today's society you can't even swear at a woman without risking arrest. What with political correctness, it would have been quite difficult for Mal to have lived in the modern world and I've found it quite difficult myself at times, too.

Gran detested Mal and I don't think Granddad liked him much either. But as I said, Mum was a rebel and she went ahead with the wedding against her parents' wishes.

Kenny and I both went to Moorside infants and juniors in Keighley Road and then on to J.H. Whitley, the secondary school in Holmfield. He was like a shining star as a kid – bright, intelligent and able to pick things up in an instant.

On the other hand, I reduced dumb to a new level. At school Kenny came just about top in everything while I was about as low as a snake's belly. I gave hope to everyone. I had special reading and writing lessons, everything . . . and the great news is I'm just as thick today. The teachers used to say: "Stand in the corner, Alan". I must say it did my self-confidence the world of good to be stood there while everyone laughed and took the piss out of me.

Kenny was always popular with the girls, too. Those sparkly blue eyes could melt

ALAN CARTER

Above: Mum and Dad, young and in love.

Right: My parents on their wedding day.

Below: Christine and Mal with Willie and Gladys. My grandparents begged Mum not to marry Mal.

Light in the Darkness

any girl's heart. I used to think, 'if only I had them', and it was one of my dreams to have his eyes and a cool name like Kenny. What were my parents thinking by naming me Alan?

At junior school I had a girlfriend called Tracey Flannery, who I walked home on many a cold night. Not sure what happened to her. All I know is, I got dumped more times than a coalman's sack.

Although he was a good brother while we were both young, as Kenny entered his early teens I soon realised that, in war terms, he was Rambo and I was the enemy. While I was playing Lego, marbles and watching *Captain Pugwash* on the telly, he was into anything that would hurt me. What a cunning mind he had.

He'd say: "Nipper, get in this suitcase and I'll bounce you up and down on the bed." It sounded like an ace idea, so I'd get inside the case and he'd zip it up before bouncing me a few times. Great! Then he'd give it the big one off the bed, almost killing me as the case hit the floor while he pissed himself laughing. And there he'd leave me, zipped up inside the case for about five minutes until I cried and pleaded with him to let me out.

Not to be outdone, I said to him: "You have a go", and I'd do the same to him. He'd shout: "I'm gonna kill yer," at which point I'd let him out of the case and run off. And that's when I'd receive a good beating from him.

While Kenny was still living at home with Mum, Dave and me, he acquired some amazing toys, including a crossbow, an air rifle and a pop-up pistol, plus a real bow and arrow set for Christmas. He'd be upstairs, straw target in one room while sat on the bog taking aim across the landing. And guess who mugged all the arrows? Yes, you got it right, me – Kenny's personal gofer.

He was a very selfish person and wouldn't let you have a shot at anything until he became bored. One day he shot an arrow that went straight through the bedroom window, so what does Kenny do? "Mum . . . mum . . . Alan's just shot the window out."

F*** me, shot it out? I wasn't even allowed a shot, let alone break the window. Here we go again, another hiding for me and I'm grounded for doing nothing. Thanks, brother.

Mum could be tough on me, too, when she needed to be. I once gave her a load of gob and, basically, was being a right cheeky, little prick. What she did – and did well – was bide her time. Anyway Mum hid a can of baked beans in her wheelchair – this was weeks after me gobbing off at her. The next thing, bang! She almost sliced my head open by throwing the can at me.

She wasn't a bit concerned about my injuries, only in making her point. As if to say, 'I might be in a wheelchair but don't mess with me!'

Lesson learned.

As a teenager, Kenny was always playing around with his air rifle. He used it mainly to shoot birds, or if there were none around I always came in handy as a target. I can see myself now, legging it over the back wasteland and just waiting for the pain as he took aim and shot me in the arse.

At the time we moved to Brickfield Lane in Holmfield, on the edge of Halifax, it

ALAN CARTER

Above: Mum and Dad with their first born, Kenny.

Right: Dad holding me with Mum and Kenny.

Below left: Kenny at Gran's house, 11 Reins Road, where we had so many happy times.

Below right: Mum, Dad and me.

was a brand new, semi-detached house with three bedrooms, a driveway and a lovely front garden where Kenny and me would pitch our tent and camp out overnight. As small kids, we'd nick sweets from the local shop and share them out in the tent. Trouble was, sometimes we'd argue so loudly over who stole what that Mum would hear us and come out to find out what all the commotion was about. When she realised we'd nicked the sweets, she made us take them back to the shop and admit our crime.

We would terrorise the neighbourhood for years. For some reason our football always ended up in the same garden, and that was Eddie's. He was right miserable bastard, nobody liked him and he always used to say: "Right, it's mine now" and take our football into his house. He wouldn't give it back to us until Dad arrived on the scene, just like Superman, and knocked on Eddie's door. He'd say: "Right, bastard, get that ball out 'ere." Eddie used to shit himself and throw it out of his bedroom window. No-one messed with Dad.

I remember one day Gran had her prized budgie, which her next door neighbour, a breeder, had given to her. Gran was amazing, all her budgies could talk. Well, one day I forgot her favourite was perched on my head and as I opened the outside door, he flew away. I cried and cried and she kept asking "what's wrong?" All I could say was "you're going to kill me" and just cried even more. Eventually I told her what had happened and that's when we all set out to catch him. And to my amazement, the budgie flew back into Gran's hands.

The local bowling club held a bingo night on Fridays. I'm telling you, I was always the first there with my 50p and it wasn't often that I didn't win something. Gran showed me and Kenny how to play bingo and many times we'd go along there with Gran, a miniature vodka and orange in her hand, and have a lovely time.

Yes, life living in the 70s as a kid was magic. After school you came home, had your tea and Mum would tell you to "piss off and don't come back 'till bedtime" and that's what we did. We played hide and seek or whatever.

My mate Dave Stewart had about 2,000 toy soldiers while I had none, so going over the road and playing at his house was like a dream come true. We played for hours and he was a great kid. His parents, Linda and John, always made me feel very welcome.

One of our favourite pastimes as kids was catching frogs – we always had plenty of them. Another great adventure was catching bees and keeping them in our jam-jars.

We used to swim in the water tanks around the back of the local mills. I once remember Kenny swimming at the back of Bulmer's mill in Holmfield, then making me have a go. I was shitting myself.

When we were young Kenny never seemed to get hurt. It was always me down at the Halifax General Hospital having something stitched up. I was such a clumsy bugger.

I loved to watch Kenny build a push bike or fix a tyre inner-tube. I'd be there all day trying to do it but he could get the job done brilliantly in just minutes.

Above left: Born to ride, Kenny outside 11 Reins Road. Above right: This one of Kenny was taken at Bridlington in 1966, when he was aged five. Below: Kenny and me with Gran at the seaside.
Bottom: This time Gran, Kenny and me are joined on the beach by her mother, Granny Moss.

Light in the Darkness

At Christmas I'd receive basic presents like Ludo and try to figure out how you played it, whereas Kenny would get a chemistry set or Meccano and make all sorts of wonderful things with them. He once had a jewellery kit from which he made Mum a pair of earrings, only for me to drop it down the toilet. That led to him giving me yet another beating.

The Spaldings were a very rich local family who lived in a mansion that our Gran used to clean. Mr Spalding was chairman of the Halifax Building Society and we were given all of his son Simon's old clothes. Yes, even the great 'King Kenny' and me started out wearing cast-offs but we had great times playing at the Spaldings' large residence.

We had a pet monkey when I was young, although I think Dad got rid of it in the end because it kept shitting too much. He certainly showed more love for his many pets than his six children. He had loads of different animals and loved his dogs.

My Christmas shopping was a fun experience. We had f***-all, money wise, so I just went to Woolworths. No wonder they went bust after all the gear I nicked from them as a kid. The security guard at the Halifax branch wore jam-jar specs and could hardly see me, let alone all the stuff I was nicking for Mum and Gran's Christmas presents. I never got caught once and as a young lad was the world champion nicker.

I could run for England, too, although that's not surprising when I think back to all the scrapes our Kenny got me into. Even the local vicar was after me after I'd been shouting abuse at him. He was the fastest person I ever came across. He'd always catch me and give me a thick ear. Then he banned me from the Boys' Brigade.

Kenny developed into a trendy kid. He dressed up as a teddy boy in his blue Elvis suit and matching blue suede shoes with bootlace tie. He looked fantastic and to top it all, the lucky bugger could even dance like Elvis. When I danced it looked like I was having an epileptic fit.

Me and Kenny grew up in an era full of great sporting superstars to look up to. We had the fantastic Barry Sheene – what a top bloke he was, a proper superstar – and motor racing driver James Hunt. Two greats who had all the girls chasing after them – yes, I sure fancied a bit of this action.

I used to watch Wimbledon ever year as a boy and loved Bjorn Borg and Jimmy Connors. And then along came this amazing young shitbag called John McEnroe. I remember thinking at the time that this was our Kenny, or his twin, but as time went on I became a big fan of McEnroe. I loved the way he used to lose his cool and go absolutely mental. As I say, he was Kenny to a tee.

There I was with Mum and Dave on Saturday afternoons watching Dickie Davies present ITV's *World of Sport* on our black and white set. We were so happy.

Darts was another sport I followed on the telly. I was crap at it but loved watching John Lowe trying to beat Eric Bristow, who seemed a cocky, arrogant prick to me. Then came Jockey Wilson, one of my all-time favourite sporting legends. Jockey would come on half-pissed and still give the world's best a run for their money. Watching Jockey leave the stage needing help because he could hardly walk for booze was brilliant – not like today's shirt-lifters drinking a glass of water. Where

ALAN CARTER

Above: This family shot taken at Butlins in the late 60s is the only one I have of all five of us together.

The other three pictures are of Kenny at different stages of his childhood. I like the cheeky grin (bottom right).

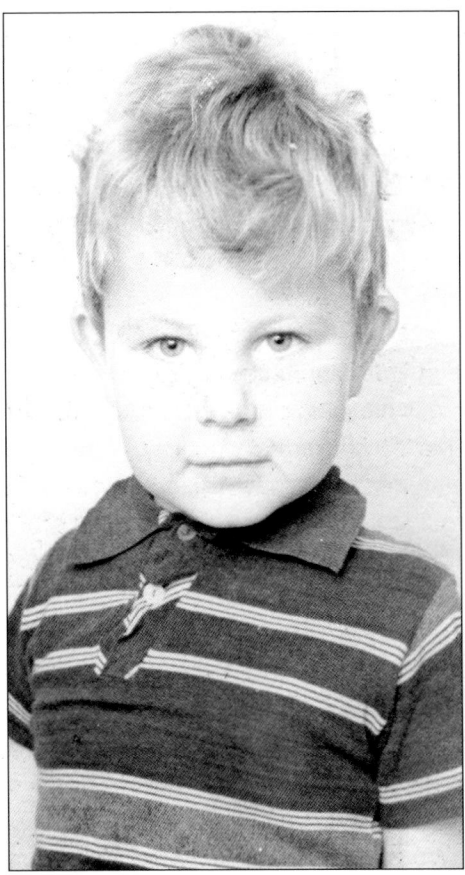

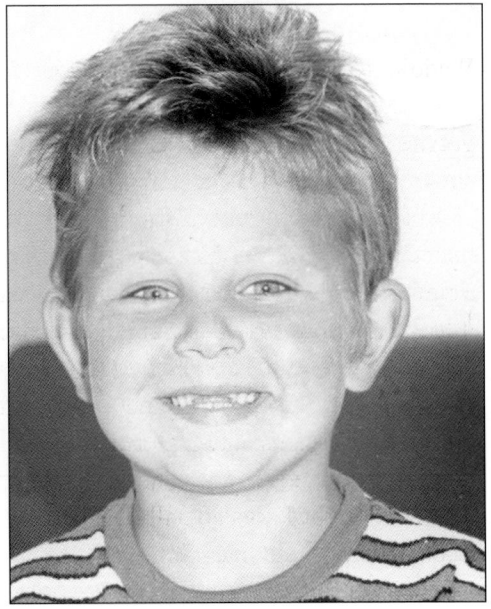

Light in the Darkness

has all the fun gone in sport?

Another favourite was the Horse of the Year show and watching Harvey Smith trying to beat the Whitakers from Huddersfield and all the rest of the world's best riders. I'd sit there watching these great riders jumping over massive fences.

I always seemed to like the grey horses and although I've never been a gambling man, just like the rest of the nation I always used to put a few quid on the Grand National an Aintree. In fact the very last time I put some money on the race was to back a grey called Dark Ivy in 1987. It was an absolute beauty but the poor beast fell at Becher's Brooke, broke its neck and then had to be destroyed. I felt sick and that was the moment I totally lost interest in the Grand National.

Moving up to senior school at the age of 11 was a big step. Luckily for me, Kenny was just moving into the top year at J.H. Whitley, so if anyone messed with me he would give them a right kicking. From torturer and tormentor, my brother became my bodyguard.

At secondary school our little gang consisted of Welsey (David Wells), Eggis (Paul Haigh) and myself. We may not have been the hardest trio but we always stood our ground and would give it a go if we had to.

Me and Welsey were always up to no good, picking on poor Chris Atkinson or Raymond Ismail. The way we treated these guys, we'd do time in today's world. I'm so glad I met Paul Haigh, because he set me in a completely different direction and calmed me down a bit. We would be friends for the rest of our lives.

The Coulters were not to be messed with and neither was Mathew Ervine, who seemed massive to me. I was the smallest boy in my year apart from Atkinson.

I became good mates with Mark Wells and Neil O'Leary, top lads at school who I shared great times with, just piss-balling about. Many times we said: 'F*** school, let's go to Ogden reservoir.' That's where the betting would start . . . 'bet you won't dive in for a Penguin biscuit'. Me and Welsey were diving in the water like a bullet just for a 10p Penguin.

My teens were mostly a great time. We rode horses that were owned by the Waddingtons on the hillside near our house. I always rode 'Mr. Head', a beige beauty of a beast who we could hire for 50p an hour – a right deal. You could never get the horses out of the yard but as soon as we were almost back there, they charged home rampantly. I fell off many a time – I was no Zorro, that's for sure.

My school report read a bit differently to those of other kids. Instead of 'could do better', mine said 'could turn up.' Once I came home with my report and was given a right shock. Mum told Dave, my stepdad, to give my arse a right beating. He gave it to me good and proper that day and had me crying like a baby.

To me, there seemed no point in going to school. I was crap at English, didn't even know my four times table and I was banned from metalwork for making kung fu pointed stars and lobbing them at my mates. And the cookery teacher, Mrs Womanlea, hated me too. She once said: "Make some pastry, Carter," so that's what I did. I thought I was actually quite good at it – and I could teach Gordon Ramsey a few things about swearing, too. Anyway, I was rolling the pastry when the bitch hit me over the head very hard and said: "Carter, you're rolling pastry, not the M62 – short, sharp swift strokes."

The only thing I was good at in school was sport. I was always in the top three at cross-country, winning many races until a Pakistani lad turned up. At 14, his pubes were longer than the hair on my head. He was massive and could run like a racehorse. I played in the school football team but was always first reserve, freezing my knackers off on the touchline. But I enjoyed all sports and was popular with the two PE teachers, Mr Robinson and Mr Robertshaw.

Otherwise, as Dad once told me, I was about as useful as a chocolate teapot and very few teachers had any time for me. There were one or two exceptions, though. Apart from the PE teachers, our history teacher Mr. Beaumont was such a lovely man that I always looked forward to his lessons.

I had my eyes on other things a lot of the time. The girls thought I was cute and funny but this didn't go down well with the lads. I fancied Jayne Blagbougher but we'd always be caught snogging in the bushes and I'd be put on detention. One of the most beautiful girls at school was Christine Bland. She was so nice, you'd nearly faint when she passed you in the corridor. Well, the Carter charm came to the fore once more and she was mine for a short time before she came to her senses and dumped me over nothing. Years later, she explained that she wasn't going to be another notch on my bedpost.

Brickfield Lane and its surrounding area was a wonderland to us kids. We had the old army camp at the top, a playground, bowling green, tennis courts, football and rugby pitches and the biggest hill to play on in Yorkshire. There was also Gee's dam, where we caught sticklebacks and frogs.

We had the best gang there was in Dave Stewart, Tony Beedon, Mark Hitchin, Baz and Peter Smith and Dale Holesworth, who was a great sportsman. Then there was Glyn Moore, the Dannylucks, the Wilsons and all the Beachwood Road and Watkinson Road clan.

We'd get our playground roundabout going so fast, I used to fly off the top. Those were the days . . . coming down the slide with a Warburton's wrapper under your arse to make you go faster – and it worked, too. We used to fight each other just for a piece of that bread wrapper.

The kids of today, sat in front of a computer or TV screen for 12 hours a day, don't know what they're missing. I consider myself lucky to have been a 70s kid playing out from dusk 'till dawn.

Kenny was expelled for fighting in his last year and he sure picked on the wrong people that day – the head teacher Mr. McDowell and his deputy head Mr Grimshaw. He punched the head teacher and at the same time *kung-fu* kicked the other bloke in the head, which is hardly a typical day's school activity. I've no idea how he got into this situation, because he was very popular and did well at school.

One day a big crowd gathered at the local bowling green, where I was meant to be fighting Graham Crouch. Kenny had set it up as he was dating Graham's sister Bev. I was absolutely petrified but he dragged me up there. I was ready to get a drilling into the earth's core but just as we began fighting, all of a sudden everyone started laughing. One of my gang had decided to smack Graham's mate, Paul, and as he went to grab his hair, Paul's wig came off in his hand! By now everyone was rolling about in hysterics and my supposed fight with Graham – who I liked anyway – thankfully fizzled out.

Unbeknown to us, at the age of 14, Paul was suffering from leukaemia, bless him. At the time it was cruel to laugh at his misfortune but his hairpiece gave us all a laugh and saved me from a serious beating.

Our Kenny was a hard act to follow but what a benchmark he set for me. It's like they say, 'aim high and if you shoot for the moon you might bag a star'.

So Kenny was Dad's golden boy while in our father's eyes I was about as worthy as dog poo. Little did they both know I had a trump card in my Gran, who became the greatest person in my life and would have gone to the moon and back for me. She loved me so much, it was just amazing.

She passed away in 2005, aged 85, and my life's never been the same since. I still miss her so much.

ALAN CARTER

Above: Dad racing in the 60s.

Left: Dad and Uncle David ready to race.

4 LET'S GO RACING

Rider killed at Dad's first meeting . . . Mal's big business breakthrough . . . helping the police . . . racing around our own 'track' . . . Kenny, the favoured son . . . Speedway pays better than moto-cross.

KENNY and I got into racing at a very young age. Dad had been a good club racer in the late 60s. He started racing on a Manx Norton after being introduced to the sport by a guy called Eric Sunderland. Eric was Dad's car paint sprayer – he touched up all his cars and, later, also fixed the ones I crashed that Dad didn't know about.

Dad would often tell me how hard road-racing was back in his day, with around 140 riders contesting different heats and only the top 40 making it to the final, which he did on many occasions and won his share of races too. But I saw Mal have some big crashes, especially in the wet.

He was once described in a motorcycling magazine as 'a reasonable rider' during his short racing career. I read that he began racing through a bet with a mate and finished when young Malcolm died and Mum was paralysed in 1970. He was noted for his hard riding on a 650cc Spitfire Metisse as a 28-year-old through to a Seeley Norton three years later.

His first race was in 1968 at the Oliver's Mount Scarborough meeting in which former British GP racer John Hartle was killed – he finished sixth ahead of Mick Grant.

I remember many occasions when Kenny and me travelled back from club meetings in the back of Dad's old van. We were only little nippers sitting on the Norton race bikes and pretending we were Agostini and Hailwood racing each other and getting down to business behind the screen. I was so small, I used to lie over the petrol tank, hang on to the bars and talk to myself.

I'd flip open the petrol tank and smell the fuel, which would make me feel 'funny'. I'd see black vaporization and pass out, then quickly regain my senses. We loved being around bikes and couldn't get enough of it.

Mal's business was buying, selling and repairing cars. He also owned a petrol station, having started up at Brickfield Motors, which was an old mill next door to where we lived in Brickfield Lane. His brother, my Uncle Alan, did all the MOTs and repair work from there and next door there was the paint-spraying shop owned by Eric Sunderland.

Dad then became involved with a guy called Wilf Denton, who was quite a slick operator. He took my father under his wing but suffered a massive heart attack in

ALAN CARTER

Above: Mum and Dad on a night out with Mr and Mrs Wilf Denton. Wilf sold his half of the garage business to Mal.

Left: Dad outside his first business premises in Halifax.

Below: A school photo of Kenny.

Below left: Kenny, on his Chopper bike, had an unfair advantage over me on my Chipper but our competitive racing instincts are already obvious.

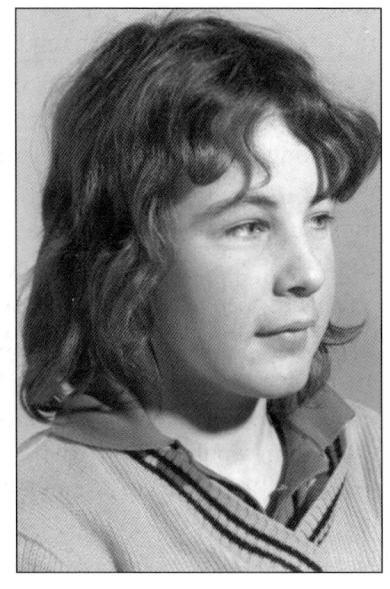

the early 70s and left his half of the business to Dad.

He owned the Pharaoh Garage in Illingworth, a filling station near Halifax where they also sold and repaired cars, plus two other garages on Keighley Road.

In the interview Dad gave *Motorcycle Racing* magazine which I mentioned earlier, he explained how he started in business in 1966. He said: "I rented a little place for 10 bob a week and in the year after I started, I sold 800 cars in one year. They were all bangers. They used to call me 'Cheap Car Carter, Bangers Galore'.

"Instead of being against the police, I ended up with a full breakdown team pulling in all the crash jobs for the police."

The article began by describing Mal as a 'gritty, heavily-built Yorkshireman who looks just like you would imagine an ex-boxer and used car salesman to be.'

Dad owned a beautiful customised V12 E-type Jaguar, worth £6,000 at the time, which he called 'The Egyptian'. Among other things, it contained a mini disco with flashing light show and cocktail cabinet, which he used for special events and charity functions.

The great thing for me and Kenny was that Dad just loved racing – cars, bangers, bikes, go-karts, you name it. At the back of Pharaoh Garage there was about 100 acres of wasteland – a rough place and an ideal place to have lots of fun. Kenny could drive a car from the age of about 10, although it took me until I was around 13. Did we rip around this land, carving out our own stock car and dirt bike tracks.

The first mini bikes we had were part of the Honda ST series. Mine was the ST50 and Kenny, as you can guess, had a top-of-the-range ST70.

Talk about happy times, we raced all weekend, every weekend, and there were always lots of different people turning up to have a go. I'm sure Dad did some deals. "If yer can beat me or any of my lads round here, we'll knock a tenner off yer new car."

I remember tearing around the field – it's now a housing estate – in an old Ford Anglia car, with me as the co-pilot and Kenny at the wheel. I used to absolutely shit myself burning around those fields and God only knows how we never had a big accident. To be honest, we were too busy having a great time to worry about the risks involved. Can you imagine having different cars and bikes to race and because we owned our own petrol station, there was always free fuel on tap. It just seemed a normal way of life to us, it's all we knew.

Looking back, other kids must have thought we were super-rich. We weren't, Mal worked seven days a week and earned his money the hard way. He had one of the most successful car sales pitches in Halifax and the 70s were boom years for him. But it was all earned through bloody hard graft.

You didn't have to be a rocket scientist to see Kenny was Dad's favoured son. I was having a great time anyway, so his favouritism never crossed my mind at a young age. It was only when Kenny would go up to the garage and come back with 20 quid – and this happened most weeks – that I became fully aware who Dad's golden boy was. Mum would see the cash Kenny came home with and go apeshit and demand to know: "Where's Alan's money?" Kenny would tell her that I had to go and collect it myself. But up until about 15 I was so shy and scared of Mal that I'd never ask for

ALAN CARTER

Above: Kenny showing his moto-cross skills in 1976, aged 15.

Left: Me enjoying the bumps and jumps on the wasteland behind Dad's garage.

Light in the Darkness

or get much from him. On the other hand, Mum always treated her two eldest sons equally.

Kenny started schoolboy motocross on a 100cc Suzuki Beamish and Dad took him everywhere to race. I was his biggest fan and he was soon going very fast and winning races. But Mal soon realised that the bike was not the best and for the start of the following year he bought Kenny a Honda 125 Elsinore motocross bike. It was the very latest model on the market and sounded unbelievable. I bobbed myself just seeing him warming it up.

Kenny was amazing, showing no fear and apparently able to do anything he wanted to on a bike. He'd say: "Let's jump over that one, Al" while I was thinking, 'I'd rather eat my own shit, thanks.' The three-and-a-half-year age gap between us seemed massive, especially from between 12 and 16. He was fast becoming a man while I was still a little kid.

Kenny had a great year on the Honda, moving rapidly through the Amateur Motor Cycle Association levels and soon getting a EMC 250 six-speed motocross bike. Now this was a weapon, the best money could buy, and Kenny went from junior, to expert, to super class – the highest grade – in less than two years.

But there wasn't any money to be earned in this form of racing, so when Kenny turned 16 and he was riding a moped and working full-time at Dad's garage, that's where the speedway thing started. Mal thought, 'where do we go from here?' It was a choice of either going on to professional motocross in the ACU or something else, and speedway on the shale tracks was where it was at.

One Saturday night Mal arranged for Kenny to go down to the Halifax Dukes and watch them in action, to see what he thought of speedway. Dad had got to know the Halifax promoter Eric Boothroyd and he became involved with the speedway by sponsoring Dukes' riders Eric Broadbelt and Chris Pusey.

Kenny had the best looking FS1-E moped in Yorkshire with its Kenny Roberts replica racing pipe and fairing – you could hear him riding it from miles away. So he parked his precious bike next to The Shay in the swimming baths car park while he enjoyed the night's racing. He came out of the stadium thinking 'I can beat these' but as he went to find his bike he discovered to his horror that it had gone. Someone had nicked it – its bare frame, minus engine and the rest was found a few weeks later.

Kenny wasn't happy but my two best mates, Welsey and Eggis, and I all pissed our pants. Get in there!

For a few years Kenny used to kick f*** out of me and my mates, he was a bully to us at times, so sweet revenge was a long time in coming. By now we were growing up too.

Kenny in his first season of speedway, at Halifax in 1978.

5 LOCAL HERO

Bunking off school to drive Kenny to Newcastle and back . . . new star at The Shay . . . The Pharaoh Garage gold standard deal . . . a snake in the office.

KENNY began his speedway career with Halifax Dukes in 1978 at 16, the minimum competitive age limit for racing on the shale.

He went straight in at senior British League level, which was a hard and fast learning curve competing against the world's best riders, such as Ole Olsen, Peter Collins, Michael Lee and Ivan Mauger. He was thrown into the lion's den but being a Carter, that's all we knew, and he was more than up for the challenge.

Although Halifax loaned him out to second division Newcastle in his first season, to allow him time to find his feet in the sport, he still rode 16 matches for the Dukes in the top flight and you could see he was going places fast. The great advantage for Kenny was that he was riding at his home-town track, where he soon became a local hero. And before long he would become a God to most of the thousands who watched the racing at The Shay on Saturday nights.

Kenny's first car was a blue Mini Van. He would rip around Halifax in it with his pet dog Tiger, a greyhound he used for rabbiting. That wasn't my cup of tea, I couldn't kill a flea. That's been my biggest problem in life – being too soft and gullible. I believed anything people told me, unlike Kenny who was as sharp as a razor.

It was a fair way up the A1 to Newcastle on Mondays but the journey didn't bother Kenny because he had his own ready-made chauffeur. Even though I was only 13 or 14-years-old at the time, he'd force me to bunk off school to drive him to the Diamonds' home meetings at Brough Park.

The Geordie fans immediately took to Kenny and he soon had his own thriving fan club run by two local girls, Maureen and Lynda. Occasionally Eggis would join us on the trip and I can still see the two of us now, sat waiting patiently on a park bench somewhere on a Newcastle housing estate while Kenny nipped off to be with a hot woman, returning later with a wink of his eye. Lucky bugger.

The Diamonds were a strong team, led by the outstanding Tom Owen who caught my eye with his smart leathers and aura of invincibility. The promoters, Ian Thomas and Bryan Larner, knew what they were about, too, and from what I understand, speedway could do with some colourful characters like them today.

A number of Newcastle's home meetings were held on Sunday afternoons, when track conditions always seemed to be dusty. It struck me how close the steel floodlight poles were to the wire safety fence and in only Kenny's third meeting there his young team-mate Chris Prime was killed when he went into the fence

ALAN CARTER

while trailing in fourth place behind my brother. You could hear a pin drop in the stadium that night.

At Halifax Kenny had a fantastic promoter and mentor in Eric Boothroyd and his wife Bonnie, nice people who put a bit of stability into his life. Then there was team manager Dennis Gavros – what a great man he was. Having older and wiser teammates around him was also good for his development. You had people like former England captain Chris Pusey, Ian Cartwright, Mick McKeon, the Danes Mike and Klaus Lohmann and Eric Broadbelt, a lovely man who I still see to this day.

Kenny rose rapidly through the ranks at Halifax and in his second season, 1979, he no longer doubled-up with Newcastle Diamonds in the National League. By then he had established himself as a star heat leader for the Dukes.

What he also had behind him was our Dad. Mal Carter wasn't one to f**k with. Trust me, when Mal said jump, you jumped very high.

He'd been around road-racing a long time and, although this is a different form of racing, he knew his stuff. He didn't miss a thing as he watched every race and every pass very closely. He could analyse everything to pinpoint accuracy.

The only thing he did wrong in my opinion was instil in Kenny – and later on me – that he had to win every time he went out to race, which is obviously impossible. No matter how well you rode, he always wanted more. I once won a race by five seconds, only for Mal to snap at me: "You're crap round Mansfield" (the name of a corner at the Cadwell Park circuit) and give me a bollocking.

I can still see Mum now, sitting in her wheelchair at The Shay and freezing as she watched her first born son winning race after race. She must have been so proud and happy for him.

Our local paper, *The Halifax Courier*, should have been renamed the Kenny Carter Times. What used to drive me crazy, after I started being successful, was that I'd win or do something spectacular at a big international meeting and get two inches, but he'd score eight points at Coventry and get half-a-page. When I did something really good, I was always known as 'Alan Carter, the brother of Kenny Carter'. I used to think, 'do they *have* to mention him in every article about me?'. I suppose it's par for the course for any son following in the footsteps of a famous father, or brothers – like the Collins boys following Peter – trying to live up to a very successful elder sibling.

Kenny and Mal could fall in a barrel of shit and come out clutching fifty pound notes. On the other hand, if I won the National Lottery I'd be denied the payout on a technicality. 'Sorry Alan, but you purchased your ticket 30 seconds too late' or 'you creased the ticket'. Talk about unlucky, I was once watching two gorgeous girls at a bus stop, thinking 'they look fine,' only to run into the back of the parked bus. I used to watch *Laurel and Hardy* on Saturday mornings, always thinking, 'that's me, the thin one called Stan – as thick as f***.'

You would certainly agree when I tell you about just a few silly things I did while working for Dad at his Pharaoh Garage. Mal said: "Go check the oil on that car." I walked over, put the bonnet up and took out the dipstick. 'Yep, he's right, needs

Light in the Darkness

Above: Mal with two of his sponsored speedway riders in 1978, our Kenny and Halifax star Eric Broadbelt, both in the Pharaoh Racing colours. To the left of Kenny is his 16-year-old girlfriend Pamela Lund.

Below: Newcastle Diamonds of 1978. Left to right: Robbie Blackadder, Robbie Gardner, Tom Owen (on bike), Graeme Stapleton, Neil Coddington, Kenny and Kevin McDonald.

some oil.'

Off I pop to fetch some oil. 'OK, let's fill the bitch up.'

Well, f*** me, what a bastard of a job that was. Could I get the oil down the dipstick hole? I must have spilt two litres of oil all over the engine and there's me thinking, 'Mal must have a good, steady hand to be as good as he is at this.'

"Dad, I can't get it in."

To my amazement and shock, he told me I was a liability and that I was to "f*** off and go play on the motorway."

The trouble was, I was doing basic things badly while Kenny was doing major things very well.

My next job.

"Oi, c***, go charge that car up."

I'm flying now, having moved up from washing cars to charging them, so I trot off with this super-duper booster thing. 'Oh, we've got a right car here,' I'm thinking. I open the bonnet and I'm like, 'so where is the engine!'

Better ask the Boss.

"It's got no engine, Dad."

This is where I get a right boot up the arse.

"You f****** thick c***, it's in the boot!"

So it's back to find the engine in the boot. 'Yes, I'm in!'

Well, it was like Who Wants to be a Millionaire. I had a red lead and a black one, so I'm thinking, 'f*** it, a 50/50 chance, red and black, just put them on and see what happens.'

There was a bang so big I nearly landed in Halifax town centre. 'F***, what's happened now?'

That's the day I learned about positive and negative leads. Unlike other kids doing car mechanic apprenticeships at college, we never did anything the right way. We did it Mal Carter's way.

We once had a giant python snake in the office, only for the thick cleaner to turn all the electrical sockets off at night and kill the thing because it couldn't survive without heating.

Dad would take anything in part-exchange to seal a deal with a customer. We offered the best service deal in town. Well, for US it was.

The 'Pharaoh Garage Service' was standard with all cars sold.

'GOLD STANDARD'.

You got:

1. Oil checked (that was just so you didn't blow the car up)
2. Washer bottle filled (screen wash Fairy Liquid)
3. Your oil filter wiped with a rag (to make it look like a new one)

Not bad for 100 quid.

Car Guarantee:

One month or one thousand miles.

The only thing we did fantastically well was clean cars. I did the best carwash in

Light in the Darkness

Above: Kenny in action in hs first season on the shale at Newcastle, where the fans immediately took him to their hearts.

Right: Fooling around on his trials bike at Newcastle Speedway during the interval break at Brough Park.

ALAN CARTER

Halifax four team tournament winners - Kenny, Mike Lohmann, my favourite Chris Pusey and Ian Cartwright.

the UK, and still do, while Katie (Dad's stepmum) and Janet (Mal's second wife) minted the inside of our cars so that they always looked great. But as they say, always read the label, don't be fooled by looks.

Mal's speciality was car finance, which included stitching you up with the highest interest rate possible. I remember one customer coming in and saying: "F****** hell, come and talk to The Midland, talk to the listening bank." That was Midland Bank's catchphrase for their TV advertisement at the time. Dad just told him to 'come in, sit down and I'll sort you some finance out, kid'.

So there he was, only interested in robbing people with the most expensive loans in history. Boy, my old man was brilliant in his day. Dad could sell anything, and he did. He was a confident character.

6 LOSING MUM

Shock and disbelief as Mum is found dead . . . Dave suffers a nervous breakdown . . . My dreadful last vision . . . Kenny makes me homeless.

AT the start of 1979 things were going great guns. Kenny was starring for the Halifax team and by mid-season he'd won his first England cap.

Dad's thriving business (aka Trotters Car Sales) was moving cars faster than he could buy them.

Me? Well, I was still the same happy-go-lucky schoolkid. I was fine.

My life would change forever, though, on Tuesday, September 18.

That's the night I was invited to the Holy Trinity School disco, which was held in a hall next to my school. There was a group of us there all having a good time. I can still remember the moment as plain as day. I was in the toilets trying to ease a very bad stomach pain – I suffered from them a lot in those days due to not eating at all most of the time.

Suddenly people were looking everywhere for me, and then someone came and said I had to go home. I have no recollection of making my way back to the house. All I knew was that, just a few months before her 36th birthday, Mum had killed herself by taking an overdose of painkilling tablets. I'm not certain who found her dead – I was told it was Kenny.

I was in shock, total disbelief. The only feeling I can remember was one of numbness. She had tried to take her own life before, only to be caught hiding the pills under her pillow by Dave, bless her.

She'd obviously suffered a lot of pain following the accident nine years earlier and had no real quality of life. She'd decided she could take no more and I think she'd reached the point where she thought Kenny was on his way, doing his own thing, a man now at 18, and I'd got to the age of 15 and would be able to cope.

It was awful and I felt so guilty, thinking I should have done so much more, but I was only a kid. As the years go by you would think it gets better but it doesn't, and I feel worse thinking, 'if only I'd done this, if only, if only . . .' but you can't change the past.

Dave Wood certainly couldn't have done any more for her. Mum really put Dave through the mill during their time together. Anyone who has looked after a paraplegic will know how tough it is, especially while holding down a full-time day job, as Dave did, and in the end he couldn't take any more. He suffered a mental breakdown and had to spend time in hospital while he recovered. Mum was still alive at the time.

ALAN CARTER

Right: Mum and Dave's wedding at Halifax Registry Office in the mid-70s. Kenny is with Gran, with Granny Moss behind Mum.

Below: Mum and Dave about to sign the marriage certificates, watched by Kenny, me and Granny Moss. No-one could have done more than Dave to put some happiness back into Mum's short life after she suffered such appalling injuries.

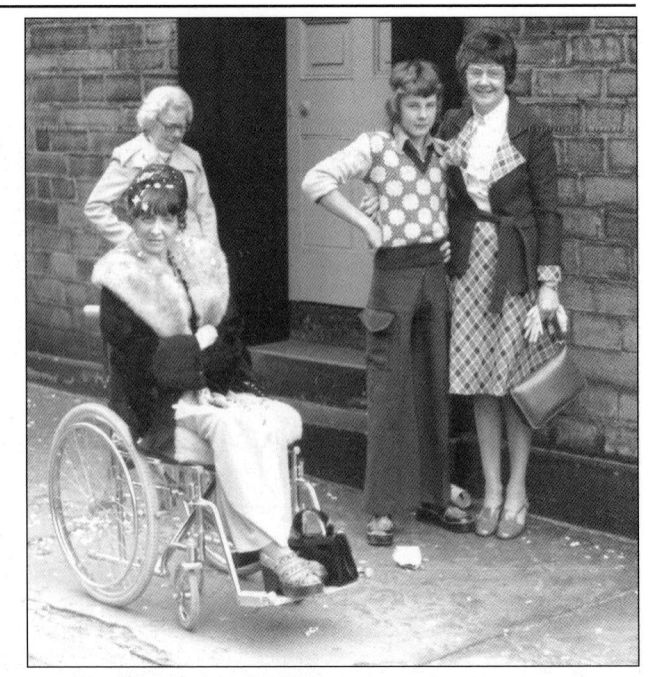

On the day of her funeral we all met up at the undertakers in Halifax. Little did I know until I arrived in the funeral parlour that it was an open coffin, allowing family and other loved ones to pay their last respects to the deceased. One moment I'm in a queue of people and then all of a sudden I'm staring at Mum's lifeless body. She looked awful, with gritted teeth, as if she was desperately trying to hang on to life, or maybe it was a sign that she'd changed her mind about killing herself? It was a dreadful last vision of her that will always haunt me.

After the funeral the first thing Kenny did was organise with Dad to purchase the

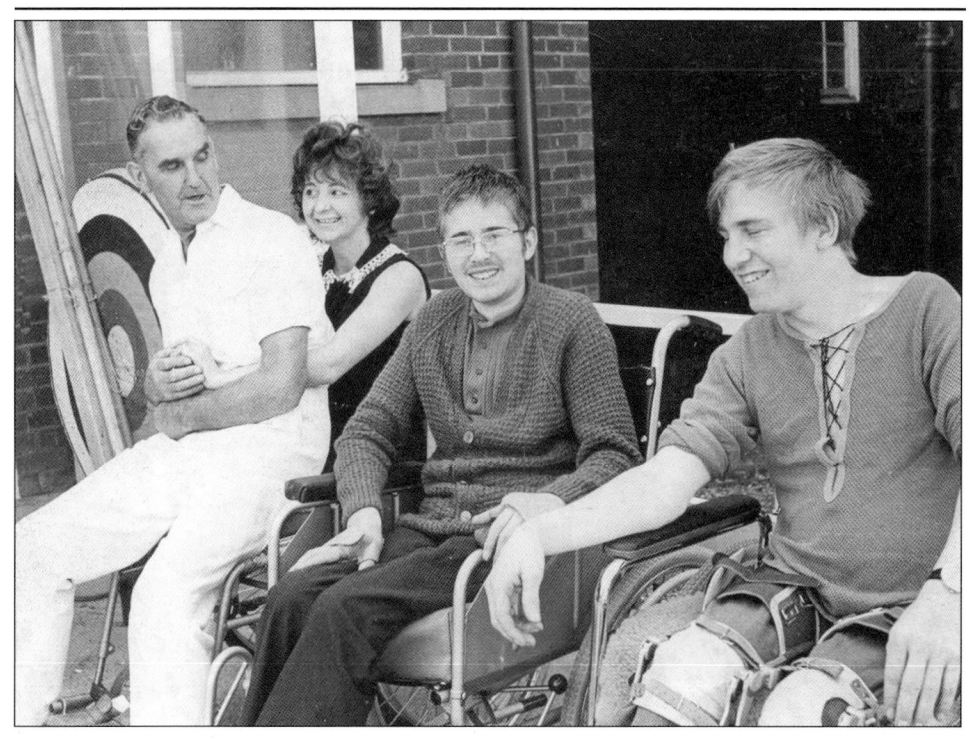

Mum with her physio and friends during the period she spent in rehab.

house. He wanted both Dave and me out of 15 Brickfield Lane, which I found unbelievably heartless of him. Kenny purchased Dad's half-share of the house to add to the quarter-share he had just inherited from Mum, leaving me with no option but to sell him my quarter. So there was Dave and me, having just buried Mum and now homeless.

Dave was in no fit state to look after himself, let alone me. He'd just lost the wife he had been devoted to and was very ill himself.

I still speak to Dave Wood a couple of times a year and we get on fine. He remarried a lady called Debbie and they had three children together. He told me he named the eldest one Alan after me.

I still often think, 'if only I could bring her back.' It's heartbreaking knowing I effectively lost Mum to a massive car crash and she had her normal life snatched away from her on one black Saturday morning when I was just six-years-old. I'd just turned 15 when she died but, to all intents and purposes, her life was taken from her back in 1970 when that tyre burst on Shay Lane.

If only I could have just one last hug and be able to tell her 'I love you Mum.'

I had no choice really but to move in with Dad at the farm in Barkisland, where he'd lived with Janet and their three daughters for about the previous 18 months, just as I was starting my last year at school. Moving home also meant a change of school, so I went from J.H. Whitley to Ryburn Valley High in Sowerby Bridge, but I hated it there. At 15, I went from being one of the most popular kids to a retard overnight. The boys there just didn't like me and my attitude to them was, 'go f***

The sadness in Mum's face is all too clear.

yourselves'. After Mum died I was in a dark place and in no mood to take any shit from anyone.

That was it for me. I left school a year earlier than I should have and started a new life with Dad, Janet and my two half-sisters.

He made me welcome at their farm and Janet did all she could for me, too. They'd got married in about 1977 and Kenny and me both went to the wedding. At least now I was being looked after and starting to eat a lot better as well, so I soon settled in with them. Janet's food was great – she was a better cook than Delia Smith and I saw more meat in a week than I had in 15 years. No wonder Dad was a big, fat pie-munching giant.

Janet could never possibly replace Mum but she was good to me and treated me well.

7 FARM LIFE

Shovelling shit and de-horning sheep . . . crashing the Chevy . . . and our abusive bird.

MOVING to Dad's farm was a life-changing experience. At Mum's house we had a black and white TV, shagged carpets, ripped wallpaper and very little money. The one thing I did have there, though, which was completely priceless, was my freedom. I could come and go just about as I pleased as long as I was in before 10pm.

Dad's was like going from the hustle and bustle of London to the isolation of the North Pole. Me and Kenny were street kids and very street-wise but at Upper Abbots Farm in Barkisland there was nothing but fields and cows – not really my thing.

I had no friends and all my mates lived 10 miles away. Plus Dad was only interested in me being a slave, not a teenage kid enjoying himself. I shovelled cow shit on a daily basis and got nowhere fast. All the other farmers in our area had a tractor, but not us.

Mal loved animals more than his own kids. I always said, 'if I go before him I'm coming back as one of his pets'. We had a buffalo called Billy, plus turkeys, horses, a llama, a fox, two monkeys, a wallaby and God knows what else. When you came home to the farm it was like Billy Smart's circus.

He always had loads of money in his pockets and he could buy and sell anything – from a Zimmer to a tandem. He made Del Boy look like a shy, retiring novice.

One day he said: "Come on, were going to de-horn some f****** sheep." I'm thinking, 'de-horn sheep, I can't even charge up a car battery!' My job was to burn the sheep's head while he held it still. F*** me, it stank! The crazy things we had to do.

Another day, we were rounding up our cows. My idea would be to carry out this task on foot, driving the cows towards the cowshed in a calm manner, so as not to frighten the animals. But not Big Mal. What he did was chase them around the fields, trying to head them off or confine them all in one corner. There were only two problems: 1) it had rained for about three days solid; and 2) we were doing about 65mph on grass in a 7.5 litre Chevrolet Blazer!

Before you knew it, we were fully locked up on the brakes, skidding uncontrollably towards a 5ft stone wall, which we took out big time. All Dad was concerned about was the damage to his pride and joy Chevy – which, to my amazement, amounted to nothing because it was built like a German tank.

Next job, Dad said: "Go start and move that Odyssey." Now the Odyssey was a fantastic custom-made van all painted by hand with pirate ships on it. This van was a show-stopper, the best I've ever seen to this day.

All winter it had been parked on a hill at the farm, facing down towards the stables. I jump in, turn it over, but there's nothing happening – just a dead battery and a little flicker on the dash. By now I was as sharp as a razor when it came to fixing motors. 'F*** this, I'll just bump it off' but still there was nothing. It didn't even move an inch. Everything was seized solid so back I went to Mal.

Now we had a massive gable end window and Dad's facing me. I'm looking out towards the window. "Dad, it won't go, it's all seized up and the battery's flat," I told him. Then, believe it or not, the van somehow managed to free itself – I must have forgot to put the handbrake on. The vehicle has rolled down the hill, and gone past the window. I've now got eyes like a Chihuahua, thinking, 'he's going to kill me'.

The van sailed right through the stables, smashing the front end. Talk about being in the shit. I was always in the shit – it was just the depth that varied.

After moving in at Dad's he converted the end barn for me. I had a room fully kitted out with a big Ferguson TV and video, a massive music player and a double bed. Next to my room I had my own shower, sink, toilet and sunbed, plus a table tennis table and a bar-cum-games room with pool table, fruit machine and a space invader machine, the lot.

On leaving school I started my first full-time job working for Dad but the only thing I was good at was washing cars – at 32 quid a week, which was good money back in 1980. Dad had about 10 people working for him – from Billy Moore the salesman, to Katie the cleaner. We also had a company mascot, a mynah bird, although to be honest it looked more like a blackbird to me.

And guess what the first and only word it ever said was? 'WANKER!' Everyone used to walk past the poor thing and shout 'wanker', so that's how it picked it up.

Kenny also worked for Dad as a mechanic after leaving school. We used to have motorbike races at the garage in Ovenden, which had a very big yard. Everyone had a go and although Dad took some beating, Kenny was the king. One day we let Granddad Willie have a go on a motorbike. He shot off at full speed with the throttle wide open and went straight through an asbestos garage. Luckily, he didn't hurt himself and all we could do was laugh.

Left: Dad and his second wife Janet. Right: Kenny riding Buffalo Billy at Mal's farm.

8 THE HASLAMS

Tragic Phil was like a son to Dad . . . blowing fish out of the water . . . 'Rocket' Ron and Howard Gregory . . . shot at by Randy Mamola . . . Donny Robinson and the scary Irish run . . . Mal falls out with Ron Haslam as factory teams take control . . . time for me to race . . . getting our revenge on cocky Kenny.

MAL began sponsoring riders through his Pharaoh Racing Team after he retired from racing in the early 70s. There were too many riders to mention them all here but the first big one he backed was Phil Haslam. Dad would tell me that Phil was the best rider he ever had and he treated him like a son.

Phil was involved in a fatal accident at the Oliver's Mount race track in Scarborough on Yorkshire's east coast in June 1974. I'm sure Dad told me that Phil's bike broke down and he was freewheeling to a halt when he started to look down at his Pharaoh Yamaha TZ250 to see what the problem was. It was in that moment that he was hit by one of his mates, Steve Machin.

In that same *Motorcycle Racing* magazine article I mentioned earlier, Dad spoke at length in the interview he gave about his sponsorship support of the Haslams. His plan was to back promising, talented riders who he felt had the ability and attitude to take on the big-name, factory sponsored riders such as Barry Sheene. By the start of 1977, when the interview was published, he had apparently ploughed about £60,000 of his own hard-earned money into sponsoring the brothers from the mining town of Langley Mill, Derbyshire.

Steve Machin was also one of the best riders in the country at the time and, as fate would have it, less than two weeks after Phil was killed, Steve also died in a racing accident, this time while testing a TD2 engine at the Cadwell Park track in Lincolnshire. Two of Britain's best riders were gone in less than a few weeks.

Dad and Phil Haslam became great friends after they raced against each other and when he talked about him it was always with the very highest regard. Mal told me he was one of the first people on the scene at Phil's accident and that his favourite rider died in his arms.

Once again, I quote from Ian Beacham's candid and in-depth interview with Dad in that 1977 issue of *Motorcycle Racing*. Mal said: "Phil Haslam was a superman, a match for anyone. The poor lad died in my arms. That was a terrible tragedy for me. It knackered my life up. I was never the same man. I had already lost a son and then it was like losing another one.

"I was like a father and I did everything for him but I always knew he'd get killed and I always felt he was too good to live. At night, when he'd be in one bed and I'd be in the other, I'd stay awake many a time looking at him and say to myself: 'You poor sod. What the hell are you doing it for?'

"The day Phil died, I walked down that 140 yards to the paddock and all I wanted was for Ron to ride for me. I wanted him to be Phil."

Mal sure did experience some horrific times.

By the time I started living at Dad's he'd been sponsoring Phil's brother 'Rocket Ron' Haslam for four or five years. Dad had got Ron flying on the 750cc Pharaoh Yamaha and pushed him into becoming one of the top riders in the country, in the premier class alongside legends like Barry Sheene, Dave Potter, Roger Marshall – who Dad also sponsored for a while – and Mick Grant. Ron went on to win four world championships, racing at the highest level for 30 years.

Sometimes Dad would take me to the Haslams' house and that was a shock. There was so many of them – talk about a big family. Ron Haslam told me that they didn't fish the conventional way. He explained how they'd fill a plastic bag with gas from welding bottles, float it down a river, then shoot the bag, which literally blew the fish out of the water.

He showed me how it was done by tying a bag filled with gas to a wall before shooting at it. Well, it shook the whole street as if a bomb had gone off. They were a rough, crazy bunch – a poor, illiterate family, but they seemed nice enough to me.

Ron liked the girls and once had three on the go at the same time. You never knew which one was going to turn up at the race meetings. No wonder he crashed a lot – come race day, he probably had no energy left to hang on to the bike!

The 70s were by far the best racing days of all. Seeing Sheene, Ron Haslam and the rest coming over Cadwell's notorious 'Mountain', watched by crowds of well over 50,000, was magical, pure heaven. And I was the luckiest kid in the world because I became the team's gofer, alongside Howard Gregory, one of the greatest mechanics of all-time. All the bikes were race-prepared on the farm by Howard, who would later be part of Kenny Roberts' team for almost 20 years. He was also Wayne Rainey's mechanic when he won his three world titles between 1990 and 1992, and established himself as one of the sport's top mechanics.

Little did I know as a 15-year-old at the time that Howard would also become my mechanic in the 80s.

But just like working at the garage, I wasn't much better as the Pharaoh Racing team's gofer. We had a big international meeting at Cadwell Park one summer and we had massive race awnings power-supplied by Honda generators. Ours ran out or fuel, causing all the lights to go out, so we couldn't see a thing.

Howard told me to go fill it up, so I got some petrol but couldn't see where I was pouring it. So what did 'Brains' do? Light a match! F*** me, the whole place went up. I don't know, maybe I should have been sectioned at birth and sent to a loony bin.

Then there was the time I pushed the bike to scrutineering, lost my balance and dropped it. I looked and felt a right knob as the bike crashed to the ground. I had a black belt in f***-ups. It's true, if pricks could fly I'd have been a squadron leader.

Light in the Darkness

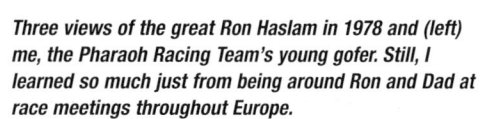

Three views of the great Ron Haslam in 1978 and (left) me, the Pharaoh Racing Team's young gofer. Still, I learned so much just from being around Ron and Dad at race meetings throughout Europe.

ALAN CARTER

Early days and how I hated wearing that orange novice jacket.

Above: With a proud Gran, my biggest fan, after a win.
Right: Two action shots of me leading at Donington.

Light in the Darkness

Dad gave me a new ty80 Yamaha, with unlimited fuel, to play on at all the race meetings. I ripped around for hours in those days, a time when there was land around the tracks for man and beast to explore. I'd ride through the woodlands, pretending to be Sheene or Giacomo Agostini and dreaming of hitting the big-time myself one day.

We had trips to far away countries like Holland, France and Italy. On one trip to Italy I was shot at by an ugly, freckled-faced kid who turned out to be Randy Mamola, who had purchased a BB air gun in his native USA. He was 17 at the time and they wouldn't let him ride. How times changed – he went on to finish world number two in the 500cc GP world championships.

We're talking about the 'good old days'. Remember pulling the choke out to start your car – and how it pissed you off as the engine fired away forever before finally bursting into life.

There was no remote control for the TV, you had to get your arse out of the chair just to turn the telly over . . . and tune into more rubbish on BBC1, BBC2 and ITV, with all three channels – yes, only three – finishing at about 11.30 before the test card appeared on screen.

When the first mobile phone came out, my mate slipped a disc carrying it. Fish and chips cost 12p but nowadays you need a Visa card to pay. All you needed as a kid was 10p for a bag of sweets. I used to say to Dougie, the bloke who owned our local newsagent's: 'How much are your penny sweets?' He'd look at me as if to say, 'f*** off, yer cheeky little sod, I've just told you they're all a penny'.

We did a big race meeting at the Paul Ricard circuit at Le Castellet, near Marseille in the south of France, where Ron was racing. I rode up and down all day long on my ty80 but I must have been driving some bloke crazy because, unbeknown to me, he tied a rope across the road. It was orange and because the sun was blazing down, I didn't see it. I was thrown off the bike, ripping my face open and knocking all my teeth out in the process. I spent two weeks in a Toulon hospital but it was no problem – I was soon back home in Yorkshire and riding my bike again. These were the most amazing times of my life.

Mal started to help a great Irish racer called Donny Robinson, a GP contender who was doing some world championship rounds as well as the UK series. Donny lived with us for a time on the farm and he was the nicest rider I ever met. He would take me on trips to Northern Ireland in his old transit van, telling me great stories about racing all over the world.

Every time we hit the A75 to Stranraer, where we'd board the ferry to Belfast, he would attempt some crazy overtaking manoeuvre on blind hills, only for an articulated lorry to be coming head on for us. While I sat there shitting myself, thinking he was going to kill us both, he just calmly whistled away without a care in the world.

ALAN CARTER

One day Mal said to me: "How would you fancy having a go, kid?"

I was like, 'sure, great!' but he said: "Well, it's like this. If yer f****** crap, forget it. OK?"

It was around this time that Dad fell out with Ron, when Honda lured Ron to them and gave him an ultimatum: either join us or stay as part of Mal's Pharaoh Racing Team. Ron chose to switch to Honda UK and he and Dad didn't speak to each other for a few years over it. When the main factory teams were no longer run by 'old school' bosses and had been taken over by a new breed of management, none of them liked Dad because of his aggressive attitude.

Honda UK used to be headed by Eric Sulley but when he moved on, Dad hated his successor, Barry Symons. I was with Mal the day he pulled into the Leicester Forrest services and saw Symons eating a meal. He resented him so much he threatened to beat him up.

When he arrived at a race track and men on the pits gate would ask Mal to show his pass, he'd simply point to his face and say: "That's my f****** pass, don't you know who I am?" Sometimes he'd threaten them. Occasionally, he might even hit them.

In the 70s and early 80s, Dad was one of just a few top road-racing sponsors on the scene, a small group of men who'd made big money through business and were now spending it in road-racing. The other benefactors were Ted Broad, who sponsored a rider called Dave Potter, Dave Orton of Appleby Glade, a company that sold fruit machines and supported John Newbold and Steve Henshaw, and then there was Harold Coppock, a Wiltshire chicken farmer who also sponsored top riders.

Dad spent a stupidly colossal amount helping the Haslams and this quote from a magazine article on Dad at the beginning of 1977 summed it up perfectly: "I work 14 hours a day to keep Ron Haslam riding. The money I throw away on that side of the job is just not true."

He was happy to plough so much cash into sponsorship of the Haslams because, as he stated, it was his ambition to "stuff the factory teams" and he was all for helping underdogs who showed drive and ambition.

The Jaguar Daimler that Ron drove around in the mid-70s was supplied by Mal free of charge, and father also sent him to America to learn more about the Yamaha engines and set-ups.

As well as backing Phil before he was killed and then Ron, the father of current world superbike star Leon Haslam, Dad also sponsored Ron's brother Terry – a sidecar racer who was killed racing at Assen, Holland in 1984.

When Dad first got behind Ron the long-haired racer was being offered just £20 per meeting to start but Mal pushed hard to get him an increase and before long he was earning £400 a start. One deal he did for Ron was worth more than £150k, only for Mal to be pushed aside when the big money came rolling in from the likes of Honda.

Thanks to Dad's loyal backing and his own racing ability, Ron had become a big star in the late 70s, earning money he'd never even dreamed of before. He went on

Light in the Darkness

to become a racing legend, winning three world championships, four British titles and countless other meetings in a great career spanning some 30 years.

But many years later, when I was skint and needed a job, I approached Ron and his wife Ann to work for them at their racing school. They didn't even have the courtesy to give me a call back, which felt like a big kick in the teeth. Without Dad, Ron would still have been a dole waller from Langley Mill.

Pharaoh Racing sponsored many riders over the years and Dad lived for it. He'd made big money in business and spent the lot pursuing his passion for racing motorbikes. But, looking back, he had been foolish and too free-spending, something I know he later regretted.

The start of my career coincided with Dad's split from Ron Haslam and it meant my father's active interest in the sport was maintained through me. Mal got me a 250cc Yamaha and a 350 Yam and off we went to Cadwell Park every Thursday for about six months to practice. In the beginning I was a bit slow – even Kenny was faster than me – but I was just a kid of 15 and had no racing experience at all.

Lots of top riders turned up at these practice days. All you did was pay your cash and start riding. There was bucket-loads of advice, help and support. You see I was a novice, no threat to anyone, so I soaked up everything people told me like a giant sponge. Just like my big brother, I was a fast learner.

I had my two new racing bikes ready to rock and I was getting faster and faster on Cadwell's practice track. One day we turned up there with a horsebox full of race bikes – you should have seen people's faces. The only reason I didn't race in the early part of 1980 was because you had to be 16 to hold a licence.

I'd been living at Dad's for nearly a year and my 16th birthday was coming up in August. By then I was very happy working at the garage and I had a new girlfriend, Mandy Slater. She was a lovely girl but she had her own problems to cope with. Her father had taken his own life shortly before we met. We were young teenagers in love, there to comfort each other. Many times Mandy would walk a mile from where she lived at Norland across Barkisland moor in the pitch black, just to visit me at Dad's farm. She must have been mad because it was a scary journey after dark, one I'd never make, and I feared the day she'd call me names, saying I was a big cissy.

We saw each other for probably just short of a couple of years. I'd gone from being a street kid to the life of a Hillbilly living on a farm and the only chance of getting a shag at that stage was with sheep! So Mandy was a great girlfriend and companion.

My first race meeting was at Cadwell Park in August 1980 and when I went out to practice before my opening race, there was carnage. All I'd done previously was ride round the practice track with a few people but the main track had a different hairpin, much harder than the practice version. You can practice on test days all you want but being in a proper racing environment is like chalk and cheese. I felt like I was just getting in everyone's way.

Race 1:

Before my first race I decided to walk near the start line in the lunch break, to weigh everything up and plan my strategy. There was a left kink into a right hairpin and I figured I'd go around it flat out, dive on the brakes, round the hairpin, and off winning my first ever race. But boy was I in for a big shock.

I came round the kink so fast I had a massive crash, although I was OK and nothing was broken. A GP racer would have picked off one rider at a time. Being very calculating is the key to being a great racer but this was my first day and I was determined to taste glory.

Race 2:

It gets better. I made a crap start and tried to pass eight riders in one go up through Charles Corner. The others looked to be going too slow to me, so I past them on the outside. Anyway I lost the front end and that was my second crash. Luckily, the only thing seriously hurt was my pride, although my brand new 350cc and me looked like we'd done 10 rounds with Marvin Haggler.

Over the years it seemed that when I crashed, I always bounced back up with no major damage, whereas Kenny seemed to break bones whenever he crashed on the speedway. I once knocked Kenny off his Suzuki 185 trail bike when we were messing about pulling wheelies and he broke his scaphoid.

So here we were, back in the pits. The bike's knackered and so am I. The only person I could see having a great day was the guy who sold the track spares – he must have been rubbing his hands with glee when I started racing.

Race 3:

The boys race-prepped the bike for the final outing – well, what was left of it because there was no fairing or screen, just half a seat and a dipshit rider.

So here we go . . . race three and Carter's on it – but not for long. By now people were saying I'd got more chance of shagging Pope John Paul than finishing a race. And you know what, they were right . . . another crash!

That was the end of my first meeting. I showed lots of balls but not much brains.

And there was worse to come – I still had to face one of Halifax's hardest men, Big Mal. I was shitting it, and all things were going through my head – from the idea of running away to jumping off a bridge. He gave me the biggest bollocking ever and told me that if I didn't calm down he'd take all the bikes away. That did the trick. From then on, I did calm down and from August 1980 to the season's end I got my head down, stayed on the bike and gained as much experience as I could.

One kid I envied at the races was John Siedel. He was a Cadwell Park track specialist but, to me, he was the fastest racer in the world over two days. He'd win 12 races – a full clean sweep – most weekends. I remember once spying on him at Cadwell. He came out of the office fully loaded with trophies and with the biggest, cheesiest grin on his face. Fair play to him, he was doing it and doing it well.

I kept thinking, 'one day that's going to be me' – and you know what? It was. I can't tell you how amazing it felt to be the man – well, at least I was as far as club racing goes.

Light in the Darkness

By the end of 1980, Kenny had become an England regular and it was obvious how proud he was to represent his country. To make the riders feel even prouder to wear the three lions on their chest, the management duo of Ian Thomas and Eric Boocock insisted their men should all look smart in new blazers, shirts and ties, which they were told to wear to all their Test matches and World Team Cup meetings.

Well, me Welsey and Eggis had all taken plenty of shit over the years from Kenny and his mates, who would either beat us up or tape our legs, hands and heads together with gaffer tape. To put it bluntly, they acted like right bastards towards us. But now we were getting bigger and stronger ourselves, all reaching the age of 16, and we'd taken enough.

One day Kenny came into my bedroom and said: "Look at my new England kit." He was wearing a dark new blazer, tie, red lamb's wool V-neck jumper, pants and new shoes. "I'm in the England team now," he says, bold as brass.

There's me thinking, 'cocky bastard, like we really give a shit'. We looked at each other and were all thinking the same thing. 'Let's do the prick', so we jumped him, ripped his shirt and jumper clean off his back and by the time we finished with him he looked like he'd done 10 rounds with Mike Tyson. We gave him a right ruffling up that night.

This is one of my greatest memories of my big brother. His face was a picture and I could see front page headlines in *The Halifax Courier*: 'King Kenny Gets Pasting From Teenage Thugs'.

Ace!

*Phil Haslam died after striking the steel frame of a bridge. His bike spluttered and cut out as he attempted to accelerate uphill out of 'Mere Hairpin'. Phil raised his left arm to indicate he was stopping and he was about three feet from the track's edge as his handlebar was clipped by Derek Chatterton, sending Phil towards the other side of the track and directly into the path of Steve Machin, who hit Phil and went right over the top of him and his stricken machine. Tragically, Phil suffered very serious neck injuries and died trackside due to heavy loss of blood, although the combination of the sun in his eyes, the track surface, and the large field all fighting for the limited space available would have attributed to his death also.

Courtesy of the website: www.tz350.net

Kenny on the pre-meeting parade before the 1981 World Final at Wembley.

9 Wembley

England's next big hope . . . Ivan Mauger helps Kenny on World Final debut . . . Mighty Mouse hits the big-time with first major win at Mondello Park . . . Kenny and Pam get married . . . Banged up in Halifax nick.

THE 1981 season was going to be a massive year for me and Kenny. By now he was already a big star, the undisputed No.1 at Halifax and set to qualify for his first individual World Final at Wembley at the end of the year.

He had a great mechanic in Richard Pickering, sponsorship from Mal and factory support from British engine manufacturers Weslake. All in all, things were looking very good for our Kenny, who became an England regular and recognised as the country's next big hope after Michael Lee, who had gone off the rails a bit by then.

I was starting my first full year of road-racing after amassing enough points at the end of 1980 to lose my orange novice jacket status, which I hated wearing. I was far too good for that but the rules were the same for everyone.

Despite a bad crash at Halifax in early April in which he shattered his jaw, Kenny still qualified through the various rounds for his first World Final in September. We all got down to London early, piled in the hotel room and had a great time. On the afternoon of the meeting at Wembley I remember going for a walk to kill time and feeling very nervous. I don't know why, maybe it's just a racer's thing.

The first thing that hit me was the crowd, it was electric. I was used to massive crowds at road-racing meetings I'd attended with Ron Haslam and Dad all over Europe – and that's what turned me on. I wanted the big-time, just like Kenny, and I was going to make it at any cost.

Kenny rode fantastically well that night and only an engine failure cost him a top three placing. He was the only rider to beat Bruce Penhall all night, although the American could afford to finish second to my brother when they met in their last race and still clinch his first world title.

Kenny had the legendary six times world champion Ivan Mauger helping him in the Wembley pits and the Kiwi legend began having quite an influence over him at the end of the '81 season. I don't know whose idea it was to bring Ivan in. It was probably Kenny's, because I'm sure Dad would have resented Ivan's presence. He would have viewed him as an imposter.

But fifth place on his World Final debut wasn't bad at all for a 20-year-old. In fact it was brilliant. But we were never happy unless we won, which spoiled some of the success we both had. We'd have raced 24 hours a day, every day, if we could. We just loved it. Winning wasn't everything to us, it was the only thing. I left the sport feeling like I'd massively under-achieved and I'm sure Kenny would have had the

ALAN CARTER

Flat out at Donington in 1981.

same feelings too.

Kenny was now someone to fear on any speedway track. He was one fast kid and his large following of supporters was growing by the day. What we Carters lacked in experience we made up for with guts. We had more front than Brighton.

I rose through the club scene, the bottom level of road-racing, faster than a dose of the shits. Towards the end of '81 Mal told me that we were off to Ireland.

By now I was going OK, doing well at tracks like Cadwell Park and Donington circuit in Derbyshire, but I was pretty average at Mallory Park, Oulton Park and the rest. So here we go again, sailing to Ireland, which seemed a faraway land. The first thing I noticed on arrival was their funny accent, which I found difficult to understand. Then there was the drinking. I couldn't keep up with the locals – two shandies and I was legless. But what a fantastic time I had in Ireland, where the people were just so friendly, the food amazing, and they know how to look after you.

My first big race was at the Mondello Park track in County Kildare, about 40kms from Dublin. The meeting featured some big names, including Mick Grant, Joey Dunlop, big, fat George Farlow (oops, sorry George!) and the rest of Ireland's racing cream.

Things didn't start too well in practice but, not to worry, we had a few days to get things right. We had a bottom end gear box problem and a top end seizure. We burned the midnight oil working through the night to fix things. Well, my lads did. I was probably shagging somewhere. Anyway, we got everything sorted for the morning of the race. Oh, by the way, I almost forgot . . . Dad gave me a great nickname. I was no longer plain Alan Carter, I became known as 'Mighty Mouse' – and I loved it. I was really small in those days, weighing only about eight stone, so I guess that's why he came up with that name.

Light in the Darkness

Going out for practice was fun. I had about as much grip as a dog on lino. Eggis, the dozy sod, had forgotten to put the oil drain bungs in the engine, so my bike was dropping oil all over the track just before the hairpin. People were going down like a plumber's tool bag. Eight crashed on this one corner alone and just about the only kid that didn't fall was me.

Back in the pits the riders were queuing up to lynch me but I just hid behind Mal. That sorted it. Things calmed down but I was a non-qualifier. Dad went off to see the organisers, to see what he could sort out, and he returned soon enough to say: "Right kid, yer in."

So here I am, the biggest race of my life. That's great news. But the catch was I had to start from the back because I was a non-qualifier. And in those days there were about 40 riders in front of me on the grid, not the 17 you see line up for Moto GPs today.

Not only did I get to start, I won the biggest race of my life from the back of the grid. How I did it, I don't know. All that mattered to me was that the Carters had come and conquered Ireland, beating some of their greatest, along with Mick Grant, a winner of many grand prix races. What a day. I'd just become the youngest ever rider to win a national race at 16.

There was a massive crowd watching that day and they just took me to their hearts because I'd put on a fantastic show. The winner's trophy was bigger than me and as an added bonus I won some cash too.

That night we had a right, old knees-up and everyone got drunk. I'd had a little taste of the big-time and I loved it.

Me and Kenny took to winning and new-found fame like ducks to water. We had everything in our grasp and nothing fazed us. And Dad was the best sponsor we ever had. When we crashed and bent our bikes, we just got 'em fixed. He was pumping in cash all the time from what seemed like a bottomless pit of money.

In '81 Dad got us both brand new Mazda Luton vans with very high roofs. We looked like Warburton's delivery boys, not tough motorcycle racers, until Kenny tried to modify his. By 'modify' I mean he pulled into a petrol station that had a very low roof and ripped the roof of his van clean off. Yeah, it was always great when Kenny f***** up instead of me.

We'd both had a great year in 1981, with Kenny near the top of the league averages and world number five and me having won my first national in Ireland. To round the year off in style, Kenny got married to Pamela Lund in Halifax on November 7, with me and her brother Adrian sharing the Best Man duties.

Kenny picked out hand-made suits for us to wear, which cost a fortune, but they didn't feel good on.

There were a couple of girls at school, best mates called Bev and Vicky, who worshipped Kenny and I would have put my life on him marrying either one of them. So it was a bit of a shock to me when he started going out with Pam. But they looked happy together on their big day.

ALAN CARTER

Kenny and Pam's wedding day In November 1981.

Right: Kenny making his point alongside Mal and me.

Below: The happy couple and Best Man. We could be laughing about our suits.

Light in the Darkness

I can't say that the wedding ended in a family fight that is typical of many weddings. Yes, Mal could start a brawl anywhere but Kenny and me weren't like him, or the notorious Briggs family in Halifax, who were always in trouble. Kenny and I could be a bit gobby but we didn't start trouble. All we cared about were motorbikes. The fame, women, fast cars and money went hand in hand with success.

I got on well with Pam's dad, Bob, who worshipped Kenny and followed him to speedway meetings all over the country. Although I found Veronica, Pam's mum, a more negative, cynical type of woman. But unlike the situation where my mum's parents tried to put her off marrying Mal, the Lunds were very happy for their daughter to be marrying our Kenny.

In the winter of '81 I continued to work for Dad at the garage and following the success I'd had on the track it's fair to say I became a bit cocky, to say the least. Mal's best mate was Brian Monaghan, Halifax's warrant officer. A massive guy, Brian had often busted Dad in his youth for fighting or something but he took a liking to Mal at some point and they became best mates for over 40 years.

One Friday I must have being gobbing off at the garage in front of Dad, boasting how I'd be out on the pull that night and again on Saturday and Sunday, too – Halifax used to be a great night out in the early 80s.

But Mal had other plans for me. He said to his pal: "Hey Brian, can yer lock our Alan up tonight, the wanker's telling me what a great weekend it's going to be."

It was about 4.30, nearly home time, when Brian walks in and says: "You're under arrest."

"What me?"

"Yeah, non-payment of a speeding fine. Come with me," Brian says. "There's no bail. You're in court on Monday morning."

Honest, my life collapsed in two seconds.

Down at the nick, it was a case of shoes and belt off and 'get in the cell boy'. I'm shitting it now and as time goes by I'm thinking, 'all my mates are out and the lovely young girls are too. What a prick I am, stuck here in a cell with tears in my eyes', thinking how much life sucks.

A few hours pass and Brian returns to check on me. "F****** hell, kid, wait till midnight . . ."

I'm like, 'f***, what happens at midnight?'

Brian says all the prozzies will be in then, plus the rapists and drunken c**** pissing and shitting everywhere!

Now I'm really crapping myself. A few minutes later Brian returns to my cell again with a big grin. "Come on, kid, it's all been a joke – yer Dad's set you up, you're free to go."

Talk about relief, I must have been the happiest kid in Halifax by the end of that night. This episode sure made me value my freedom. But Dad and Brian were a right pair of bastards and I sure kept on the straight and narrow for a very long time.

Many times the local police would call in at our garages just for a coffee and at

ALAN CARTER

Above: To see Pam and Kenny as happy as this makes the tragic events of four-and-a-half years later even harder to comprehend.

Right: Kenny and me at the church.

Christmas they'd all have a few drinks at Pharaoh Garage. Some even got a little tipsy on these occasions and the bobbies would get out their breathalysers and test each over to see if they were too pissed to drive home. And many times they were, but that's what it was like in those days.

10 THE MONEY MACHINE

CB radios by the lorry load . . . spoon-fighting parties . . . riders who visited the farm . . . gone fishing with Big Mal.

THE period from around 1979 to 1982 was known to us as the Mal Carter goldrush days – and Dad hit the jackpot with a new craze that began sweeping Britain.

Dad had been doing great in the 70s, wheeling and dealing, and we never knew what was coming and going next – from fruit machines to wild animals. One day four brand new Range Rover engines appeared! But this was small fry to what was about to happen.

It was the dawn of CB radios.

Mal being Mal, we didn't buy just a few, we took delivery of them in arctic truck loads, mostly arriving at night after dark.

CBs (Citizens' Band Radios) became massive in the UK and, naturally, Dad became one of the main players when it came to selling these devices that enabled individuals to communicate with each other over short distances while on the road.

Unbeknown to me at the time, this was an illegal operation and all I ever did was help to unload the trucks and count the money that came rolling in from sales. We had bin liners full of cash. Talk about pikies, we had some right characters coming to the farm to pick up their stock and make plenty of money for themselves.

Dad's CB 'handle' – the name a person used on the two-way radio service – was 'Rough Diamond'. Mine was 'Superstar'.

The parties we had were legendary. Janet would put on a spread fit for a king and I'd watch some of Dad's party games. 'Spoon fighting' involved two drunken men sat on chairs with about 50 people watching them and a dessert spoon in their gob. They both took it in turn to bend over and hit each other over the head with the spoon. It never hurt because you couldn't grip the spoon with your teeth to get any power into it but, as usual, it was all a set-up.

I would get hit and fake severe pain from the blow, then glare at my opponent as if to say: 'Right, you bastard, yer having it now'. When it was my turn to strike, some poor pissed-up guy would bend over and then one of my sisters would appear from nowhere and whack them over the head with a chef's industrial serving spoon, which hurt like hell.

One party ended like a shootout at the OK Corral, with Mal pasting several of the invited guests in the barn. They never came back again, although I never knew what that was all about.

Dad became great mates with a guy called Oliver Tobias, some sort of actor who

ALAN CARTER

Big Mal wheeling and dealing.

Light in the Darkness

looked like a scruffy pikie to me.

One day I was teasing our pet llama in the field on my xr75, as I did most nights. I always got away from it just in time but not this particular time. It had been raining hard and I had no grip, so I slipped off the bike and the llama took a big chunk out of my back. I fully deserved it because I'd been tormenting the animal. When I told Mal all about it, he said he'd "sort the bastard out" – and he did. He shot its head clean off with a gun while I just stood there in shock.

We had a very aggressive cockerel that kept going for us, so Mal said: "One day I'm going to sort that bastard." We were working on the race bikes with the doors open and Mal walked past with the dead cockerel over his shoulder. He must have wrung its neck. We all looked at each other and knew not to f*** with Big Mal or we might be next on his hit list. That's how scared we were of him, and many other people were too.

If you wanted to ride for Mal Carter's racing team you needed to be a hard bastard, I can tell you. Talk about make or break you, if you survived Dad you were on your way. He gave backing to many racers, including Alex George, a nice Scottish guy and a top TT racer who Mal sponsored for a while.

One day some young Aussie kid called Wayne Gardner turned up, so me, Donny Robinson and Wayne took off in the van to go racing at Knockhill in Fife, Scotland. We went up so many bloody steep hills to get there that I kept complaining: "We're only doing 20mph – I can run there faster." Pissed off by now at my constant moaning, Wayne said: "Well, get out there and do it," so I did. To my amazement, I wasn't fast enough to keep up with the guys in the van, so Wayne and Donny pissed off and left me in some remote part of the Scottish mountains. Me and my big mouth again.

One racer who turned up at the farm was John Williams. The thing about John was that he was black – and no-one had ever seen a black racer before. Mal gave him this fantastic greeting on arrival: "Now here, you black bastard, what do you want?" In today's politically correct and multi-cultural world he would have been locked up for life.

John had come over from the USA seeking fame and fortune. We took him down to Cadwell Park to give him a try out and he was fantastic. He weighed the track up instantly and posted superb lap times. Watching him ride on those practice days was pure magic. He had a fantastic riding style, just like Freddie Spencer.

Mal signed John for his team and for a time on the farm he called him everything – soap dodger, coon, the lot. I felt really sorry for John but you could never say anything to Dad. He only had one answer: "Shut up or I'll give you a right crack, too."

John raced in the UK but with Mal pushing him far too hard, he started to crash his brains out every meeting before losing confidence and returned to the USA a broken man. John was a really lovely person whose company I enjoyed. It was such a shame for him that he didn't fulfil his potential.

Chris Guy was another top rider, super-fit, very dedicated and with dreams of making it big. The girls loved him, too, the lucky bugger. One day Chris said to Mal:

Dad getting his message across to Kenny, who seems to be surrendering under the pressure.

"Fancy a day out sea fishing, my dad's got a big boat in Cornwall?"

Dad and I met Chris at Salcombe Bay in south Devon. There's me thinking we'll be going out on some little shit boat but it turned out to be a massive sailing boat, the kind Columbus would have picked to go around the world in. All I'd ever been on before this were the rowing boats in Shibden Hall, a historic place near Halifax, but now I was sailing in the English Channel thinking I'm Captain Pugwash, king of the seas.

We got the fishing tackle set up but Chris and me caught nothing, not even a tadpole, and we were as sick as dogs all day. Not Big Mal, though. He caught what seemed like half the fish in the Channel on that sunny day in the west country.

That night Mal filleted the fresh mackerel he'd caught and made me and Chris one of the tastiest suppers I've ever had. Dad loved his food and fishing was a great hobby for him. When he had the time, he particularly loved sea fishing in Florida, and going for the biggest catch in the ocean was a challenge he always relished.

11 THE ART OF SPEEDWAY

It's harder than it looks . . . big crowds and flying shale . . . writing off Kenny's bike . . . and crashing his car . . . a hard case who nutted 45 gallon steel drums . . . pulling strokes in the pro-am series . . . single-minded approach . . . and why speedway wasn't for me.

BY the start of the 1982 season Kenny and I were raring to get back out there. I was moving up to national level, where most of the top guys raced as a kind of warm-up before they went on to the world championships and big international meetings around the world.

I did well to finish in the top 12 because, to be honest, I was out of my league when it came to winning races. Some of these guys were qualifying right at the sharp end of the world championships and I could see that I had a long way to go to get to the very top. I would practice each Thursday and did two meetings every weekend. And sometimes I'd ride at two tracks in a weekend, so at that stage of my career I was getting more track time than anyone else in the UK.

Kenny would practice and test his bikes as often as possible too. He could use the fast steeply-banked Halifax track just about as often as he wanted.

Kenny and I made regular Saturday morning trips to Ellesmere Port Speedway to test his bikes. One day we were there and some kid pulled a wheelie down the back straight and it was my turn next to have a go out on track, so I told Kenny and my mates: "Watch this, I'm now going to pull the greatest wheelie in speedway history."

Not quite. I hit the floor like a bag of shit, writing off Kenny's number one bike in the process.

The first thing about a speedway bike that I could never get to grips with was the fact that they have no brakes or gears. It was just a 'drop-the-clutch-rev-it-and-go type of thing. I didn't really see any art to it at first but when I tried it for myself, I realised that it's nowhere near as easy as it looks.

I'll try and put the difference between speedway and road-racing in layman's terms. With a road-racing bike, you come into the corner and peel in, whereas with a speedway bike you throw it in, flicking the back end out. The closer you go towards the safety fence, the more you need to wind on the throttle so that the bike takes you *away* from the fence. But in my experience as a road-racer, whenever I headed towards the outside of the track, the more I panicked and would shut the throttle off. It was the natural thing for a road-racer to do.

So when I tried to apply the same technique at Ellesmere Port that I used in road-racing, I got into trouble on the corners. I found speedway to be a lot harder than it looks. The four riders come into the corners flat out, with their back wheels spinning and then have to look for the dirt to find more grip . . . I just couldn't figure it out.

ALAN CARTER

Kenny and his Halifax team-mate Steve Baker leading Belle Vue's Louis Carr at The Shay in 1982.

I crashed on Kenny's speedway bikes while practicing at Ellesmere Port, Halifax and Belle Vue. I found the fence intimidating and more often than not, I went through it or under it.

Funnily enough, Mal told me that the first time Kenny went round Halifax on a speedway bike at the age of 15, I went quicker than him when I had a go at The Shay for the first time a few years later.

After having a got at it myself I certainly had more respect for what it took to be a good speedway rider but the shale sport still never appealed to me from a riding aspect. You get mucky and it's all over and done with in a minute.

In road-racing, I could screw up the start and know that I still had 18, 26 or 32 laps to work my way through the pack and pass the other riders. If you make a cock-up at the gate in speedway, you're knackered – your race is effectively over before its really even begun.

At speedway, the pits were usually dark, dirty places. Riders were cramped together with puddles and muck all around them, while having to make adjustments

Light in the Darkness

to their bike. This never appealed to me. I'd get out of the bad weather by retreating to my motorhome or relax in a posh caravan while drinking coffee and reading a magazine.

What I loved about speedway when Kenny was riding were the fans and the whole atmosphere they created inside the stadium. I liked the shale coming over the fence and hitting me. I'd stand right next to the boards on the fourth turn terracing and then duck down as the four riders flew past, just inches away.

The times I spent watching him race at The Shay were some of the best nights of my life.

At Halifax, I'd go to the track shop and enjoy looking at the little badges and rosettes. Chris Pusey was my favourite – he was known as the 'Polka Dot Kid' in his younger days and had distinctive spots on his leathers and looked real cool, if a bit rough and ready.

I also loved watching the likes of Bruce Penhall, Erik Gundersen, the Moran brothers, Kelly and Shawn, and Tommy Knudsen.

Kenny took over the souvenir kiosk at Halifax once he'd become the big star there and fans could buy just about anything with his name on it. It was great at the time but it seemed a bit eerie seeing Dukes' supporters walking round Halifax wearing a Kenny Carter Racing jacket 20 years after he died.

The only personalised merchandise I sold in road-racing was 'Alan Carter Mighty Mouse' T-shirts, which is what many of my fans wore to race meetings. One of Ron Haslam's sisters used to sell them for me.

We had some fun up on Merseyside at Ellesmere Port, where there was a rumour going around about a guy called Bobby Bell. He was a massive bloke, a member of the track staff, I think, and a real character. His speciality was nutting 45 gallon steel drums. I was like, 'no way – bollocks he can' and, being the cheeky little sod that I was, I challenged him to show me his party trick. He looked at me with sheer rage in his eyes and I almost died on the spot.

But he proved the rumours correct. We were at the back of the pits when he threw this drum 10 feet in the air and nutted it a distance of some 20 feet. I was gobsmacked, we all just stood there in amazement at what this hulk of a man could

ALAN CARTER

do with his forehead.

Apparently, Newcastle's Kiwi rider Graeme Stapleton was giving Bobby Bell some lip at Ellesmere Port one night and he just laid him out with one punch. He was mad.

Kenny and me were very competitive and our racing rivalry wasn't confined to the track either. One day he said 'let's race to The Shay' and it was like Santa Pod as he beat me by about 50 yards. 'Bastard's done me again,' I thought. Going up to the stadium gates he did a handbrake turn to the left, parking sideways next to the gate.

I was thinking I'd do the same as our Ken, so the front ends of our cars would be nearly touching, but I got it wrong and wiped out the front of a parked Capri and smashed all the back of my new VW Scirocco. Once again Kenny laughed at my expense.

Kenny had the best cars all the time and boy could he drive. One day I asked to borrow his XR3 Ford Escort so that I could go for a spin in it with my mate Doug. "OK, but don't crash it," he said. Just like me, Kenny was right funny about his stuff, it always had to be in tip-top condition. So off we went, me and Doug burning around having a great time in this mint blue XR3.

We were on our way to Gran's for one of her tasty milky coffees. I was co-pilot when I decided to rip the handbrake on for a laugh. Well, we hit the curb, bent a wishbone and f***** the rear alloy wheel. All day Doug and I dreaded breaking the bad news to Kenny but then we decided to see if we could nick a replacement wheel instead and fit it without him knowing any different. We tried the car park of a squash club and – bingo! – someone was in for a shock. We jacked up this XR3, nicked a rear wheel and did one as fast as Geronimo on horseback. Sorted.

I can just imagine some old giffa coming out of the country club, starting the engine and then – bang! – his car dropping to the ground. I still feel bad about what we did that night. We didn't even put our cracked wheel on for him, we just pissed off as fast as we could and that was the end of that.

In July 1982 I rode in a national meeting at Cadwell Park. I was racing a 350cc Yamaha against 500cc bikes with riders like Paul Iddon and Rob McElnea and many more on semi-factory bikes. They would pass me down the straights, only for me to be all over them around the bends and sometimes out-braking them. This happened until I suddenly crashed coming up The Mountain and broke my collarbone.

Two weeks on and I had another big crash, when my gear box locked up and spat me down the road at Oulton Park. It put me back in Halifax Hospital for a right talking to from the nurses, who tried to stop me racing again so soon after my crash at Cadwell Park. At least I had Eggis, my best mate, looking after me, bringing me sweets, crisps and videos most days. We joined a video club, the first one in Yorkshire, for 20 quid, which was a week's wages for many. What a guy Eggis is. He's stood by me for over 20 years, being a rock in my life.

In 1980 Mitsui Yamaha introduced the legendary 350 Pro-Am series, a televised championship at major British race meetings to promote the then recently launched

Light in the Darkness

Kenny congratulating me at my 18th birthday party in 1982.

Yamaha RD350LC. Twenty four riders – 12 established and 12 rookies – were chosen by a panel of experts, then given a completely free season of racing with a very generous prize fund thrown in. Yamaha provided everything – all you had to do was turn up and ride.

All the bikes were meant to be the same. You pulled a key from a hat and they were all numbered and that was it – you kept that bike for the weekend. I took a liking to a certain bike, so I asked one of the guys at Yamaha if I could put my hand in the bag while already holding the key of my choice in my hand. "Yes, no problem at all," he agreed. It was amazing what people would do for you if you just got along with everyone. I don't think anyone suspected.

I was a cheeky little bugger but I could get away with murder, especially with the girls who conducted the ballots for starting grid positions. If I pulled out one that I didn't like, I just dropped it back in the bag and picked another one – and have a giggle with them as I did it.

To keep everyone in the dark about this secret deal with Yamaha, my mechanics changed the number plate on the bike so that it corresponded with the key I was holding. The Yamaha Pro-Am series produced some amazing racing and I just loved the bike too.

Just to make sure I got plenty of time on one, Dad got me an rd350lc to use on the road and zip about on. Just remember, there's no such thing as a level playing field. Dad could pull more strokes than the Oxford rowing team, and we were always one plan ahead of everyone – or so we thought.

ALAN CARTER

*Kenny loved racing against and beating the Americans. These first bend action shots were taken at the England v USA Test at Belle Vue in 1982. Above: Kenny (outside) and Andy Grahame challenge Shawn Moran.
Below: This time Kenny and Andy are getting the better of Bruce Penhall (outside) and Bobby Schwartz.*

Light in the Darkness

My first race in the pro-am was at Cadwell Park. Most of these races were won by inches. I loved winning and everything about it . . . waving to the fans at the end of the race, getting the winner's laurel wreath around my neck, collecting the trophies, and then being interviewed by TV and radio commentator Fred Clarke . . . it was like a fairytale. I once won a race and Fred asked: "What was the hardest part, Mighty Mouse?" I told him I had a problem getting my chin strap undone at the end of the race. God, I was a cocky little beggar.

Just like Kenny, I'd say I was going to win and pull it off most of the time. I had a good team around me and Mal's bottomless pit of money, so we couldn't fail. I had to be single-minded too and wasn't going to help other people, especially ones who could possibly beat me. It wasn't because I was nasty or anything, it just seemed pointless telling people my bike set-up and then trying to beat them on the track.

Riders and mechanics would ask what gearing I was running and I'd fool 'em by saying silly things like: "1066, but it's a bit of a battle." What they didn't work out was that I was actually referring to the Battle of Hastings, not my gear ratio. Or they'd ask: "What carburettor jets have you got?" and I'd reply sarcastically: "Brass." They were all made of brass.

It sounds selfish, but I'd think: 'Go f*** yourself. I've been here testing for two days and working damn hard to sort this bike out, so why should I make it easier for you by telling you my secrets?'

You need to be single-minded to reach the very top.

ALAN CARTER

Down and out . . . Kenny's forlorn look in the LA Coliseum pits tells its own story about the '82 World Final.

12 KENNY AND BRUCE

Disgraceful scenes in LA . . . Big Mal's interference proves costly . . . what Ivan should have told my brother . . . why I changed my mind about who was to blame for Kenny's crash . . . my brother's big mistake . . . Penhall quitting did no-one any good . . . and what I'd tell Bruce if we ever meet.

I WAS way too busy with my own racing commitments at the end of August 1982 to make the World Final in Los Angeles but I felt very excited for our Kenny's hopes of coming home as the new world speedway champion.

He could overtake in places on the track where no-one else dared to go. He had guts in bucket loads. He was no Michael Lee out of the traps, more like a snail and gating was something Kenny never perfected, but he won loads of races from the back through sheer skill and willpower.

He was my hero.

He wasn't at all well before the '82 final in California and really shouldn't have been there due to the big crash he had at Ipswich a few weeks earlier that left him with a badly damaged lung. But with the Carter never-say die attitude, nothing was going to stop him from lining up in his second World Final and trying to take the crown from his arch rival Bruce Penhall.

According to Ivan Mauger, Kenny was half-a-second faster than the rest in practice. Ivan was Kenny's manager and mentor at the time and knew what he was talking about but then Big Mal turned up and tried to take over. Dad was a very intimidating and controlling man and Kenny would have been fearful of going against him.

Between practice and the meeting itself, and very much against Ivan's wishes, Mal demanded Kenny ditch the superior American-made Carlisle tyres that most riders preferred to the British-made Dunlops, so the psychological advantage my brother had over his 15 opponents during practice had been lost, or thrown away, in an instant.

Mal's interference before the '82 World Final marked the end of what should have been the start of a great relationship between Kenny and Ivan, who had won the individual world title six times and everything else in the sport worth winning in a brilliant career.

My personal view of Bruce Penhall at the time was one of pure admiration even though he was by then Kenny's sworn enemy after a couple of heated and high profile on-track clashes between them in the build-up to LA. Bruce was one of the most popular riders in the sport at the time. He was fast, the reigning world

ALAN CARTER

Kenny and his team in LA – the great Ivan Mauger plus mechanics Graham McKeon (left) and Richard Pickering.

Wrong place, wrong time – Kenny outside Bruce Penhall in their brutal battle.

Light in the Darkness

champion and one of the slickest operators in speedway. As they say, you're only as strong as your weakest link and Bruce had a great team around him.

For Kenny to have become world number one in California that night it meant him having to play a very clever chess game. Unfortunately, he and his team, including Ivan, failed to make the right moves at the correct time.

After the riders had all taken their first three rides there was only one who had a maximum nine points – and that was Kenny. Penhall, the local hero, was on eight after finishing behind Les Collins in his second race.

Kenny met Bruce in Heat 14, the one that was always going to decide the whole thing and it's a race speedway fans everywhere still talk and argue about to this day.

This is where Kenny should have been prepared to lose the fight in order to win the war.

Ivan should have told Kenny: 'By all means win the race if you can, but don't get involved in a physical battle with Penhall. Don't take any chances whatsoever in trying to beat him and, if necessary, be prepared to accept second place. If you get into a fight with him and he takes you out, we're f*****.'

If Kenny and Ivan had adopted this more cautious approach, the most likely outcome is that he would have had a run-off against Bruce at the end of the night to decide the world championship. If I'd been Ivan, I would have said: "Look son, this isn't do or die, it's not shit or bust, the result of Heat 14 doesn't matter now. Think of the bigger picture."

Penhall had already dropped one point, so Kenny could afford to lose one himself and, providing he won his last two scheduled heats, would still have got a second crack at Bruce in a run-off. And that really *would* have been shit or bust time.

And if it had panned out that way, with Kenny and Bruce tied on points at the end of the night and having to race each other again in a run-off to decide the championship, then that's when Ivan should have told Kenny: 'Now do whatever you want to win it, even if you crash trying to win the world title.'

The infamous bitter battle Kenny and Bruce had in the LA Coliseum was one of the most unsporting speedway races I've ever seen. Much has been said and written about who was to blame for Kenny's crash that effectively handed the title to Bruce. Personally, I thought the referee should have put both riders back in a rerun after warning them both to clean up their act, although I accept that wouldn't have been fair on the other two riders in the race, Peter Collins and Phil Crump, who were the innocent victims in all this, along with Englishman Les Collins who was challenging Bruce and Kenny hard for the title.

Unfortunately for Kenny, speedway rules stated that someone had to be excluded as the cause of the race being stopped, and it was my brother the Norwegian official Tore Kittilsen blamed. It was Kenny who fell off, or got knocked off depending on how you saw it, so the ref didn't really have any option other than to throw him out of the race. After all, Bruce didn't fall off his bike, did he?

But I thought the way Kenny and Bruce both turned into each other down the straights was a disgrace to the sport. There are times when all riders push things to

ALAN CARTER

Penhall stops after the race to see what happened to Kenny, who is trapped under the fence.

Kenny protests his innocence to his manager Ivan Mauger as Big Mal and mechanic Richard Pickering look on.

Light in the Darkness

the limit but what they did went way beyond sporting competition.

Watching it on TV at the time, I thought Penhall eventually wiped him out. But then I saw a different camera angle – shot from behind them as they came out of turn two – and from here it looked like Kenny had washed the front end out and Bruce had not actually touched him.

My conclusion having viewed the incident from the rear camera angle on the bend is that Kenny lost the front end and had nowhere to go.

His big mistake was to allow Bruce to control the race from the position he was in. He allowed Bruce to run him wider and wider until he went through the fence, which is technically a 'professional foul'. Bruce knew exactly what he was doing and I've done the same.

Later on I'll tell you about a similar situation I found myself in with Nigel Bosworth, where I ran him off the track. I did it on another occasion to Alex Barros, too. Alex was trying to come round me and, to be honest, he was just a kid and I f***** him because he was inexperienced. He should have tried to pass me on the inside but he went the other side instead, so I turned right and put him on the grass.

I knew at the time what I'd done and I did it because Alex was a 16-year-old and I wanted to win this important race in Brazil. The kid had a big crash but he was OK. It was the kind of thing I only ever did two or three times in my life.

But getting back to Kenny, he made the same mistake as Alex Barros by putting himself on the wrong part of the track, which was a surprise coming from an experienced professional like my brother. He couldn't control the race from the outside and Bruce did what he had to do – and fair play to him, he got away with it.

I wouldn't blame Penhall for that. I would have done exactly the same in his position.

What's more, Kenny would have done exactly the same to *him* if their positions on track had been reversed. I have no doubts about that whatsoever..

Penhall went on to retain his world title in the LA Coliseum and for Kenny it was the first of several disastrous attempts to win that coveted crown. Bruce collected the trophy and then immediately announced his retirement from racing to pursue a Hollywood acting career. It was a great shame for the sport but I understand why he decided to quit at the top. Who knows what would have happened to him if he'd continued racing. He might have ended up in a wheelchair like my mate Garry Stead.

As well as being a great loss to speedway, Bruce quitting was bad news for Kenny, too, because I think he lost a bit of edge for a while after his main rival left the sport. Fact is, they both brought the best out of each other.

A lot has been made about Kenny's so-called hatred of the Americans but how could he hate the Yanks when he liked both Kelly and Shawn Moran as much as he did? Fact is, Kenny was at his best when Bruce was at the top and my brother was trying desperately to knock him off his perch.

People continue to debate that Heat 14, which sparked one of the greatest controversies in world championship history, but I still believe Ivan was right when he said Kenny probably lost the world title that year when he chose Dunlop tyres instead of the Carlisle. That was the biggest reason he didn't win the '82 final.

We shouldn't forget that the consequences of Kenny's crash and the decision not to exclude Bruce also had a big effect on Les Collins, who might have gone on to win the meeting had Penhall not won the rerun of Heat 14. In the end, Les had to settle for second place overall to Bruce on the night, which was still a fantastic achievement.

In 2010 I attended a 25-year Ellesmere Port Speedway reunion and was privileged to meet Les Collins, who I found to be a lovely man and a pleasure to talk to. I asked Les about the Los Angeles final and he said he thought the referee should have excluded both Kenny and Bruce for what happened. We agreed that both riders had way overstepped the mark.

Les said the problem with Kenny was that he was all out for himself, and he told me how Kenny once put him through the fence and smashed his bike to pieces when they were riding together on the same team as a pair for England. Les said it was just uncalled for and I can only agree with him. The main thing Les pointed out to me when we met up was that Kenny had no friends on the track – apart from Neil Evitts, his Halifax and Bradford team-mate – and that he was a loner who only cared about himself. He made too many enemies. I don't understand why he did what he did and to so many. You've got to have respect for all your rivals.

I've been asked if Kenny would perhaps have been better suited to road-racing, which is more of an individual sport than speedway. But even in road-racing there are teams and there is a pecking order. One guy gets all the best goodies while the other can be treated second-rate, so it's not really much different to speedway in that sense. The only reason Kenny went into speedway was to make money. He was a top moto-crosser and could have become the British or even world moto-cross champion but there was no money in it, or so he was led to believe.

I was a completely different person to Kenny during our racing careers. He seemed to rub his competitors up the wrong way. It was hard enough beating them anyway. I just kept my head down and was much more interested in winning races and chasing the girls than making enemies on the track.

I loved my brother but I still have a lot of respect for Bruce Penhall, too, and I'd love to meet him one day. Like me and Kenny, he had to cope with tragedy when he lost both his parents in a plane crash before he made the big-time in speedway, so I can relate to him in that sense.

And maybe Bruce will have a slightly different opinion of Kenny once he has read this book. I expect he will still hold the same views of him as a person but when he knows the full extent of what Kenny went through as a young boy and in his youth, perhaps he will now believe that my brother over-achieved in terms of what he did in speedway.

What Kenny thought of Bruce was up to him but I'm my own man. Opinions are only opinions. They're not facts.

I'm dying to meet Bruce and if I ever do, I'll shake him by the hand and tell him how much respect I have for him for what he achieved.

13 OVERNIGHT SENSATION

Armstrong-CCM, the sweetest thing I ever rode . . . Doug Holtom, a mechanical genius with the will to win . . . Caravan capers . . . what the f*** is a Pernod? . . . 'the next Sheene'.

IF our Kenny couldn't pull it off in LA due to being robbed, bad luck, his own poor judgement or whatever else you want to call it, I was about to shock the world of road-racing.

The 1982 season had been getting increasingly better and it was about to get a whole lot better when Mal bought me one of Kawasaki's factory vans. It had everything and was so good, you wanted to live in it. The awning alone was massive, half the size of any race paddock.

To my shock, Dad also got me a second-hand, but good as new-looking, bike to race – the British-made Armstrong-CCM 250cc fitted with an Austrian Rotax engine. It was the sweetest thing I ever rode.

And to top that, he recruited a young, hungry GP spannerman called Doug Holtom, who worked for the CCM factory in Bolton. We would become lifelong friends.

After several impressive showings at national level the season was coming to a close. The world championships had finished and there was a new 250cc world champion in France's Jean-Louis Tournadre. He and all the other grand prix stars were coming to England for the last big international of the year, the Jody Sheckter World Cup, at Donington Park. All the big names were there . . . Kenny Roberts, Barry Sheene, Randy Mamola, the lot, plus all the top 250cc GP riders.

Dad agreed my start money with Donington owner Tom Wheatcroft. My starting price in 1982 was £2,500, plus prize money, and Dad footed the bill for everything. Boy, I was a high-flyer now. I'd hit the big-time - Vegas here we come!

Oh, by the way, caravans were supplied by Mal with a bit of a twist. You didn't enter them in the conventional way, via the door with a key. This is what I was told to do.

"Nipper, I've lost the f****** keys, so get up on that roof and f****** rip off the skylight, climb inside and open the door."

So that's what I did. My next job was to go up to Goodalls, our local caravan dealer in Huddersfield, near Whitham's airfield, and buy a new lock and skylight. I'll leave the question of where these caravans came from to your imagination.

We left for Donington all kitted out with a new van and a caravan in tow, the works. Under strict orders from Mal, his wife Janet filled it with enough food to feed an army, so my mates, Kev Mitchell and Eggis, and I were well set for a wonderful weekend. But not for long. We were zooming down the M1 as happy as Larry when,

ALAN CARTER

all of a sudden – bang! – one of the caravan wheels fell off. How I managed to control the van that was pulling it was purely down to luck.

The undercarriage was badly damaged and, basically, we were in deep shit. Well, when you were in the shit you only did one thing – ring Big Mal.

He knew everything but his solutions to problems were not always what most normal people would arrive at. Instead of sending for a rescue and repair vehicle or phoning the police for help, Dad took a much more basic approach. He told us to get everything out of the caravan, rip the number plate off, leave it on the hard shoulder and, in typical no-nonsense style, to "f*** off as fast as you can."

So we abandoned the caravan right there at the side of the M1 and continued on our way south to Castle Donington, Derbyshire in the customised Kawasaki van.

On arrival at Donington for practice I was a relative unknown in this GP paddock, so no-one really took much notice of me – even though I think I'd finished among the top 10 in practice. We had problems on the Friday and Saturday, blowing two engines and to top that the experienced Frenchman Christian Estrosi was absolutely flying. He was half-a-second faster than me and no way was I going to beat this man. Plus he was riding a Pernod. I mean, what the f*** was that? I thought it was a drink. And I only knew that much because Pam, our Kenny's wife, used to drink it on a night out.

Doug went back to CCM's factory in Bolton that Saturday night with two engines that had basically been destroyed but he worked all night, bless him, and made one good engine. He came back on the Sunday morning, fitted it and we were going racing – all thanks to a genius who had pure dedication and the will to win, just like me. That was the best engine I ever raced – so thank you, Dougie.

Things got even better for me. The only guy I didn't think I could beat, Christian Estrosi, had a giant crash in the morning on cold tyres down the Craner Curves. This was a fifth-gear-120-mph-plus accident. If you crashed there, you weren't getting up and they carted him off to hospital.

I couldn't believe my luck. I won every race that day, beating new world champion Jean-Louis Tournadre and I don't know how I did it. I just got stuck in, passing and going through them like a knife through butter. I was flying.

I'd become an overnight sensation, the hottest young property in the world of grand prix motorcycle racing. The press went into frenzy, everyone wanted a piece of me. I was now being billed as the next Barry Sheene.

On that Bank Holiday weekend in August 1982 I became the youngest international winner of all time.

But looking back now, I wasn't ready for GP racing. At 18 I was still too young and needed to gain more experience of different tracks. I was just like a big lump of coal that needed lots of polishing into a fine diamond.

But I had no choice the following year, 1983, I was going grand prix racing. And you know what? I neither feared nor respected anyone. I was The Kid and these old-timers were having it.

Boy, was I in for a shock. Talk about naive.

14 WRONG CHOICE

Burning my bridges with Armstrong-CCM . . . the Mitsui mistake . . . night they feared Kenny had been killed . . . my first ban . . . 'Pizza face' Kenny's golden words.

THE CCM-Armstrong factory tried to sign me with the best deal I was ever offered in my racing career. Having just beaten the new world champion at Donington on one of their bikes, they offered me an unbelievable deal to ride for them in 1983. Basically, it was a full works ride in the world championships and a lot of money for me personally.

In hindsight, this was the best option. I'd have been able to continue building the great relationship we'd formed with them in '82 plus there was the continuity of staying on the same bike. It's no good changing teams and bikes every year, it just doesn't work.

But, at the eleventh hour, Mitsui Yamaha UK offered Mal, my manager, a good deal to race for them – all the gear, plus expenses but no cash for me. They were on a tight budget but if I did well they said they would use it as a grooming year before switching me to their 500cc bikes the year after. That's what swayed it for Mal, so we went for it with Mitsui.

The people at CCM were absolutely gutted and so was I. I'd really been looking forward to continuing with them, especially working with Doug Holtom. Their bike, developed by Barry Hart, was so easy to ride. I felt I'd really let CCM and Doug down but Mal was the boss. He didn't even mention that I had a choice. I'd just turned 18 and had no say in it.

Rotax supplied engines to both CCM-Armstrong and a very small company in Italy called Aprilia. I believe I would have won a few world titles for CCM and gone on to great things with them in the early 80s days but Rotax pumped more effort into Aprilia instead. Within a few years CCM had practically fallen off the end of the world while Aprilia became a massive company and remains so to this day. History was being made and I was in at the start of it where these two motorcycle companies were concerned.

It's weird but Kenny was so busy racing himself most Sundays that he rarely watched me race. We were just busy doing our own thing. But if I wasn't racing, you could always count on me being at The Shay on Saturday nights – I just loved watching him because you knew you could see something very special at any given time.

The night at The Shay, in April 1981, when Kenny hit Hans Nielsen's back wheel before crashing into the solid fence, was a bad one. Everyone thought Kenny had died on the track that night – there was total panic on people's faces and deadly silence on the terraces as anxious Dukes supporters held their breath.

That night at the hospital it was a bit touch and go with Kenny. I remember walking into his hospital room, looking at him and saying to myself, 'who the f***'s that, it's not our Kenny' and walking out . . . only to ask staff where he was and be sent back to the same room. Honest, his head was three times bigger than normal. I was scared, unable to even recognise my own brother.

Thankfully, after smashing his jaw in about eight places, he made a full recovery and almost won the British championship on his comeback. Kenny blamed Hans for causing him to crash and Birmingham's Danish star said it was Kenny's fault. All I know is, Kenny was sure looking for revenge.

He always seemed to have a grudge against most of the top riders. I mean, come on, there is room in the world for more than one great rider. When you read about how Peter Collins, Michael Lee and Bruce Penhall used to hang out and travel overseas together, it must have made life so much more fun and exciting for them.

That's what I was doing in road-racing, having the time of my life with racers just like me. We had a common goal and bond to become the next World Champion, or at least give it all you had. I was having unbelievable times with fantastic people. What a great feeling it was to wake up on the morning of the Dutch Grand Prix at Assen and then perform in front of more than 120,000. It made the hairs on the back of your neck stand up. I didn't need motivation to go fast. No way was I going to make myself look a t**t in front of any fan.

I used to look in the mirror and say to myself: 'This is it, Sunday, performance day. I will put on a performance far superior to everyone else'.

I wasn't just going fast in road-racing. I was also driving cars at full speed everywhere I went, which landed me in trouble with the police. One day I was coming down the M1 towards Donington in a brand new Peugeot 205GTi and the next thing I saw flashing blue lights in my rear view mirror. I only looked about 15 and the copper who nicked me said: "I've done 145 to catch you, son, so how fast were you going?"

"I don't know," I replied. "F*** me, it wouldn't go any faster."

It wasn't the diplomatic answer PC plod was looking for, so that's when I had my first court appearance for motoring offences.

A few weeks later my mate Matt Wroot and I were racing each other when we saw the coppers chasing us. They stopped Matt and I should have split but I thought it best to stop otherwise he'd only have grassed me up. Matt jumped out and I'm thinking, 'go on Matt, say something amazing, like me wife's having a baby and we're rushing to the hospital . . . '

But what does he say instead? Matt started: "I'm a silly c*** and we were just having a burn-up . . . "

And I'm like, 'no way'. So just like Buzz Lightyear, I jumped in to save the night. I cockily told the copper: "I'm a professional motor bike racer and I know what I'm doing. Who the f*** are you, sergeant?"

Light in the Darkness

Above: With my new Mitsui Yamahas at the start of the 1983 season.
Below: Pushing my luck.

Collecting my thoughts after another fall.

He said: "I'm only a PC – but we'll see you in court."

And he did, too. I received my first 12-month driving ban for speeding at more than 135mph.

Being as bright as a button, one day I decided to have a drive whilst disqualified, only to be pulled over again by the police near Halifax.

Copper: "What's yer name?"

"Paul Haigh." (My mate Eggis.)

"Where do you live?"

"15, Keswick Close, Sidal."

"Oh, right, what's yer date of birth?"

"19th of the twelfth, '63."

"Right, what's yer wife's name?"

"Nanette," I replied.

"No, you're Alan Carter – and yer coming with me!"

He must have recognised me from my picture in the papers. The price of fame, eh! Anyway, the police at Halifax nick held me in a cell for about 12 hours for wasting their time.

Now I was well in the shit. I was given another 12-month on top of the previous one, plus my best mate Paul wasn't too happy either.

Talking of bullshit, our Kenny could talk plenty of it at times, too. I remember him

Light in the Darkness

telling one reporter all about his new training regime and how he had this new drop handle push bike and was doing 40 miles a day on it – which, by the way, I was doing. The lying little sod, but this reporter believed every word Kenny told him.

The only exercise the lazy prick ever did was walk from his house to the car.

His idea of 'sports nutrition' consisted of fish and chips every day – no wonder he had a spotty face. In fact, my nickname for him was 'Pizza Face' or 'The Topex Kid', after one of the most popular acne creams of the day.

Dinner for Kenny was either fish and chips or a fry-up at the Braziliana Cafe in Halifax owned by a Greek guy called Stanley. Kenny would meet up with Jimmy Ross, one of his closest mates and the best bloke he ever met, plus the rest of the gang. Jimmy loved and treated him like a son and had Kenny's best interests at heart. He also did me and Welsey a favour when he arranged a mortgage for us and got me a helmet sponsorship deal.

The people around Kenny during this period were proper mates, not the hangers-on he surrounded himself with towards the end of his life.

One Friday night Kenny and I had a few drinks at his house in Bradshaw and it almost ended disastrously. We were just shooting the breeze, talking about business and racing and having a few drinks, and it was two o'clock in the morning before I left his place and sped off in my brand new black Mini Metro Turbo.

I was half-pissed and thinking 'just take it easy – chill man'. I'm only half-a-mile from home and going through Mixenden when I pass a copper going the opposite way. "Oh shit!" So I turn it on to warp speed, thinking 'just get this baby home' and flattened it.

By the way, it was pissing it down.

I came towards the Stone Chair Inn, where it's a bit off-camber, doing about 85-90 mph, when I aquaplaned and lost the front end. It was like a river running across the road and as well as wiping out the scaffolding that had been put up in front of the pub ready for refurbishments, I badly wrecked my car. Somehow I managed to make it home the last 500 yards on the rims, with glass all over me.

I rang Kenny to tell him what had happened and, although he was half-cut as well, he came straight away. And, as always, he just couldn't stop laughing at my expense when he saw the damage I'd done to my new motor.

"Nipper, this is no good," he says. "Not sure if they'll write this off. And you don't want this back anyway 'cos it's f*****".

I'm like, 'so what are we going to do?'

"Don't worry, I'll sort it," Kenny says.

That's when he found a giant boulder and dropped it onto the roof of my car.

"Sorted now, kid."

Dad and Kenny were so alike, they could sort anything.

Many times Kenny and I would go to the pub for dinner but mainly to play pool. Trouble was, a quick 30-minute get-together always turned out to be a four-hour marathon. You see, he just wouldn't be beaten, so I'd usually lose 17-16 or something just so that I could go home. And there was always the standard deal –

ALAN CARTER

Left: Young and carefree.

Below: Kenny with the Golden Helmet that he felt belonged to him.

loser pays for the food.

I'll tell you how confident and cocky Kenny was in his prime. The Golden Helmet was a big thing in speedway back then, a prestigious competition with a lot of history and all the top riders wanted to win it. Each month the holder would defend the famous Golden Helmet against a nominated challenger, or the top rider in the opposing team depending on what era you're talking about. Whoever won the race, or best-of-three series, went home with the Golden Helmet. Kenny took a lot of pride in being the holder and it took a lot to get it off him.

Anyway, I can't remember who he was riding against this particular night at The Shay but what I do recall is me asking him: "Where's the helmet?"

He just winked at me and said: "I didn't bring it . . . what's the point? I'm not going to lose."

What a man.

Light in the Darkness

15 GLORY IN FRANCE

Debut season in the GP . . . making history at Le Mans . . . ones that got away.

THE 1983 season promised to be a great year for me and that's how it proved. I had everything going for me. I was in the 250cc grand prix series for the first time, the youngest kid on the grid, I had a great coach in Mal and one of the best GP mechanics in the world in Howard Gregory, while the cream of Yamaha had produced a gem of a bike for the '83 season.

The 11-round '83 world championship campaign began on March 19 in South Africa, where I felt great in practice and was doing even better in my first-ever GP race. There were five riders, including me, swapping places until I ground to a halt after the chain snapped. Although out of the race, I'd at least shown that I could run with the fastest guys in the world on a track I'd never seen.

On the trip to S.A. I noticed a stunt rider at the track wearing all black. I didn't recognise him at first until my great friend and team-mate, Ireland's Donny Robinson, pointed out that it was in fact Eddie Kidd, the then golden boy of stunt riding and a right good looking chap. On the flight home Eddie was sat two rows behind us so, being a big fan of his, I introduced myself and chatted to him all the way home.

After the disappointment of South Africa, we were off to France. For some reason we were late getting to Le Mans, where Yamaha had produced a factory upgrade kit for their top riders. We'd been blown away in Kyalami by the straight line speed of Patrick Fernandez's Hummel cylinder Yamaha and you couldn't slipstream the rapid Chevallier Yamahas of Balde, de Radiguès and Espie.

We paid the price for arriving late because Christian Sarron, Carlos Lavado and the other factory riders got first pick of Yamaha's new go-faster kits, while me and Donny got what was left, which wasn't a lot.

If I felt robbed of a podium position in Jo'burg, that was nothing compared to the disastrous start I had in France, where my bike seized – both cylinders – on each practice day. Talk about being on a downer. I qualified in 32nd place – or, to put it another way, last. On the start line for the race the front guys were so far in front on the grid, I couldn't even see them.

Another problem was that Dunlop made all the new tyres we used in Europe way too hard. The tyres were identified by numbers – 8 was soft, 16 was medium and 32 hard. All week everyone had been crashing their brains out because the front tyres were too hard. And believe it or not, it snowed on that morning of the French GP.

Warm-up before the race went well for me, though. I got the bike set-up right and had some valuable track time. My trump card was that I had one tyre left from the previous year, a 724 super-soft front. Well, Dunlop got wind of this and asked if

ALAN CARTER

My greatest achievement in racing – winning the French Grand Prix. I still have this trophy.

we'd give it to Lavado, who was on pole position. Dad being Dad, he said: "Go get f*****," so it was on my bike for the race.

When Sunday, April 3 dawned, no-one expected anything special from me that day. But I made a good start – in the days when they still used push-starts – kept out of trouble and picked riders off one at a time.

I remember catching Tournadre, the World Champion, and pushing him so hard that he lost the front and crashed out. I was lucky to miss him. Next Sito Pons was leading but when he missed the first turn, out-braking himself, he ended up going down on the long Mistral straight.

I kept passing riders on the start and finish line but was so focused I didn't see my pit board. Three laps from the end, it started spitting with rain and Rapicault, a young French rider, slowed too much just before the last lap through the esses, so I dived under him at a rapid pace and passed him.

Starting the last lap, I didn't even know I was leading, I just felt assured of a place in the top three. I was so excited. I was on it, setting a new track record and winning the French GP – all from the back.

Donny Robinson, my team-mate, had crashed on the first corner in the race and as I passed him on the slow down lap, I remember thinking how happy he looked for me to have won, jumping up and down as if he'd won the race himself.

As I pulled into the pits veteran journalist, the late Norrie White, a giant of a man, was the first to reach me. I took my helmet off and asked him excitedly: "Who won?"

He looked at me dumbfounded and said: "You did!"

It turned out I'd finished just less than two-and-a-half seconds ahead of the Swiss, Jacques Cornu.

Light in the Darkness

FRENCH GRAND PRIX
Le Mans, Sunday, April 3, 1983

Pos.	Rider	Nat	Bike	Time/Gap
1	Alan CARTER	GB	Yamaha	42' 29.910
2	Jacques CORNU	CH	Yamaha	+2.430
3	Thierry RAPICAULT	FRA	Yamaha	+2.990
4	Didier DE RADIGUÉS	BEL	Chevallier	+3.720
5	Tony HEAD	GB	Rotax Armstrong	+18.570
6	Patrick FERNANDEZ	FRA	Bartol	+19.690
7	Jacques BOLLE	FRA	Yamaha	+25.870
8	Harald ECKL	GER	Yamaha	+26.810
9	Thierry ESPIÉ	FRA	Chevallier	+27.210
10	Jean Marc TOFFOLO	BEL	Morena	+27.450
11	Jean Michel MATTIOLI	FRA	Yamaha	0 Lap
12	Pierre BOLLE	FRA	Yamaha	0 Lap
13	Sito PONS	SPA	JJ Cobas	0 Lap
14	Ivan PALAZZESE	VEN	Yamaha	0 Lap
15	Jean Francois BALDÉ	FRA	Chevallier	0 Lap
17	Christian ESTROSI	FRA	Pernod	0 Lap
18	Reinhold ROTH	GER	Yamaha	0 Lap
20	Paolo FERRETTI	ITA	Yamaha	0 Lap
21	Carlos CARDÚS	SPA	JJ Cobas	0 Lap
	Not Classified:			
	Donny ROBINSON	IRL	Yamaha	25 Laps

I created history that day by becoming the youngest ever 250cc GP winner, a record that stood for well over 20 years and not even the greatest rider of all-time, Valentino Rossi, could beat it.

There were other GPs I could, and should, have won and many people in later years said I was a 'one-race wonder'. Just to put the record straight, here's a brief summary of the ones that got away . . .

GPs THAT GOT AWAY

1. South Africa GP, 1983: Was in the leading group when the chain snapped.

2. Swedish GP, 1983: The frame snapped in half when I was placed third within the leading pack.

3. South Africa GP, 1984: It rained like you have never seen before. I held a 10-second lead but the sun came out, my tyres disintegrated and I finished 10th.

4. French GP, 1984: One of the best rides of my life. Came from mid-pack to fourth when the engine failed.

5. British GP, 1985: Leading by 13 seconds, crashed, got back on and finished seventh.

6. British GP, 1986: Rev counter stopped working after two laps, which made it very hard to ride. Placed second and going for the win until last lap crash.

7. Belgium GP, 1986: Lying second and waiting to pounce until water in the electrics reduced the power of the engine, so had to settle for fifth.

There were others where I was in contention but fate restricted me to that one GP victory at Le Mans.

After winning the French grand prix we had a great night, drinking with our team and other teams' sponsors and some amazing new fans. I think we were all in shock and just drank until we all dropped. It was like a fairytale and I was all over the papers on my return to England. A new star was born, with the press again building me up to be 'the next Barry Sheene'.

16 SHATTERED CONFIDENCE

Helmet scam . . . babe-magnets . . . Donny dies.

VICTORY in the French GP at 18 was like American tennis star Tracey Austin winning the 1979 US Open at 16. People were so shocked to see inexperienced youngsters achieving such great feats, because it was largely unheard of in that era. But for me, it was just too much too soon. I'd raised everyone's expectations of me to a massive level and the pressure was surely going to get a lot tougher.

In fact, the biggest high in my life was soon to become the biggest low point. You see Mal seemed to focus on the now, the instant, not the future. Decisions like turning down CCM, when the deal was all but done, meant I'd burnt that bridge forever and in such a small community you just couldn't afford to burn any bridges.

Also, for the 1983 season, we switched helmets. I went from a fantastic-fitting AGV to the Swiss 'Kiwi' helmet, which was about as much use as tits to a bull. After telling Dad that the Kiwi helmet was causing me bad headaches, he said: "No problem, we'll paint an AGV helmet and make it look the same – and put Kiwi stickers on it."

'What a top idea' I was thinking, except for one problem. On the visor there was a tiny AGV logo, which we'd missed! I mean, come on, I was on the front cover of every motorbike mag worldwide, so of course Kiwi picked up on it and terminated my contract with them worth £5,000. And you know what, fair play to them. It wasn't nice what we did, but I just couldn't use their helmets because I found them uncomfortable.

To my surprise, Dad then sorted me out a new sports car, the latest Mazda RX7 in blue with my Mighty Mouse logo on the bonnet. It was a fantastic car and I loved it. "That's eight grand, kid." Cheers, Dad Knowing Mal, he probably paid 7k for it.

I travelled to all the grands prix in it and was on cloud nine. I had some great laughs with Keith Huewen, the ex-GP racer and now Sky TV's speedway GP studio host. Keith drove a blue 2.8 Capri and we once raced each other all the way from the Spanish GP, near Madrid, to Salzburg in Austria, hitting speeds of over 140 mph.

The greatest part was the bit before we reached the pay booths on the autostratus. Just before braking we'd look across at each other, smile and then slam the brakes on, sliding and snaking the cars to a halt with rubber burning smoke everywhere, and then trying to give your cash to the attendants, who must have thought they were witnessing an armed robbery. If you got out first, it felt better than winning a GP!

Not that the Mazda lasted long. One day Dad told me to pick our Lucy up from school. It was snowing cats and dogs but little sis had a great idea: "Shall we go to the pub car park and spin around in the snow and ice?"

We were doing big 'donuts' in the snow, it was ace, but then I lost control and hit a corner wall at full speed. The car was a right-off and so was I after facing Dad.

Mal said it needed a new shell from Japan because I'd given it a right bananaring. "You're the biggest prick that walked the earth, all you're fit for is a banger," he told me. So my next car was a Mini Traveller in orange, which cost 150 quid and the only way it started was by bumping it. It meant I always had to park on a big hill. What a babe magnet of a motor this was. Almost overnight, I'd gone from owning a flash sports car to pulling the choke out of the dash on a banger of a mini.

I love people and the funny stories you hear along the road of life. I had a sponsor called Bob who used to tell me things about his dad that would crack me up. He once told me how, one Father's Day, he invited his dad to his place for a barbeque. He explained how his dad always had a problem chewing meat and that many times he'd nearly choke to death before they managed to hit him on the back very hard and a piece of meat would fly out of his mouth, much to everyone's relief and no little amusement.

Well, on this Father's Day Bob's Old Man did actually choke to death on the meat that his son had cooked for him. I know this sounds awful but I could see the funny side, too. Imagine the headlines: 'SON KILLS DAD ON FATHER'S DAY'.

After arriving home from the French GP I got a hero's welcome at Donington Park the next weekend, where they staged a big British race meeting. But from here on my confidence took a big battering.

I made a very bad start, became impatient and was pushing way too hard on cold tyres before having a massive crash on the very first lap and knocking myself out cold. Talk about being brought down a peg or two.

The third round of the GP was Italy but because I was still suffering from the injuries sustained at Donington, I wasn't up to it. In the cut-throat 250 world championship, if you weren't on it, you simply weren't going to qualify. It was held at Monza, the most famous race track in the world, and it's true that when you go under the tunnel there, the hairs on your neck stand up. It's a very eerie feeling indeed.

Practice at Monza went well and now it was race day. I'm just about to start my first Italian Grand Prix, only my third ever GP, and I get a flier of a start. I'm in the leading group going into the first chicane, where Sarron goes down and I run him over, ending up in the gravel trap on my arse. And that was it, my Italian GP debut all over in the first corner. That's racing.

One of the things I loved about my career was my racing kit. I liked to look like a gladiator, immaculate, and I was always cleaning my leathers, boots and gloves, and my helmets had to look beautiful, too.

On the bikes we always tried to do things to baffle our opponents. All the barrels on the race engines that came out of Japan were in black, so Howard Gregory would put them in a bucket of paintstripper overnight and then clean up in the morning so

Light in the Darkness

that they were now a silver colour. So everybody thought I was using 'trick' barrels from the factory but it was a load of bollocks. All we'd done was change the look of them, and maybe ground some numbers and letters on the side to try and confuse them even more. It was so funny watching other mechanics taking a close look at my kit during the pre-race inspections.

After Italy I was on a mission to show people what I could do. I felt like I should have been leading the championship by now not just finishing one race.

Next stop was Spain's Jarama, one of the best tracks. It suited my style – short and twisty and no giant straight. I was 10th fastest in practice and gunning for a podium place but had another big crash – although no broken bones – which again put me out of the race.

On to Salzburg in Austria, one of the fastest tracks in the world and pretty dangerous, too, but nothing compared to the circuits Sheene and co. raced on in the 60s and 70s. We didn't do well here, our bikes were too slow, but that was irrelevant because this was the weekend my team-mate Donny Robinson had his career-ending accident in which he suffered serious breaks to both legs.

But he didn't have the giant pins removed and made a fatal comeback. In 1999 he crashed and was killed at the North West 200 – held on public roads in his homeland of Coleraine, Northern Ireland and the second most famous road-race in the world after the Isle of Man TT.

Donny was a great guy, I loved him just like a brother. He was one of Ireland's most successful and popular racers and more than a match for Joey Dunlop on his day. Poor Mrs Robinson. She and Donny's dad were both such lovely people and would lose all three of their precious sons to road-racing. I often think about her and how sad she must feel, bless her.

Road-racing is obviously dangerous and accidents will happen but the tragic loss of a team-mate and many other riders through the years never put me off doing it. I never considered quitting.

We set off for Yugoslavia for the next GP and it turned into a long trip. Mal and I travelled there in the Mazda but the gearbox broke, so we could only use second and fourth gear.

I crashed in the first practice at Rijeka. It was a strange one – I lost the front end, something I'd never done until then – it was always the high side for me. I broke both ankles that day and Mal made me put them in freezing cold buckets of ice for 20 minutes at a time. He then took me to see the famous Dr Claudio Costa to see if he could do anything to help. The Italian 'Medicine Man' made some small pots for my ankles. I couldn't walk in them but I could still throw my leg over the bike, so the next day Mal sent me out for practice in total agony. I did a few laps but it was useless, I couldn't go on and we were on our way home.

So my GP record for 1983 now read: One win and five dnfs and lucky to be in one piece.

After a few weeks off we were back on the road again, this time heading to Holland for the Dutch GP at Assen. Remember, every track was new to me. I'd

With my 1983 team-mate Donny Robinson, another sad loss to the sport.

never even been outside the UK until now. I should have been learning all about GP life and getting to grips with the new tracks, not being pushed to win every GP at the age of 18. My sensational early season victory in France was fast becoming a heavy burden to bear.

But I adapted quickly to the Assen track and loved it. I always did perform a bit slowly in the early practice sessions but this was going to be my best GP practice placing so far. I was running about ninth going into the final practice when Mal offered me an amazing bonus – a free 'shopping trip' to Groningen if I made it onto the front row. And boy, was I up for it!

The grid positions at all GPs by then saw five riders on the front row, four on the next, etc, with 40 riders lined up on the wide tracks and 36 on the narrow ones. There were so many trying to qualify – about 65 riders in all – they split us into odd and even practice groups.

With one minute to go after three days' practice I was in fifth place, heading for the front row and feeling like the man again. Later that day we received the grid sheet for starting positions and saw to our disgust that it was 4/3, not 5/4 as expected. Never! So I'm the first man on the second row and feeling gutted.

But this time Mal appreciated the effort I'd put it and how well I'd ridden, so he said: "You did fantastic, kid, so go shopping in Groningen – and enjoy it."

In the race the next day I'd made a great start and was up to third place when, on cold tyres, I had another massive crash at the chicane just before the start and finish

Light in the Darkness

line. I'd got on the gas too hard.

I really hurt myself that day, my second big crash of the year and my fifth in about seven races and a non-qualifier too. Now my confidence had been shattered again.

Before my first British GP, at Silverstone, eight rounds of the world championship had produced one win, one breakdown, one mid-field finish in Austria, plus four crashes and another one at Donington. And in the last round, the Belgium GP at Spa, the most dangerous track in the world, I didn't even qualify due to a complete lack of confidence.

On arriving at Spa I remember saying to Barry Sheene: "This is a bit dangerous, Barry." But he just laughed at me, saying "here, get in," so I jumped in this big, flash Merc, just like Dad used to drive, and off we went.

Barry was taking me for a lap of the old track at Spa – at warp speed. Now this was a bad track and he told me how lucky I was to be riding on the new Spa and not the circuit he used to race on. He was right and I felt lucky to get out of the car in one piece after the speeds he was doing.

Barry was a great guy and his wife Stephanie was the princess of the GP paddock. The lucky bugger, Barry, he had it all – and I wanted it too.

To be honest, I think by now even my head had gone and I don't even reckon I could have won a club race, let alone a GP. I had no confidence at all at Silverstone, the other guys had got their stuff going even faster and that was basically it.

But, unbeknown to me, I'd caught the eye of three times 500cc World Champion Kenny Roberts, which I'll come on to later in the book. The funny thing is, I was also keeping a close eye on him at the time, hoping he'd kick Freddie Spencer's arse. Their own fight for the 500cc title was going down to the wire and it was Kenny's last year in the GPs.

I qualified mid-pack at Silverstone. That's when Mal came up to me and said: "Look, yer f*****, miles back on the grid." I'd be starting in about 19th position but Dad added: "I've sorted the start out with Bill Smith." He was a top ACU official at the time and a friend of Dad's. Mal said: "Look, when Bill drops his handkerchief, start pushing and get a flier."

"OK Dad." Remember I was only just turned 19 and wet behind the lugs.

Bill Smith dropped his hankie and I'd passed two rows of riders before a guy grabbed me and ordered me to go back to my original starting position. As I was pushing the bike back, the race starter dropped the flag and that was me knackered – stone last.

I finished the race in mid-pack but, given my record at the time, 11th place felt as if I'd won a GP. On the last lap of the race you could've covered six or seven riders with a blanket. A young French kid called Jacques Bolle won his only ever GP race ever with a fantastic performance.

It was now down to the final race of the year, at Anderstorp in Sweden. As usual, we set off from Yorkshire and headed for the North Sea ferry at Hull – it made much more sense to depart from there rather than go all the way down to the port at Dover in Kent. We always had a great night on the overnight boat disco and enjoyed everything else that was going on. The last race in Sweden was going to be a

ALAN CARTER

Light in the Darkness

cracker. I loved the track and Roberts and Spencer were only two points apart in the 500cc championship.

I qualified well and could easily have finished in the top three in the race but my frame snapped in half. It was shaking violently but I wasn't going to stop at any cost after such a nightmare season. I'd been among the leading group but dropped back to fifth due to the bike shaking like you have no idea.

Afterwards, Howard Gregory checked the bike over and initially could find nothing wrong. It was only when he took the petrol tank off and pushed the suspension down that he saw a two-inch gap. The frame had snapped clean in half down the tubes and only stayed in one piece because of the shock absorber.

In the 500s there was a titanic battle, with Kenny Roberts on the Yamaha leading Spencer all the way, then on the final lap Freddie ran Kenny off the track to win a race that is still disputed by these two great rivals to this day. Freddie Spencer, on the Honda, had snatched his first world championship by two points.

My new mate Christian Sarron had just won the 250 GP race and we all celebrated by jumping in the pool at Anderstorp. Seeing the joy on the Frenchman's face that day made me want to become World Champion even more.

In 1983 that honour deservedly went to Carlos Lavado – and what a great guy he was. On many occasions during the year most riders would just shut off the throttle in practice, not letting me follow in their tyre tracks while I was trying to learn how to ride the tracks, but not Carlos. He was a true gent and tried to help me whenever he could.

I also became good friends with Ivan Palazzese, Carlos' team-mate, who was killed in the German GP at Hockenheim in 1989.

This one hurt a lot after I got on the gas too much at Assen. The two Frenchmen who managed to avoid me in picture are Thierry Espié(35) and Herve Guilleux.

113

ALAN CARTER

Above: Kenny on the outside of his World Pairs partner Peter Collins (10) in the final at Gothenburg, Sweden in 1983. Their victory proved to be our Kenny's only FIM gold medal success.
Below: The 1983 individual World Final at Norden with Kenny alongside one of his mechanics, Graham McKeon, and walking the German track that was tailor-made for the home favourite Egon Müller.

17 GOLD FOR KENNY

Love-hate with the Americans . . . the wild west . . . Kenny's fit for nothing . . . and all this for a mankie ham sandwich.

KENNY had his sights set on qualifying for his third individual World Final. Once again, he narrowly failed to win the British title that year but at least he collected his first FIM World Championship gold medal when he and Peter Collins won the World Pairs Final at Gothenburg, Sweden in June.

Kenny scored 15 points on the night, with Peter getting 10. This was a great pairing on paper. You had PC, the most experienced top guy in England, partnered with a young upstart in Kenny, and they pulled it off by winning the title just one point ahead of the Aussies. Kenny and PC could have gone on to win several more World Pairs titles together but they fell out big-time the following year, which I'll talk about later.

It's a shame Kenny never developed a lot of close relationships with his fellow riders. Many times he'd overstep the mark in team events by focusing on himself instead of the team, which didn't gain him much support from the others. It's different when you're racing for yourself in individual meetings where you have to be selfish to succeed.

Maybe Kenny carried a lot of insecurities from his childhood, which certainly wasn't the best. Personally, I find it hard to trust anyone and my close friends have often told me to relax a bit and chill out more.

His well-publicised so-called hatred of the Americans was blown out of proportion, though. Kelly and Shawn Moran had no problem with Kenny and all three were good friends. I think it was Bruce Penhall and his close circle of rider mates, including Dennis Sigalos and Bobby Schwartz, who Kenny didn't like, because they were Bruce's mates. Kenny just cut them all off and that was it.

Kenny sold things from his souvenir stall at The Shay that were, let's say, not very appropriate. Badges that said 'Stuff a Yank' and 'I Hate Americans' and other distasteful anti-American items.

Bruce badly damaged his own reputation in the eyes of the British public when he deliberately finished last in the 1982 Overseas Final, a World Championship qualifying round at London's White City. He poodled around at the back, pulling wheelies, so that the other three riders in the 'race', Dennis Sigalos and the Moran brothers, would finish ahead of him and collect the vital points they needed to reach the next round.

It was a joke and things like that would piss anyone off and did him no favours with his fellow riders. The fans, even those from Bruce's British League team

Cradley, booed him and they were not happy at all. Kenny would never have done what Bruce did that day.

Maybe Kenny could relate to Kelly and Shawn, who were just like down to earth Yorkshire kids, whereas Bruce and the rest seemed to come across as being a bit more upper crust-types above him. I mean, when Bruce came in after a race he looked like he'd just been on a film shoot, not ridden a hard-fought speedway race, and it was the same with the American road-racing star Freddie Spencer. But when I finished a race I always looked like I'd been shovelling Yorkshire coal for 10 hours.

I loved the Yanks in road-racing. They all had a winner's attitude, were larger than life, fitter than everyone else and set a great benchmark for me to beat them. They were always 100 per cent prepared and on top of their game, so they raised my game plan too. All in all they were great stuff.

Speedway's World Championship has been run along grand prix lines since 1995 but in those days the World final was still a one-off, one-night meeting and the hardest thing was qualifying for it. There were so many rounds held all over England and other parts of Europe, you knew that if you'd made the final 16 you really were one of the best riders in the world.

Kenny won several championship qualifying rounds along the way but always seemed to come up short on the big one, the World Final, and most important meeting of all. It happened at Wembley in 1981, Los Angeles in '82 and again at Norden, Germany, where the final was staged in 1983.

Let me tell you the story about Norden, which began like a scene from the wild west. We set off with some heavy artillery, led by big and intimidating men like Mal Carter (The Daddy), John Silcox, a well handy guy who was Dad's sales manager at Pharaoh, and Peter Garside, a giant of a man, plus a few other heavies and all of Kenny's mechanics.

We boarded the Holland-bound North Sea Ferry at Hull and everything was going great. We all booked into our cabins and then it was evening dinner – a feast fit for a king . There was an amazing buzz on the ship, because it was half full of speedway fans.

After dinner we all hit the bar and the disco and things were going as sweet as a nut. The drinks were flowing and I was dancing with some girls when this big German guy pushed into me. It was no big deal at first but when he knocked into me again, that was when Mal said "hit the bastard", so I gave him a big right-hander. Before you knew it, everyone was fighting, it was sheer madness. We were only going to the speedway final, not to watch Bruno v Tyson.

One of Kenny biggest fans got a right roughing-up by one of our team and had a black eye in the morning. The poor chap thought he was only coming to watch Kenny win his first World final, not get a pasting on a ship, but he was fine the next day and we all shook hands.

Departing the ship at Hook of Holland, we were all rounded up by the Dutch police who wanted to form an identification parade to catch the instigator of the trouble.

Light in the Darkness

Kenny leading Danish star Hans Nielsen and Germany's Karl Maier at Norden.

The German pointed out me as the ringleader and the cops stood there in amazement, laughing at this parade of menacing looking men that made Vinnie Jones look like Peter Pan, so we were all allowed to carry on our journey to the final we nearly missed. In the fight we all lost our gold chains – about four grand's worth back then – and I nearly broke my wrist punching the giant German.

After checking into our hotel at Norden we went to look at the track, which was in the middle of nowhere – a million miles from the class of Wembley and the LA Coliseum. The track itself looked OK, though, and Kenny was flying again. With Penhall now retired, my brother was odds-on favourite to win the vacant title. He was looking great and once the bikes were set up it looked a foregone conclusion that he was going to win.

But on arriving at the track on race day, we immediately noticed they had put about a million gallons of water on the track. It was a right bog and meant setting up the bikes for these conditions became a lottery.

Many people will tell you the track was especially set-up for the German star Egon Müller but to be honest, I just don't know. All I can tell you is that I've never seen a guy win five races so easily. He made everyone else look like they were on the old two-valve Jawas because Egon rode fantastic that day on his GM rocket ship to win with a 15-point maximum.

For Team Carter it was the same old, same old . . . fantastic in practice followed by a very poor race meeting – another fifth place for Kenny with 10 points. For the third year in a row he was fifth in the World Final. Now trust me, that's unacceptable when you go there thinking you're going to win.

Kenny was absolutely gutted to the bone. And little did we know at the time but due to badly broken legs in the following two years, Norden '83 would be his last

World Final of his very short life. It's heartbreaking for me to think that two of the most naturally talented kids ever to race bikes, both with fantastic support in our early careers, never became world champions.

The great three times world champion Kenny Roberts said: "It's not easy to become a world champion regardless of your talent."

Never a truer word has been spoken.

Not that Kenny was down for long after his failure in Germany. Back home, he tried to prove to me how fit and strong he was, which gave me a laugh.

I was working out in my gym when he phoned to say he was on his way round. I fully loaded my bench-press with weights and had a practice go before his arrival. I could just manage to do one rep with about triple my body weight on the bar.

"Let's have a go then – OK no prob, let's go for it," he says.

Talk about funny. Well, he puffed and panted then gave it his all – but the bar didn't even move off the stops.

I'm like, 'come on then' and he said: "I'm just, er, er, warming-up."

Warming-up, my arse. So he tried again and screamed out loud to try and get some extra power into the bar, but it still never moved.

"Get out of the way, you lamo," I screamed at the top of my voice before doing one rep. I could only do one because I'd piled on about 10 times more weight than I'd normally push. I knew I could do it after the practice I had before he turned up.

Kenny's face was a picture. Despite another desperate attempt, he still couldn't even move the bar holding the weights and had to finally concede that I'd beaten him again.

I worked hard on my fitness, doing bench-pressing, curls, tricep pull-downs, leg work and use a treadmill. I'd usually spend at least an hour in the gym most days and also did a lot of running and cycling. Kenny did nothing to maintain or improve his fitness.

He ended the '83 season on a winning note by taking victory in the Brandonapolis individual meeting at Coventry – it was three times World Champion Ole Olsen's farewell to British speedway and all the top blokes were riding. I remember it for different reasons.

Kenny rings. "Fancy coming to Coventry, Al?"

Which translates to 'basically, I'm f*****, no-one else can come, so can you help me?'

"Yeah, no prob," I said.

That was my problem. All I could ever say was 'yeah, no prob' because I was too nice. On many occasions I should have told him to piss off and hung up but I didn't, and I'm still the same with people today.

"Get to my house for one," he says.

"OK, bye."

Ten minutes later, he's on the phone again. "Can we use your van?"

"Yeah, no problem, bye."

Light in the Darkness

Another 10 minutes goes by and the phone rings again.

"Oh, forgot to tell yer, fill it up and I'll give yer the cash back when we get there."

Talk about a tight bugger, he squeaked when he walked. He was about as tight as a duck's arse, and that's water-tight.

As you can guess, Lord Kenny slept all the way to Coventry but I'm OK. I'm thinking how cool I look and how all the girls will be after me 'cos they sure won't be chasing Pizza Face.

On arrival at Brandon Stadium the cheeky t**t pulls out a pair of £3.50 overalls that looked like they'd come from Wilkinson's and tells me I'm his dope-and-oiler for the night. I'm like, 'great'.

So King Kenny scores a 15-point max and I'm like 'get in there, son', while looking forward to a nice slap-up meal after the meeting.

No such luck. In the dressing room after racing he rips in half some mankie ham sandwich and says "have a swig of me orange pop if yer want."

Dad always said he had two sons – one a miser and the other a poseur. And he was right.

I got home from Coventry without grub and it cost me £30 in fuel to chauffeur the Brandonapolis winner there and back. What a deal that was.

The next time Kenny rang asking me to come with him to Wolverhampton, I said: "My name's Tommy Tucker, not Silly F*****" – and hung up.

ALAN CARTER

Above and right: The great Kenny Roberts invited me to become part of his new adventure.

Below: American Wayne Rainey was my little known team-mate in 1984.

Light in the Darkness

18 INVITE FROM KENNY ROBERTS

Splitting from Big Mal . . . running scared . . . meeting Wayne Rainey . . . home alone at 18.

I'D just finished 14th in the 250cc world championships and now the 1983 season was over. Not only did I feel I'd massively under-achieved, in hindsight Mal had pushed me way too far for my own safety.

We had no firm plans for '84 after our sponsor, Mitsui Yamaha, pulled the plug after one year of GP racing. They failed to pay Dad money owed to me on time, which he wasn't happy about. He was always chasing them for money on the deal they had agreed and ended up paying a lot of our unbudgeted expenses out of his own pocket, and I've got to say he really did a fantastic job in organising our world championship team.

It was all about to change, though, both on and off the track.

We got a call late in the year from Kenny Roberts. He said: "I'm going to be running a team with sponsorship from Marlboro cigarettes and would like Alan in the team to partner a young American called Wayne Rainey. Could you come down to London and meet us?"

When Dad told me the news, I couldn't believe my luck. We set off from Halifax one cold December day to meet Kenny Roberts and chatted all the way to London. Mal said: "Leave it all to me, son." I felt so excited.

We met up in a restaurant in the Chinatown area of London's West End, where Kenny Roberts was accompanied by Wayne Rainey, who, unbeknown to me, had become the AMA Superbike Champion in October '83. I didn't know anything about him at the time, never checked his record to see how good he was, and the truth is I didn't really care. Wayne, who is four years older than me, was very quiet at our meeting but he came across as a nice guy.

Everything seemed to go fantastically well and the deal was done. I was getting $25,000, a huge increase on what I'd raced for in '83, although I was happy just to be in the world championships. They paid it all to me upfront – the dollar was worth 1.5 times the pound, which would pay for a few fillet steaks and dover soles – and I felt like I'd become a millionaire overnight.

At end of the night, we all shook hands and Dad and I were on our way back up the M1 to Yorkshire.

This turned out to be my last journey with Dad as my sponsor and manager. I fell asleep on the way home and, for some reason, he wasn't happy with me. I have no idea to this day why. Maybe at the meeting he had a premonition of what was to follow or I'd missed something that was said at the meeting. I know he had the hump with me a bit because I wouldn't eat the 'foreign food' – crispy seaweed and all that crap. It wasn't for me at the time but I've become multi-cultural with cuisine since then.

We travelled more than 500 miles that day. It was a long trip, I was exhausted with excitement and, as you know, it's not easy to stay awake when you're the passenger and feeling tired.

A few days passed and I got a call from Kenny Roberts pointing out that it was his team and that he really wanted me in it. But – and this was the crux of the matter – he didn't want Dad to have anything to do with it. That was the deal – take it or leave it. Fair enough.

I can see how Roberts probably took offence at Dad's mannerisms and cocky demeanour, and telling him how things were going to be. And on the other hand, Dad probably resented Kenny Roberts having such a big say in my career. I couldn't see it at the time but, looking back, I now realise it was probably the case. Mal was a kingpin in British road-racing at that time, a powerful character who saw himself as a bit of a Ross Brawn/Ron Dennis, and he wouldn't have taken kindly to me joining a team run by the legendary Kenny Roberts.

I dreaded telling Dad what Kenny had said on the phone. He'd just built a new luxury flat in the basement of the house next door to the garage, where his father Lionel and his partner Katie were living above, and I was living there rent-free. I'd also put a lot of hard work into doing it up myself. I knew Mal was not a guy to cross at any cost but I couldn't turn down this once-in-a-lifetime offer to join the triple World Champion's racing team.

I told Roberts I was in and then approached Mal to inform him what the American road-racing superstar had said. Instead of wishing me all the best, he just did what he always did. He ripped into me, calling me all the names under the sun.

I felt very bad but as far as I was concerned this had nothing to do with money. I would gladly have given Mal 25 or 50 per cent of the $25,000 Roberts was going to pay me just to have him by my side. After all, I appreciated that he was the guy who spent a fortune on getting me up there in the first place. As it happens, I found out years later, while reading Rainey's book, that Roberts had paid him $40,000 to ride for him. Good luck to Wayne. If that's what he negotiated for himself, there are no sour grapes from me. If Kenny could have got him or me for 10 grand a year, then obviously he would have.

Looking back, if Dad and I could've worked something out, that would have been great and the ideal solution for me. I'm not the sort of guy who likes to fall out with people.

So there I was, still only 19 at the time, and on my own. Maybe Kenny Roberts did me a great favour by making that call, I'm not sure. What I do know is that Mal always said to everyone after our split that I was "f****** rubbish and a no-hoper."

The fact is, I went on from being number 14 in the world with Mal to number nine in 1984, then number seven the following year, so he was talking bullshit and just being a bitter man, although I truly understand how he must have felt. He would have viewed my decision as an act of betrayal.

Kenny Roberts invited me to the USA in the winter of 1983-84 for what would

Light in the Darkness

have been a great opportunity for me to practice on his farm, along with Wayne and other riders, on different types of dirt bikes, but it was just not possible. I was scared that Dad would kick me out of the flat and I'd find myself homeless. I also felt that he had it in him to beat me up, which he'd threatened to do on several occasions. If ever you gave him any back-chat he'd threaten to hit you. And if you didn't shut up, he would do. You had no chance of winning an argument with him – or our Kenny for that matter, although my brother never threatened me. I've become very wary of people who, like Mal and Kenny, are very opinionated.

At one point Mal did actually tell me to get out of the flat but by then I'd seen it coming and had made alternative plans. My main focus now was not on the 1984 world championships, but to move out of the flat.

I found a brand new detached bungalow in Mount Tabor, a semi-rural location about five miles from Dad's garage and some three miles from our Kenny. It cost me £29,995 and was ideal. I moved in at 2 Whernside Way just before the 1984 world championships started in March.

Kenny also split from Mal about the same time as me. By then he'd made his own money from speedway and was no longer as reliant on Mal as he used to be. Kenny and I never spoke about splitting from Dad, we just grew up into young men and needed to branch out and do our own thing. I think, deep down, Kenny was just as scared of Mal as I was.

It's a sad thing to say but I feared my father until he passed away in 2009. There was never ever any love or compassion shown by him, not even a hint of a caring side. He was a person to be feared.

People will possibly point to Mal's tough upbringing as the root cause of his own bullying behaviour and the fact that he was so unloving but I don't go along with that. Take his elder brother, David, for example. He's a lovely man. And Dad's

The bungalow that became my first own home in 1984, with my red Fiat Strada Abarth parked outside.

younger brother, Alan, is also a nice guy. It's just the way Mal was and I put it down to his own insecurity.

These traits often go in generations. Perhaps Mal thought that because his father had neglected him and treated him so badly as a child, then it was OK to treat me and Kenny the same. He often used to say to me: "You've never done a day's work and you've lived a charmed life." He'd hold out his hands and say: "Look at these, you don't know what struggling is."

He'd say this to me even though I'd lost my Mum, my little brother and my eldest brother, all in very tragic circumstances. And then when my baby died, he brushed it off by saying it was just like a cow or a sheep dying. We'll get on to that last tragedy in my life a bit later.

Anyway, I drew a line under his bullying nature and decided I wasn't going to continue the Carter pattern. I went the opposite way to Mal and vowed that my own children were not going to be treated as I was by my Dad.

I think both Kenny and I should have sought some form of counselling after all we'd been through with Mum but in those days it was just unheard of. You just got on with what you had to do and that was it.

The more I think about the terrible way Kenny and Mum's lives ended, the more I think that what happened to her must have had a major psychological effect on his brain. He was 10 and I was seven when she came out of hospital a quadriplegic. She would scream our names out very loud for us to go and help her in the middle of the night. It was awful.

Some of the sights we saw were not pleasant – finding her on the floor after she'd fallen out of bed trying to get to the toilet, then shitting herself many times. Even the two of us didn't have the strength to pick her up off the floor and God only knows how we managed to do it and clean her up.

Sometimes I look back and think: why us? What did we do wrong? We never hurt anyone. But we were robbed of a proper childhood and it just wasn't fair.

To be honest, how Kenny and I achieved what we did in racing under these circumstances was a miracle.

19 CHANGE IN KENNY

Moving to Grey Horse Farm ... old friends and a first class mechanic cast aside for glorified gofers ... Kenny's riding crap bikes ... how I cheated Rainey and Lawson ... and when Roberts did a runner.

OUR Kenny had purchased a run-down old pub with some land off Taylor Lane, Bradshaw, just south of Halifax. It had been empty for many years with only an old man living on the grounds in a ramshackle old caravan, so my brother had a lot on his plate having to rebuild it more or less from scratch.

When he'd finished the renovations early in 1983 the stone-built house at Grey Horse Farm looked fantastic. He had his own workshops and also carved out a moto-cross track with a proper speedway starting gate, where we'd occasionally race each other. It used to piss him off that I'd out-trap him every time, although he'd soon come flying past like a madman.

Around this time things were changing for him on a large scale. Out would go Richard Pickering, one of the best speedway mechanics in the country, along with most of his childhood mates who were there for him in his early days. Richard was older and smarter than Kenny and very meticulous. He'd been Chris Pusey's mechanic and had been around. The friends he discarded included Graham 'Dunny' Dunn, who was his best mate, and Gary 'Gaz' Docherty, a former neighbour of ours from just up the road in Brickfield Lane.

As far as I was concerned he brought in glorified gofers, people like Phil 'Ollie' Hollingworth and Bryan Larner. I'm not saying they weren't nice people, but they weren't capable of looking after the number one rider in England. Kenny needed a solid team around him, just like Bruce Penhall had, not a circus act. It just goes to show that Dad and Kenny were so much alike – tyrants, dictators or whatever else you want to call them.

I just couldn't believe what he was doing but, like Mal, you could never tell him anything. At times he was just pig-headed beyond belief.

Kenny could see, and so could everyone else – riders and fans alike, that Bruce had a slick operation and there were no weak links in his chain. So what on earth was Kenny thinking?

I'd always wanted to be the ultimate superstar, to look immaculate with everything looking great. I really loved the way Bruce conducted himself, the way he spoke. He was just first class. But I thought Kenny's machine preparation was shoddy by comparison.

I worked for Kenny as his mechanic at one meeting and took a close look at his bikes. Some of the bolts holding them together were a complete joke. I noticed a 70-

ALAN CARTER

*Kenny outside his new home, Grey Horse Farm at Bradshaw, surrounded by machinery, equipment and mechanics.
Below: Happy family: Kenny, Pam and baby Kelly-Marie.*

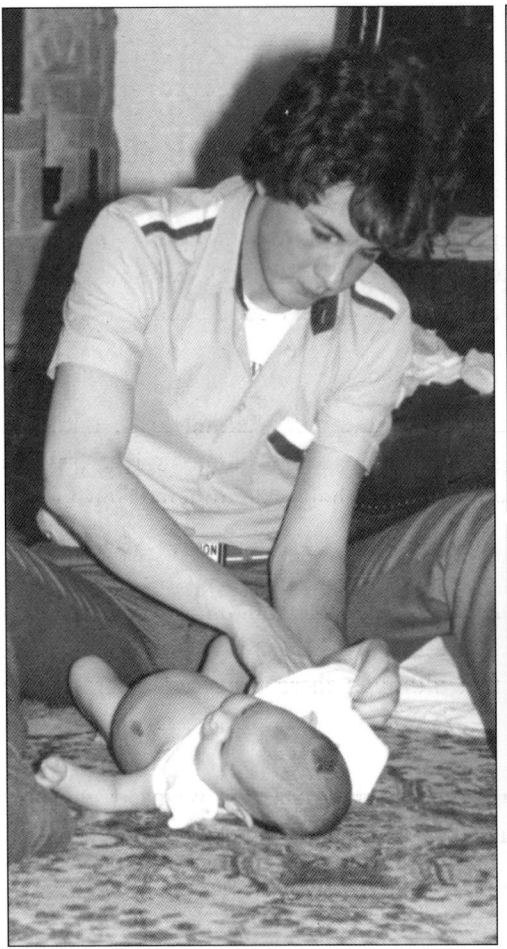

Light in the Darkness

80mm bolt through the back mudguard, when it should have been no more than 35mm in length. It was nearly touching the tyre and I thought, if this tyre was to expand, as they do, it will rub onto the bolt and could lead to a puncture. I pointed this out to Kenny but he took no notice.

The bolt came loose after every race and I had to wind it back in, but there were no washers or locking nut. It was shoddy. As a rider, I was operating on a much higher level than Kenny, supported by some of the best people in the world of road-racing.

So from about 1984 to until his death in early '86 Kenny was riding crap equipment – well, good stuff but badly put together. I think this also had something to do with the broken legs he suffered and which wrecked his world championship dreams in both 1984 and '85. This period became a downward spiral in his career.

Sure, Kenny still had moments of sheer brilliance, just like Michael Lee did, but he should have had a top manager and a brilliant back-up team to push him on to become World Champion. But I could see it all slipping through his fingers and there was only one person to blame – himself.

My own preparation for the start of the '84 season was not the best either. I'd missed all the winter training in the USA at Kenny Roberts' ranch and was still fearful of Dad calling around and giving me a good hiding, or bumping into him in the bank or somewhere else around town. It was a bit unnerving for me. I'd trained hard on my personal body and was in good physical shape. Just wasn't as strong, mentally, as I would have liked.

I flew to South Africa for the first GP of the year. Kenny Roberts had arranged for us all to stay at his rented private house in Johannesburg. On meeting up, Kenny was keen to see how fit we were, so he organised a four-mile running race involving myself, Wayne Rainey and Eddie Lawson, who had been Kenny's team-mate on the Marlboro Yamaha 500s the year before and was also a very good buddy of Wayne's.

I was right there with them at the halfway point but, to be honest, I was knackered. I don't know if it was the altitude or them being super-fit – probably the latter. I stopped for a few seconds to catch my breath and, not wanting to be outdone, flagged down a pick-up truck carrying a load of trees and hitched a ride back to Kenny's place. The driver drove me to within about a half-mile from the finish when I jumped off and ran into the house in first place. You could hear a pin drop, everyone was astounded that I'd kicked Wayne and Eddie's ass.

But my moment of glory didn't last long. As soon as they got back they said: "You cheating little prick!" I was busted but I still gave the team a great laugh.

It didn't take long to become clear that although there were two riders in the Roberts team, only one was receiving 100 per cent support while I was basically given a standard bike for the year.

But no Yank was going to beat me without a fight. I was the youngest ever GP winner, I'd had a year's world championship experience and this was my fourth season riding 250cc two strokes, proper racing bikes. Wayne did fantastically well

ALAN CARTER

Kenny, the barman, entertaining friends and family at Grey Horse Farm.

Kenny and me got ready to have fun riding around his home-made moto-cross track.

Light in the Darkness

Kenny (nearest camera) and me take a break from our respective sports to enjoy the jumps and bumps of his moto-cross circuit on the farm. Below: Kenny showing off again.

to qualify in fifth place for his first GP but I grabbed fourth spot to show him that I was the main man, not him.

It pissed down all morning on race day and I was like, 'get in there, this is going to be an easy win.' Tyre choice was easy – I went for 100 per cent full wets while all the Europeans picked intermediates.

I was gone like a bullet out of a gun, pulling out a 10-second lead and the race was in the bag, but then it stopped raining. Once the sun came out the track dried in just a few short minutes. My tyres began to over-heat and fell to bits – I was down to the steel belt by the end of the race. Basically, I kept losing the front end. I would normally have pulled into the pits but I carried on and finished 10th on the basis that one world championship point was better than nothing.

But I just couldn't believe my luck as yet another GP went begging.

As a manager, Kenny Roberts treated me fine, although the team he ran in that first year was cliquey. There was Kenny's mentor and former manager Kel Carruthers, the 1969 250cc World Champion, plus Wayne, Eddie, the tuner Bud Aksland and another guy working with them called Bruce.

Kenny liked to let his hair down and socialise with the rest of us. He was funny, a bit of a piss-taker. One day, Rainey said to him: "Hey Kenny, look at that blackbird." And Kenny says: "It's a crow, dickhead!"

He once came out of a bar in Holland with Eggis, my mechanic, and a few other guys and crashed their car into a number of other parked vehicles before doing a runner. The cops paid us a visit the next day but our team manager, Paul Butler, who is now the race director for MotoGP, sorted it.

I wish I could have ridden for Kenny Roberts later in my career, after gaining more experience. My only disappointment with him came years later, when I was trying to get a ride and hoped he might be able to help me. I phoned his home in California and waited on the line to speak to him, only for the person who answered my call to hang up. That hurt. Maybe he never got the message? I'll probably never know.

20 CHAMP WITH A BROKEN LEG

Kenny at centre of major track row . . . his passion for fast cars . . . sleeping with Rainey
. . . mischievous girls with a porno mag.

THE 1984 season began in a blaze of publicity for our Kenny when he was controversially appointed the new England captain at the age of 22, despite his unpopularity with team-mates.

But his joy was short-lived. Within days of the start of the season he crashed while riding for Halifax at Cradley on Easter weekend and sustained a compound fracture of his right leg. Most riders would have accepted that their season was over there and then, but not my brother.

He hobbled around the pits on crutches and still somehow managed to get through the British semi-final – his first qualifying round of the world championship – at Oxford just five weeks later. But he was still nowhere near fit when the tough British Final qualifier was staged at Coventry in June, when track conditions were a joke.

Rain had fallen heavily on the Brandon circuit before the meeting and, to me, it looked like it should never have started. Most of the 16 riders didn't want to risk their necks and after watching the video, I don't think I would have either. Kenny and one or two others wanted the meeting on, though.

The slippery conditions caused several riders to crash in the first few races and the meeting was held up for around 45 minutes as the arguments raged behind the scenes. In the changing rooms five or six riders, including several of his England team-mates, ganged up on Kenny and swore at him as a major row erupted.

If I'd been the ref and there were 13 riders who wanted it off and only three who were happy to race on, I probably would've gone with the majority vote and called it off. PC and Chris Morton had been around a long time and they were probably right when they said the track was unfit and too dangerous to ride. The track did look bad, although it got better as the meeting went on.

Kenny was in a pretty bad way, having to be pushed around in a wheelchair before the meeting and between each of his five races. With his broken leg encased in a plaster cast and wearing a specially-made oversized protective boot, I've no idea how he even got clearance to ride from the track doctor.

I wondered what was going through his head as he sat in the pits in a wheelchair. Surely Mum must have been in his thoughts – it was as if he was going to do this for her.

ALAN CARTER

The winter weather at Kenny's place was nothing to the icy blast he got from his rivals at Coventry.

Light in the Darkness

I liked racing in the wet and Kenny probably fancied his chances of qualifying in conditions that were far from ideal, although he was taking a risk that another fall could damage his leg even more. Come rain or shine, he didn't really give a shit about track conditions, though. His only focus was winning races. Maybe some of this blinkered attitude stemmed from his schoolboy motocross days when you raced whether it pissed it down all day or not.

It wasn't his decision anyway. With a 10,000 crowd inside the stadium and the ITV cameras present to record it for national television, the referee decided the show had to go on.

From the re-start of the meeting, Kenny was hell bent on becoming British Champion and he knew that victory in his last ride would clinch the title he craved so badly. He had to beat the former World Champion Peter Collins, his World Pairs-winning partner from the previous year, and PC's younger brother Les.

Kenny made a howler of a start and it was looking like a costly third place finish until he passed Les Collins and came hard under PC to take the lead and win his first British Championship. The crowd went crazy and he became a national hero.

The cheeky little bugger, who nicked a Jack Russell pup and sold it to me for a tenner when I was a nipper, sure had come a long way.

It's funny, but throughout the first six years that Kenny rode for Halifax Dukes they never finished higher than sixth in the final British League table and failed to win any major honours – even though they had probably the best English rider in the country. Kenny was local born and bred but I wonder if he ever thought about leaving them to join a better team. I know *I* would have. I can tell you that if ever he did consider trying to better himself elsewhere, he never mentioned to me about any dissatisfaction with Halifax. He was Halifax Dukes to the bone.

Having said how loyal Kenny was to his home-town team, it's fair to assume they probably couldn't afford to sign another big-name rider to spread the load because they were already paying him a lot of money.

I think he earned a lot more from racing than I did. While I rode once a month, he was often racing three, four or even five times a week in England and abroad. I could easily go all the way to, say, Yugoslavia, crash or break down in my first race and then wait a month for my next ride. My schedule was 12 GPs a year but he had more than 50 meetings more or less guaranteed.

In road-racing, you were paid an allowance from the FIM to cover air tickets and accommodation but no start money was paid. To earn, you had to be in the points. When I won the French GP in 1983, my prize money was £2,500. It's difficult to say how much I earned at my peak but it would have been somewhere between £10,000 and £30,000 a year. Some years I made nothing. In 1982, '83 and '84 I did OK and even though I finished seventh in the world in '85, I blew it all.

My best year, financially, was either 1983, when Dad paid for everything, I got a bit of sponsorship and kept all my earnings, or my last year in racing, 1992, when Hein Gericke, a German clothing manufacturer, paid me £12,000 and Honda gave me £2,000 and I received other bonuses here and there for things like helmet deals.

I was always one or two rungs from the top of being signed up for a six-figure deal, due to politics rather than lack of ability, so I can't say I ever made any real money out of road-racing.

Although the deal with Kenny Roberts was that he paid me $25,000 a year to race for his team, and I was allowed to keep my own prize money to fund my lifestyle, I still had to pay my personal expenses –meals, etc – out of that annual sum.

Our Kenny was always one step ahead of me. When I got my Mazda RX7 sports car he had to buy one too – but his had to be the turbo version. You could never have anything better than him. But I wouldn't say he was flash with his money. He liked making it, not spending it. His only indulgence was his love of fast cars – he had a Scimitar, a Ford Escort RS2000, a couple of Mercs and a Rolls-Royce. He drove fast, flat out wherever he went, but he was a good driver.

One day I happened to meet a delivery man called Pete, who was working for Knight Freight, a firm that used to deliver stock to me around 2007 when I was supplying the florist trade. Anyway, we got talking one day and, as we both came from Halifax, we got on to speedway, but little did he know at this point who I was.

He said: "I'll tell yer a story about that Kenny Carter . . . "

I was like, 'oh yeah, carry on . . .'

Pete said: "I was playing pool in the Prospect Inn (the speedway hangout in Halifax on Saturday nights when it was jam packed) and me and my mate were playing pool with a few 10ps on the table when this cocky c*** came up and said: 'I'm on next, do you know who I am?'

"I told him; 'I don't give a f*** who you are, you're on after us'."

Light in the Darkness

Above: Funny, it was normally me the police were after. Below: Kenny had to be helped onto his bike after deciding to bravely race on with a broken right leg in 1984. This was taken before a practice ride at The Shay.

ALAN CARTER

At that point I laughed and told Pete who I was. You should have seen his face.

If South Africa was a complete washout, for the second round of the '84 GP series in Italy I descended to a new level. I had no confidence in the front end of the bike and didn't qualify for the race at Misano. I was first reserve but didn't get to start. But I rode a blinder to finish fourth in the Spanish GP – Rainey came 10th this time following his third place in Italy – and now the confidence was returning at last.

While all the mechanics slept in the transporter truck with our bikes the night before race meetings, Wayne and I shared a caravan – me on the top bunk and him on the bottom. Can you believe it, two superstars in bunk beds!

One day Linda Davis, our team cook, and her best friend Stephanie Sheene (Barry's wife) decided to play a joke on me and Wayne. Each month Kenny Roberts would bring along a copy of the porn mag *Hustler*, which ran a regular article called 'Arsehole of the Month'. It was a feature about a famous person ridiculed by the magazine.

What Linda and Steff did was cut the heading out of the magazine and place it inside my helmet, along with picture of me that had been superimposed. They did the same with Wayne's helmet, with his picture showing beneath the same magazine headline.

When we went to put on our helmets, neither of us had any idea who had put the contents there – and at first we both suspected each other. Rainey wasn't happy and when he asked the two girls who was responsible for the prank, they told him it was me.

And when I found the same thing in my helmet and asked them who'd done it, they pointed the finger at Wayne. I never got the impression that Eddie Lawson liked me, so I thought he was the one to blame.

It was so funny after the penny had dropped and we all realised that it had been a big stitch-up by Linda and Steff.

I had to have the last laugh, though, so, I approached Barry Sheene's dad, Franco, with a plan. He and his wife Iris were almost as famous in road-racing circles as Barry and Stephanie. I said to Franco: "I need Stephanie's clipboard."

She would sit on the pit wall armed with her clipboard and stopwatches to record the riders' lap times. Franco lent me her clipboard. I found a picture of a naked woman showing her fanny, which I cut out and then stuck a photo of Stephanie, which Franco also gave me, over the girl's face. I then slipped my handiwork inside Steff's clipboard before shutting the door to the motorhome behind me.

It was only hours later, when 'Sheeney' was on the start-line as the 500cc GP was about to start, that Steff opened her clipboard and saw what I'd done. She took it well!

I liked Barry and Stephanie. Dad had told me in the past that, basically, Barry had only won his 500cc world championships in 1976 and '77 because he was on a four cylinder engine when his rivals were all still using three cylinder motors . . . he said he was on a superior bike to the rest and he was this and that. But everything Mal said about Barry was bollocks.

Apart from my old mate Donny Robinson, Barry Sheene was the nicest road-racer

Light in the Darkness

I ever met. Bruce Penhall had a hell of a lot of charisma and charm but Sheeney had 10 times as much as the American.

A couple of times I drove down to his luxurious Manor House, at Charlwood in Surrey, and he'd take me up in his helicopter. When we went to nearby Gatwick Airport to fly out for a meeting somewhere, he'd inevitably be booked into business class while I'd slum it in dogshit class. But then an air hostess would come down the aisle and say: "Mr Carter, would you like to follow me to business class, where Mr Sheene is waiting for you."

Despite his long and loving relationship with Stephanie right up to his sad death from cancer at the age of 52 in March 2003, he had a reputation as a playboy and womaniser. Barry worked hard and played hard like no other.

At one time they said I would be 'the new Barry Sheene' and for a while I thought I was, too. Before I'd even got into the GPs, in 1981 and '82, not long before he retired from racing in '84, Barry offered me good advice and plenty of encouragement. But I wouldn't listen because I thought I'd become better than him.

I badly wanted to be the next Barry Sheene. I had a big spread in the News of the World, where in an interview I stated that I was going to make Barry look like a monk.

If I'd made it big, I've no doubt that I would have behaved much as Barry and Georgie Best did in the 70s, when they were sporting superstars in the spotlight with girls falling at their feet. Barry put road-racing on the world map, took it into the mainstream. Fame and money go hand in hand. While Barry will always been remembered as one of the greats, I never made it to the very top, although I was close to it.

While he could walk out of the front door of another home he had, in Russell Square, central London, and into swanky West End hotels do business deals and meet sponsors, I was living in the wilderness on a remote Yorkshire farm.

It was heartbreaking that he died so young but the legend lives on. There will only ever be one Barry Sheene.

Two legends I've been proud to know – Kenny Roberts (left) and Barry Sheene.

ALAN CARTER

On the Marlboro Yamaha in 1984. But the bikes weren't good enough in Roberts' first year as team boss.

21 SPECIAL TREATMENT

*More breakdowns and heartbreak . . . Roberts shows us how it's done . . .
too many DNFs . . . stolen clothes.*

EVERY season of racing presented new problems and it wasn't long into '84 that I started to notice that Kenny Roberts' team was becoming a bit one-sided in favour of Wayne Rainey. Suddenly, he appeared for one round with twin front brake discs – a good idea copied from Carlos Lavado's Yamaha – but where were mine?

Anyway, he crashed on them – it was raining and he had too much front brake. I must admit after turning up in South Africa having not even sat on any type of motor bike in the winter of 1983-84, while Wayne had been racing around Roberts' ranch all winter, beating him in qualifying gave me a real buzz. I feared no-one and I had a point to prove too. I wanted to prove I was the number one in the team but it soon became evident that was never going to happen.

The Carter/Rainey spearhead that Roberts set up looked, on paper, like an unbeatable dream team. With backing from Marlboro, we were red hot favourites, or at least I was. Wayne was an unknown quantity in the 250cc GPs at this stage, although he'd soon show that on his day he could more than match anyone.

Bizarrely, Roberts only turned up at about four meetings that year. And when he did show, he always had something new for Wayne's bike – special barrels or something tuned by Bud Aksland – but never anything different for mine.

One day they even appeared with a full alloy frame for Wayne but it turned out to be no good. He was the team guinea pig but, luckily for me, most of the things he was given didn't work, or at best they were no better than a standard bike.

This preferential treatment affected me mentally, though, because it hurt when I wasn't getting anything new from Roberts and the team. It made me feel unwanted and inferior and I was also getting very angry inside, although it gave me a burning desire to beat Wayne even more. That's just how racing is. One rider usually gets the works while the other receives little. There has never been such a thing as a level playing field – well, at least not in my day.

The best thing I had was Howard Gregory, my long-time mechanic, and best friend Eggis, so we was a strong, tight little British unit and we just kept our heads down and continued to work hard.

The next few GPs were a flop for me, though. We were either at the sharp end or breaking down. The crankshafts were rubbish, although it didn't help that I was over-revving them a bit. But we'd had no problems with them in '83 and I wasn't doing anything differently. We even tried welding the cranks but that made little difference, so in the end we started using a different crankshaft, produced by a company called Hoekle.

Looking back now, it's easy to see I was inconsistent – either right up there with the leaders or breaking down. With Mal well out of the picture, one positive change in '84 was that I was no longer crashing because the only guy pushing me now was . . . me.

A year had passed since the greatest day of my racing life and I was very excited as we headed back to the French GP. This time it was at a different track, the Paul Ricard circuit in the south of France.

Roberts put in an appearance for this one and a good job too because me and Wayne had lost ground a bit and were both on a bit of a downer regarding our race bikes. At best they were very average and our competitors had raised the bar – their bikes were going much faster by now.

Wayne complained to Kenny, saying the bikes couldn't pull the skin off a rice pudding, and I backed him up. Roberts said: "Right, OK lads, let's go see what the problem is."

He rode three laps at Paul Ricard – remember he was well retired by now, but you would never have guessed it. Roberts knocked a second off both mine and Wayne's best track time before pulling back into the pits. What could we say to that? I just wanted to crawl off and die in some faraway place.

Roberts said: "Look, you f****** moaning pair of dickheads, this is what we have now, just go out there and ride the wheels off it."

I can only speak for myself, but this kick up the arse was just what I needed from the boss. It was like working with Mal again, only Kenny had a much smarter way of going about firing you up.

After the previous disappointments – I was 16th in Austria, where Wayne failed to finish and then he finished one place ahead of me as we came home sixth and seventh in Germany – I was ready to retain my French title.

If ever there was a career-defining moment, this was it. On this hot summer's day at Le Castellet I rode like a true genius. Inspired by Roberts' earlier humiliation, I came from mid-pack, right up to the leading group, passing some of the world's best. I was in fourth place, ready to blow by them and win the French GP again, when the engine ground to a halt. I was out. Heartbroken. Again.

How many bad knocks can one man take? When you look back in history, I won one GP but I feel like I was trapped in a nightmare in which I was mugged over and over again. I should have won more than 30 GPs and become a three times World Champion at least.

There was never the sponsorship or the support for riders in England to enable us to compete with the rest of the world. People like Sito Pons were getting massive money from the Spanish oil giant Campsa – even the king of Spain attended the GP at Jarama. Team Italia was giving it a massive push through the Italian organisation plus there was the likes of Rothmans cigarettes backing some of the top foreign guys, who had been great but were now well past their sell-by date.

What did we have? The f****** ACU – a bunch of old giffers doing f*** all.

Light in the Darkness

When I approached people for sponsorship they thought I was a greasy biker in black leathers or something. It was like pissing in the wind. People would give you products – helmets, oil, etc – but mention money and they were gone as fast as Linford Christie.

Rainey would also have his own problems in his first year of riding the 250cc two strokes bikes. He couldn't start the thing at the Yugoslavian GP, having ridden fantastically in practice to put his bike on pole position. On race day he was last away again, which must have been so frustrating for him, and he did well to finish fourth, three places ahead of me. I really did feel for him but it was a dog eat dog world and you just looked after yourself.

There are so many aspects you have to get absolutely right on the day to win world championship races, let alone season-long championships. It was easy winning meetings in England but in the GPs I was up against multi-GP winners with years of racing experience. They had bikes that were so fast and light compared to my Yamaha, I just couldn't run with them on the fast tracks, at places like Monza, Spa, Salzburg.

After Holland and Belgium, we were back at Silverstone, where we were so well down on top speed I knew we had no chance in the British GP on what is a fast track. That's when a guy came into our race team garage saying: "My name is Bob and I am from Germany."

He was an engine tuner, he had some barrels with him and he asked if we'd like to try them. Roberts said he was not interested but he said I was OK to try them if I wanted to, which is what I did.

After running them in and then getting down to some fast lap times in practice, the bike felt as if it had just had a jumbo jet engine fitted – it went like a rocket ship, the fastest thing out there. Then, you guessed it, it seized and destroyed both barrels, so we had to put the stock Yamaha ones back on for the race. I was gutted again – they were the only pair of barrels Bob had.

By the start of the race I was on another downward spiral. I was in the mid-pack when my bike ground to a halt yet again. If '83 was the year I crashed my brains out, '84 was the year of the DNF – Did Not Finish – due to repeated mechanical breakdowns.

Now we were off to Sweden for the penultimate GP of the season. I spoke to Steve Webster, who was one of the best sidecar racers in the world championships and asked him if there was any chance of a lift to Sweden, so I met up with Steve and his team. They were boarding the boat at Newcastle and when I asked Steve how much my tickets cost, he just smiled and said: "Don't worry about that."

As we arrived at the dock and were about to go through customs, Steve said to me: "Just hide in the sidecar and keep quiet, we'll cover you with a blanket and give you the nod when we're on the boat."

'OK, ace, a right cheap do here,' I thought.

The boat was fully booked, so all the cabins were full and even the chairs had all been taken, so where was I to sleep as we sailed across the North Sea?

I devised a plan to take the curtains down in one of the rooms on the boat. This was going to be my new sleeping bag for the night. I found a nice, little quiet place to kip too. After neatly folding my clothes, I placed them next to me and all I had on was my underpants. I was out like a light.

I awoke in the morning to find that some wise guy had stolen my clothes. I was going to look a right fool, so I had another bright idea. I ripped a hole in the curtains and made a 'poncho'. There I was, England's number one 250cc road-racer, walking around a luxury liner looking like some weird drifter – no clothes, no shoes, only a pair of curtains wrapped around me. As I entered the dining area, I received a reception fit for a king – everyone pissed themselves laughing as it became clear to me that Steve Webster had nicked all my clothes.

Practice went fantastic at Anderstorp, where I qualified in the top 10. On race day, I was so excited because I was now on a track that I loved and felt I had a good chance of a top three placing, even a win if things panned out right.

I made a great start and was running with the leaders. I equalled my best result of the season, another fourth place, just missing out on a rostrum position but happy to finish 10 positions ahead of Rainey.

We headed to the Muggelo race track in San Marino for the final round of the world championship on September 2. It had one of the longest straights in grand prix racing and once again we were down on power. Even so, practice had gone well and I was happy with my bike set-up.

On race day I made another great start but got stuck behind four times World Champion Toni Mang. To be fair, I was much faster in the turns but his bike was just so fast in a straight line. It was making things difficult for me as the leaders were getting away, so I knew I had to pass him. I dived under him, only to lose the front end.

I broke one of my fingers in the process and had to settle for ninth place overall in my second season of 250cc world championship racing, just one place and four points behind Wayne Rainey. France's Christian Sarron won the title, despite four GP round successes for the German Manfred Herweh.

I could go on and talk about 'if this and if that' but like they say: 'If ifs and buts were candy and nuts we would all have a merry Christmas.'

22 BROKEN DREAMS

Injuries take their toll ... Team Carter ... underhand dealings ... Donington fall guy.

MINE and Kenny's dreams of becoming World Champion were slowly fading away. The broken leg he sustained at Cradley in the early part of 1984 was now getting worse, not better, and it was all his own fault – he wouldn't give it a chance to heal properly.

I know how he felt, though, as I came back too soon after a bad injury in the early 90s. He'd just won his first British title and in treacherous conditions that were unfit for racing, and as a racer all you want to do is get back out there and do what you love most – racing.

Kenny pushed as hard as he could to try and make the World Final in Sweden but, after scraping through the next qualifying round at Belle Vue, he was eliminated from the title race during the final qualifier in Denmark after the pain became too unbearable.

Several of the screws in his lower right leg had come loose due to him racing on it when he should have been resting at home. He'd suffered a very serious compound fracture which needed time to heal but, being very impatient, he never gave it a chance.

After his troubled first season as boss of his 250cc world championship team, Kenny Roberts pulled out of racing, just like Mitsui had at the end of '83, so I had nothing to ride with the '85 season fast approaching. Our Kenny thought he had the answer.

Like Dad, Kenny had a sharp business brain and was always looking at ways to make his next fast buck. He was a wheeler-dealer while I focused 100 per cent on my racing. With a lot of time to kill over the winter of 1984-85 as his broken leg finally had a chance to heal properly, and with Mal completely out of the picture regarding our racing careers, he came up with a plan.

We had a meeting at Kenny's house and as we chatted he asked: "Alan, why don't we work together? I think, from a marketing point of view, we are a much more saleable package as the world's most famous motorcycle racing brothers."

It sounded like a good idea, so that's when we agreed to form Team Carter.

Kenny was going to take care of everything and all I had to do was race the bikes, which suited me fine because I didn't like chasing sponsorship – I always felt like a beggar.

The deal I had with Kenny was just like the one I'd previously had with Dad. I'd give him 25 per cent of everything he got for me, which I had no problem with at first. One thing I have to say about Dad was that I trusted him 100 per cent – he never did anything underhand on that front, unlike our Kenny.

Maybe I was too naive and trusting, my guard was down because he was my brother, but that's when he took advantage of my good nature.

First we set up an office on Kenny's farm. When it came down to business we had long discussions about the best way to approach potential sponsors. I would supply him with details of all my contacts and do the groundwork on them before passing everything on to him. The plan was that he would come in and close the deals. It was a brilliant, bullet-proof plan. All we had to do to make it work was stick to it.

I made one massive mistake. The 25 per cent 'commission' I gave Dad applied to all the cash sponsorship and prize money we received, not free products. They were regarded as a 'little tickle' on the side, a much needed and appreciated bonus.

Well, I'll tell you what my loving brother did to me. And to keep the record straight, I want to say that no matter what Dad and Kenny did to me, all I ever did was love them both with all my heart. They were family, people I trusted.

Since 1980 I'd always had a deal with Dunlop Tyres. They looked after me through thick and thin, they were my rock in racing, along with Shell Oils. These deals were all set up by Dad when I was a kid starting out in racing.

My standard deal with Dunlop was that they'd supply me with 100 tyres per season free of charge, and after that I got them at a discount price. But I can tell you, no matter how many tyres I used, sometimes well over 100 per year, they never charged me a penny. They recognised that we were a team, working towards the common goal of winning,

After passing all my contacts to Kenny he sorted out the Dunlop deal for the 1985 racing season – 100 tyres free for me, which was my standard deal. The normal price of each tyre was £100 each, so that's £10,000 worth of free product. So far, so good.

But, get this, Kenny then sent me an invoice for £2,500 – his 25 per cent commission on my FREE tyres!

I was completely shocked. I didn't have a pot to piss in and was suddenly now two-and-a-half grand in debt to him.

I basically told him I couldn't pay and that he could have 25 f***** tyres at the end of the season instead. I wanted to hit him and should have. He wasn't a happy man and neither was I but this nonsense went on and on.

Next, he told me he'd got me four helmets for the new season – that's £1,000 worth. In the post I received another invoice, this time for £250. I told him: "You're getting a f***** helmet from me at the end of the season and if I stay on and don't damage any of them, yer can have a new one. But, basically, f*** off you rotten, manipulative, piss-taking c***."

The only good deal he did for me was to persuade the owner of Donington Park, Tom Wheatcroft, to sponsor me – and that became a total balls-up, too. Tom was a good friend of Dad's and a big fan of mine. He was a lovely man and really wanted to look after me.

Kenny thought the money would just roll in but it was hard and, to be honest, he

Light in the Darkness

was no better at getting backers than me.

Tom said he would buy me two new bikes and all the spares I needed for the season. I would have to give the bikes back to him at the end of the year but it was still a very good offer. The bikes would have cost Tom about £10,000 new and he'd probably be able to sell them second-hand for around six grand. I think Kenny announced to the press that we'd done a deal worth around £100,000. But that was him – a champagne lifestyle on lemonade money.

All I had to do in return for Tom's backing was race in the British Championships as well as the GPs.

But instead of taking everything Tom was offering us, Kenny told him we'd take the bikes only and not to worry about the spares. He said we'd be getting them from Honda free, so that's how the deal with Tom was done. Tom then diverted the money he was going to give me in spares towards a car racing project, which meant his budget had now gone for the year.

But Honda weren't as forthcoming as Kenny believed they would be. In the end, I ran two of their bikes for the '85 season and when one broke down, I had to take bits and piece from the other one to keep one good machine in running order.

Thankfully, I received no further invoices from Kenny. Maybe he was getting the point that he shouldn't be f****** me over.

Before the start of the 1985 season we had a big Team Carter launch at Donington Park. It was the usual razzle-dazzle occasion, just how Kenny and Dad liked it, but not me. I'd have preferred a much more sophisticated launch. Anyway here we were again, all fur and no knickers.

Launch day was a cold, damp February morning. Kenny invited anyone who had a camera and there was a large media turn-out. I was thinking, 'never mind this

The infamous Team Carter launch day at Donington Park, as Kenny cracks open the champagne.

All's well (above) as we cruise around Donington .. until (below) Kenny gives the media their picture.

bullshit, where's all the cash?' And 'how am I going to get to South Africa in a f****** rowing boat?'

At Donington, Kenny was not as clever as he thought he was. We both did a few laps of the track using my two new race bikes and as it was very wet I picked the bike with the full wet weather tyres on. Kenny was none the wiser – I sent him out on the one with the intermediate tyres. Well, much to the delight of all the photographers and press in attendance, he slid off and made himself look a right prick – and the media had a field day at his expense.

Despite everything, I really did love my brother. He was my friend and hero and the guy who taught me how to ride a motorbike. I was pretty crap at that, too, in the beginning but it's amazing what some tenacity and hard work can do. I'm living proof of what you can achieve in life.

Light in the Darkness

23 MY BIGGEST MISTAKE

Saying 'no' to Honda's top man . . . rubbing shoulders with Fast Freddie Spencer . . . owing money . . . helpful friends . . . missing Mal . . . my British GP agony . . . why a lack of cigarettes in England can seriously damage your wealth . . . British Championship giveaway . . . Tom Wheatcroft, one of the good guys.

MY team for the 1985 season was built around Howard Gregory. We'd been working together for more than five years and this was going to be our third stab at the world championships together. I think I was paying him about £200 per week at that time but God knows how I was going to afford him, because we had no money behind us at all.

I talked my old school pal Welsey into coming on board as the team gofer on 25 quid a week, plus free grub and the chance to see the rest of Europe.

So we got a van and a cheap caravan and we were rocking and rolling.

Round one of the world championship was in South Africa and although Wesley couldn't make it, Howard and I were joined on the trip to Jo'burg in March by brother Kenny. To be honest, he did a good job helping out.

During qualifying Honda Japan unveiled a one-off bike for Freddie Spencer, their main challenger for both the 250cc and 500cc world titles, which had 100bhp and weighed only about 90kgs – the weight limit that year was 95kgs.

As well as Spencer's special, there were lots of factory-kitted Hondas in the paddock, too, but my RS Honda was a standard bike out of the box – with about 70-75bhp and weighing 103kgs.

One of the worst and most embarrassing aspects about the weight issue was the ritual of the pre-race inspection. Everyone would turn up for these because it was one of the few times you could really get close to your competitors' bikes and see what they had, and maybe copy a few things.

All the bikes had to be weighed before passing inspection. When the officials put mine on the scales – or should I say used a crane to lift the bastard on – people would piss themselves laughing. That is apart from the smart technical boffins who thought I was tricking them, as if I had a full tank of fuel in it. But we never did, it was always empty.

My bike was about as fast as a turtle with no legs. The speedtrap times on the long straight at Kyalami clocked Spencer as the fastest at 249km, with me the slowest on my garden-gate-pile-of-shit at 228km.

When the race finished I was last and just avoided being lapped by Fast Freddie. I was gutted.

The biggest mistake I would ever make in my life was about to happen. The boss

ALAN CARTER

Right: Howard Gregory, my loyal and trusty mechanic, and me enjoying some oriental spices.

Below right: With double World Champion Carlos Lavado, a top man as well as a great racer.

Below left: Fast Freddie Spencer.

Bottom: An early season ride at Cadwell Park, my favourite UK track, in March 1985.

148

Light in the Darkness

of Honda Racing Corporation (HRC), Yoichi Oguma, had been watching and as he came towards me, he looked at me with startled eyes and asked: "How you like ride 500cc?"

Spencer had caused them lots of problems by not turning up for testing at venues all over the world and they were pissed off with him. Honda were looking for the next superstar he was offering me a golden chance. Oguma wanted me to test their bike and if I'd gone fast enough on it, Honda would have signed me up on a deal worth a million dollars-plus to me. But I choked.

I've no idea what I was thinking and I've cried many times since at the thought of me wasting this great opportunity to become a true superstar like Barry Sheene. My dream could have become reality if only I'd said yes to the top man at Honda. But instead of living a millionaire lifestyle in Monaco, I'd struggle to make ends meet for the rest of my career and beyond. I'd totally f***** up this time.

Why didn't I jump at HRC's amazing offer? Maybe it was due to me finishing last at the South African GP or the frightening memory of Mal sending me out on 190mph 750cc Yamahas, which had had scared me at the age of only 15. I'm not sure what it was.

I never even told Kenny about this amazing offer. Had I done so, he would have been round to the Honda hierarchy like a rocket ship, saying: "Get that bike warmed up, the little bastard's going out right now."

I don't know why I did so well in racing. Perhaps it was pure fear of Dad. As if I had no option. I had to win.

The bottom line is, Honda never offered me another factory ride and that was the end of that. Another door closed for life.

When we came home from South Africa Kenny was constantly faxing Japan, demanding help from the Honda factory and telling them that my bike was too slow. His pressure must have worked because when we arrived at the next round in Spain, there was a full factory engine waiting for me. Honda UK's Barry Symons said: "This is for you" – it was the biggest breakthrough I ever had, or so I thought at the time. Howard bolted it in and we had two sets of carbs to try, too. And we were at one of my best tracks, Jarama, near Madrid.

I did very well in practice and finished fourth in the race. Now I had some real power under me. Maybe not as quick as Freddie Spencer's kit, but I was happy with what I had. In fact, I came in five places ahead of the brilliant American in Spain. I'd gone from stone last to a very solid fourth place, which put me back on a big high.

At the next round, in Germany, I again finished fourth, beaten only by home favourite Martin Wimmer, Spencer and another German, Toni Mang.

Then came the next hammer blow. After the race at Hockenheim, Honda Japan said their engine that I'd used to such good effect in the previous two GPs had to go back to Japan for one of their other riders. I was like, 'no please.'

For the next few rounds of the world championships we were just not there. And Kenny's great idea that Honda would give me all the spares free of charge never happened. Honda did have a great racing spares service at all the GPs – this was their big comeback year in 250cc GP racing – but everything you took from them at the track was billed and had to be paid for.

I started to run up big bills with Honda. Their spares were keeping us going but I was starting to panic that we wouldn't have the money to pay them.

I was thinking how stupid that brother of mine had been to shun Tom Wheatcroft's previous offer to provide free spares and how that decision had put us in this awful situation. I was now in debt to the biggest motorcycle company in the world.

I was in the public eye and putting on this grand facade that all was great. In reality, my life and finances were crumbling faster than the banking system in the 2008 credit crunch. It got to the point where I owed Honda around £5,000 and it wasn't nice ducking and diving around the GP paddocks trying to dodge the people I owed. I wanted to pay them but I had no money and my self-worth plummeted. Eventually, Honda stopped my credit and wouldn't allow me to purchase any more spares. In the end, I think they actually tore up my bill – but they still wouldn't supply me with more spares.

Because I was well-liked in the GP paddocks, two of my competitors – or should I say new 'sponsors' – started to help out. There was the German legend Toni Mang, a great guy who went on to win five world titles and 42 GPs. He was competing against me on factory Hondas but that didn't stop him from lending me parts on many occasions, at times when we were close to giving up.

I was like one of those irritating, scrounging kids at school: "Toni, I've crashed, can you please lend me a gear?", or "can I borrow a silencer?", or "my fairing's knackered, have you got a spare screen?"

I was a pain in the neck but Toni never turned me down, he was always there and helped as much as he could. He was old school from the 70s – an era when fellow competitors did help each other. No wonder they still talk about the 70s as some of the greatest times in racing.

Then there was Dominique Sarron, a young kid like me who had an elder brother – in his case Christian Sarron – who was a fantastic racer and a World Champion. I became good friends with Dominique, who was riding a similar bike to mine. Several times I'd ask him for some parts and he'd kindly sneak them out for me.

At one GP our crankshaft broke and Dominique happened to come round to our pit for a chat. I was near to tears again and he asked what was wrong. I told him we

Looks like this one was taken at the Italian GP.

were going home, that the crank had gone and we were finished.

He disappeared and about 20 minutes later he was back with a little wooden box with rope handles and a big cheeky grin. "Here," he said, giving me a brand new crank. "Alan, just give me the old one back after Howard has re-built the engine . . . I will tell Honda the broken one was mine."

We were back on the floor after Honda's factory engine was taken away from me but I had to pick myself up again – and I did. Howard worked no end of hours on the bike and we all kept pushing as hard as we could to get results.

Nowhere did I come closer to a GP victory in '85 than in my home grand prix at Silverstone in early August. Howard had got the bike going nearly as well as the factory engine. Howard was amazing – God knows why he stayed with me all those years, because he was one of the best in the world and could have enjoyed more success elsewhere.

I qualified on the second row of the grid and the mood in the camp was electric, there was a real buzz in the air. On race morning you wouldn't believe how much it rained and rained and rained but I was determined. It had now been two years since my French GP win and I was having this one at any cost.

I made a fantastic start to the 22-lap race and kept pulling further away on every lap. I was so far in front, I could've made a pit stop and still won. I never had one slide or blip or anything, it was pure perfection. My pit crew were going mad on the

ALAN CARTER

On the start line before the Spanish GP with Ray Bailey of AP Lockheed

pit wall, trying to get me to slow down. The only problem was, my vision was so bad I couldn't even see them.

On lap 13, after coming down the Hanger Straight at near 150mph in the pissing rain, as I tipped it into the right-hander I lost the front end and skidded about 75 yards, taking out two rows of hay bales.

But thanks to the Carter never-say-die attitude, I dragged the bike out. It was full of shit but despite the front brake lever having half gone, a broken right footrest and a bent handlebar, I somehow got going again and finished seventh.

On the way home I cried my eyes out. I'd just thrown away victory in the British GP in front of 90,000 home fans, all of them as gutted as me.

Despite the frustration at trying to score points on a sub-standard bike, I had to keep telling myself what I could achieve given quality machinery and the right breaks. I'd finished ahead of Freddie Spencer in a 1985 grand prix and he made history that year by becoming the first – and only – racer to win both the 250cc and 500cc world championships in the same season.

Despite the setbacks and heartaches, there were highlights too. I qualified on the front grid – in fourth place – at the Swedish GP and had a fine race, battling all the way to the finish line and narrowly missing out on the top three.

Like many sports involving machinery, especially cars and motor bikes, and this must apply to speedway as well as road-racing, it's not always the most talented guys who win races. Having a lot of money, good sponsors and being mounted on top class equipment counts for an awful lot. To be beaten by riders of lesser ability, but who had faster and more reliable bikes than me, was heartbreaking.

Looking back after nearly 30 years have passed, it's clear to see that other teams had very slick operations funded by sponsorship and massive budgets. Companies with global brands were now starting to pump big money into the sport.

We, on the other hand, looked like a poor club racing team. It was impossible trying to beat the world's best when they were wining and dining and spending more money in one day on hospitality than I had to get me through a full season.

One of the areas I went wrong was that I never used an engine tuner, I just used standard stuff between 1982-84. The expensive factory-backed teams started to come in big-time around '85 and because it was specialist equipment you didn't really need to tune it. But Toni Mang used a top German tuner called Sepp Schloegl, who got his bikes flying like rockets. I could never afford to use a tuner.

I started to realise how important Mal had been in the early days. And I can honestly say Dad was the best sponsor I ever had, and that I was missing him. I'd frozen in a complete panic over the Kenny Roberts situation, scared and with no idea how to face Dad. It was all a big mess.

I found to my cost that politics and marketing can also have a big say in important decision-making. Shortly before the end of the '85 season when I'd finished seventh overall in the world championships at the age of 21, Rothmans announced that I was on a short list of four riders to join their full factory Honda team for '86. I was all set to grasp the opportunity. Now seventh in the world, I had proved myself the fastest and most successful privateer of the season, and I was ready for the big-time.

ALAN CARTER

But, instead, I lost out on this golden chance to my mate, Dominique Sarron. Not because he was any better than me – he wasn't. It basically came down to the fact that he was French . . . and Rothmans were selling a lot more cigarettes in France than they were in England at the time. I'd lost out purely on a marketing decision.

1985 250cc Grand Prix Final Standings (Top 10)

Pos	Rider	Team	Machine	Pts	Wins
1	Freddie Spencer	Rothmans-Honda	NSR250	127	7
2	Toni Mang	Marlboro-Honda	RS250	124	2
3	Carlos Lavado	Venemotos-Yamaha	TZ250	94	2
4	Martin Wimmer	Lui-Yamaha	TZ250	69	1
5	Fausto Ricci	Rothmans-Honda Italy	RS250	50	
6	Loris Reggiani	Aprilia	Aprilia-Rotax	44	
7	**Alan Carter**	**Donington Park-Honda**	**RS250**	32	
8	Manfred Herweh	Massa-Real	Real-Rotax	31	1
9	Reinhold Roth	Römer-Yamaha	TZ250	29	
10	Jacques Cornu	Parisienne Elf-Honda	RS250	25	

For my 21st birthday in August '85 our Kenny arranged for us to enjoy a top night out and a meal in a Bradford club called Cloud 9. There was Kenny, his wife Pam, myself and Nicola Dickinson, the prettiest girl ever to have come out of Halifax. Let's face it, I was hardly going to go out with Nora Batty, was I? I pulled Nicola in a bar in Halifax and she later became my first wife.

Kenny issued his instructions: "Nipper, get the drinks in, I'm off for a piss. I want a Seventh Heaven."

'OK, no problem,' I thought. I'll have my usual bacardi and coke, plus a Pernod for Pam and a lemonade-wine for Nicola. I asked the barman for a Seventh Heaven and he looked at me a bit strangely, before saying: "Are you sure, only they're 70 quid?"

Once again KC had well and truly stitched up.

By the way, a Seventh Heaven consisted of a giant rosebowl filled with a cocktail of champagne and all sorts. It looked amazing and it should have because it cost me more than my first car. Kenny wasn't much of a drinker, though. He went through a phase when he was into Piermont wine but I can never remember him getting drunk.

He didn't have much class or good taste, come to think of it. He liked tomato soup and Compo, out of Last of the Summer Wine, had better dress sense than him.

The extortionate cost of Kenny's drink aside, we had a wonderful night out in Bradford. Pam was always really quiet when out socially and, I'm not being funny, but she could put a glass eye to sleep.

But she was a lovely lady and would go on to become a fantastic mother to their two young children. I never heard Kenny say a bad word about her.

On top of the demands of the grand prix campaign, as part of the deal with Tom Wheatcroft we'd also agreed to compete in the 1985 British Championships. I won the first four races before having a big crash at Snetterton. I was coming on to the

Light in the Darkness

Nicola, the prettiest girl in Halifax who became my first wife.

back straight when I crashed and the bike burst into flames and was completely destroyed. The fire was so hot the crankcases split.

My massive lead in the championships had been reduced to nothing. My main rivals for the title were Niall Mackenzie and Donny McLeod, who were both riding for Armstrong – the same team Mal suddenly changed his mind about me joining on the eve of the '83 season. There I was struggling to beat two good lads, who I felt were not in my league on the race track but they had a great package behind them. I had the chance to have benefited from the same deal as them but Dad f***** that one up.

For the final round of the British Championship we headed to Oulton Park, a tricky track and one I didn't have much experience of, and a circuit I didn't really like to be honest. Our gearbox was knackered, too, it was jumping out of gear, but there was nothing we could do. We had no spares and it was the last race of the year.

It came down to Mackenzie and me for the title. Although I knew we had no chance the way my bike was performing, we got lucky. It pissed it down on race day and Mackenzie just cleared off, and he was winning the race easily until he crashed. The title was mine now . . . or it should have been.

When he fell off, Mackenzie cleverly hid his bike behind the hay bales and with very little vision, I couldn't even see that he'd crashed or that my pit crew were giving me signals that he was out of the race.

It turned out that all I had to do was stay on and I would be the 1985 British Champion, but would you believe it I crashed, too, leaving Mackenzie the champion.

At the end of a typically rollercoaster season, another massive bridge was about to be burned. Between Mal, Kenny and me we must have burnt more bridges than the British Army – and all without intent.

Tom Wheatcroft wanted the bikes back so he could sell them. I explained that basically all there was left was one bike and a frame and that if he would send the money needed to fix the second one, I promised him they would both come back to him as good as new.

But I think he thought we were taking the piss and told us to just bring them back in the state they were. So that's what happened and our relationship was never the same again.

Tom was such a great person. I remember listening to him talking on many occasions, laughing and joking in his private suit at Donington, where he was always the life and soul of every party. He was great man who I owed so much.

24 WILL TO WIN

Double British champ . . . pipped in the Pairs . . . hopes and bikes go up in flames . . . another bad break . . . from zero to hero in Oz . . . last Christmas with Kenny and Pam.

IN 1984 Kenny had won the British Final when most riders just wanted to go home. Well, 12 months on the meeting was cancelled on the Sunday due to a waterlogged track and re-scheduled for the following Wednesday. Kenny turned up with one only one thing in mind – retaining his British title, even though the right leg he'd broken the year before was still not in good shape to say the least.

In perfect conditions, Kenny rode fantastically well to win all five races with a thrilling performance. As usual, he made hard work of it but the fans loved to see a tenacious rider coming through the pack to win in determined style.

He was now the double British Champion and, fair play to him, he was magical to watch on a motorbike. By the mid-80s there were only a few riders who had that amazing talent and bravery to come from last to first against the very best. Kenny was one and Shawn Moran another. I once saw the American pass my brother around the outside on turn two at Sheffield. It was pure magic, because not many did that to Kenny.

His victory at Coventry helped to further promote Team Carter. Although we were competing in different motorcycle sports, the original idea was that we would look and dress much the same when racing.

At the start of the year Kenny announced we'd both be wearing Hideout Leathers. But when they arrived they were as thin as paper, offering little protection. That might have been OK for speedway but it certainly was no good for road-racing – I'd have been killed in my first crash.

I told him I wouldn't be wearing them and rang Dainese, the Italian leather manufacturer who had sponsored me in 1984, who supplied me with the very best for the '85 season.

Kenny nearly became a World Champion again in the Pairs, when he teamed up with Coventry's Kelvin Tatum for the final at Wroclaw, Poland. But in a tight finish, it all came down to the race when they met the Danish duo of Erik Gundersen and Tommy Knudsen and were pipped to victory. The Danes dominated world speedway in the 80s and England had little answer to them.

After the meeting, Kenny and Kelvin were booked on a flight back to England but their mechanics were driving Kenny's Mercedes van through East Germany when they were involved in a terrible accident. The driver fell asleep on the long journey home and although the three people in the van mostly escaped unhurt, the impact of

ALAN CARTER

Above: Kenny (left) and his World Pairs partner Kelvin Tatum at the starting gate at The Shay in 1985.
Below: The top three in the '85 World Pairs Final in Poland – Denmark's Erik Gundersen, a rider our Kenny always liked, and Tommy Knudsen, Kenny and Kelvin and the Americans Bobby Schwartz and Shawn Moran.

Light in the Darkness

'King Kenny' looking for the opposition on the way to retaining his British crown at Coventry in 1985.

the crash caused the vehicle to burst into flames. The fire totally destroyed Kenny and Kelvin's four racing bikes plus all their other equipment.

Disastrously, the green card carnet had just expired, so they had no insurance cover and now no bikes or equipment left either. Kenny rallied round, setting up a disaster fund and trying to get sponsors and other people to help them get back on their feet. The British speedway authorities offered no help at all, even though Kenny and Kelvin were in Poland representing England in a FIM World Championship final. Kenny reckoned the accident cost him about £18,000.

I lent Kenny a set of leathers for a meeting at Coventry and he scored a maximum in them. I also had a full set of tools that were my pride and joy. I'd never used them but liked to have a set of the best just in case they were ever needed. I gave them to Kenny, as a brother and great friend would, to help get him back to normal as soon as possible.

Despite retaining his British crown at Coventry, Kenny failed to reach the World Final again in '85. It was a bitter blow because he was desperate to win the World Championship on home soil, with Bradford's Odsal Stadium hosting speedway's biggest night that year for the first time.

His leg was still in a very bad way and although he did give it everything he had left in the qualifiers, once again the pain became too much. The final straw was a three-man crash in his second ride at the final round in Sweden, where he was

ALAN CARTER

*Above: The crash that effectively ended Kenny's world championship hopes in 1985. He is seen flying through the air and about to land on the slippery Vetlanda track as John Davis (inside) and Andy Smith try to avoid him.
Below: Afterwards, a consoling arm round the shoulder from Pam as the leg suffers another break.*

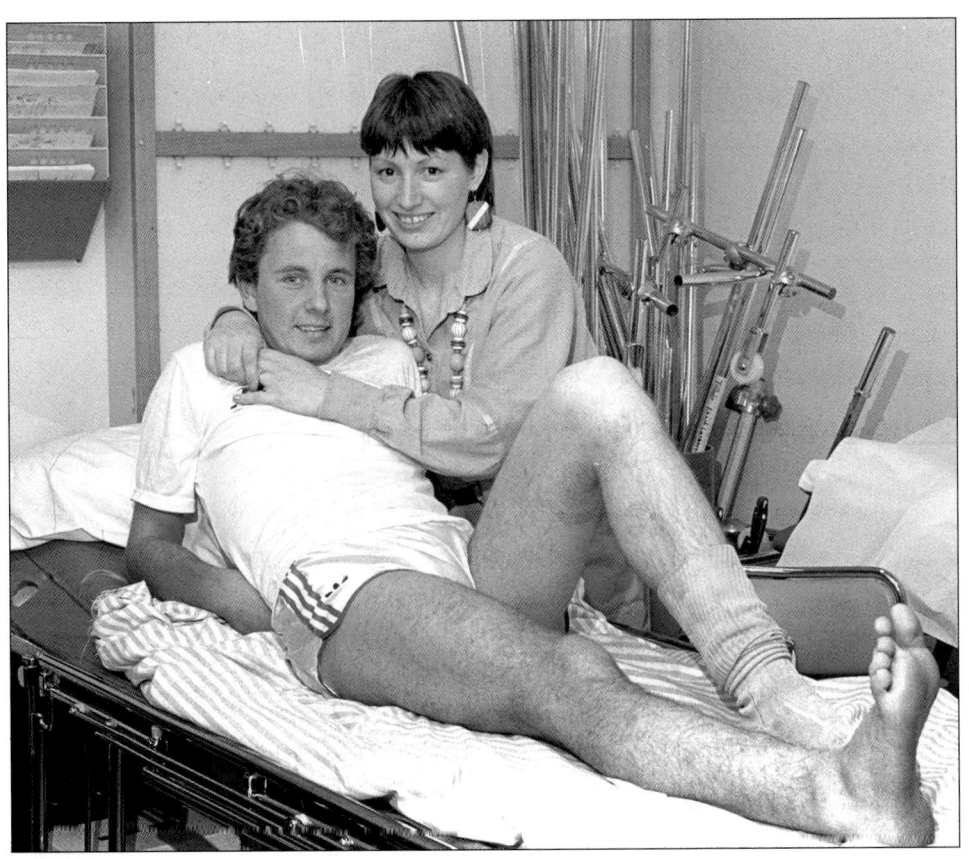

Light in the Darkness

carried from the soaking wet Vetlanda track in agony.

He later found out that he'd re-broken the same leg he busted 18 months earlier. For the second year in succession, his season had ended early with a serious injury.

His right leg was in a very bad way. The second crash had bent the plate inside and Kenny even considered suing Dr Carlo Biagi, the Scottish medic whose great work to repair the original bone damage in '84 had enabled him to pursue his world title dreams for two seasons.

Biagi examined Kenny's leg again when he returned from Sweden and dismissed the Swedish doctors' diagnosis that the leg had been re-broken – he said he thought they had been confused by the fact that the 1984 break had shown up on the latest x-ray.

But it was some seven weeks later, after he'd been hobbling about on the leg, that Kenny visited a local clinic for a third opinion and it was finally confirmed that his right leg definitely had been broken again in the Vetlanda crash.

That's when Kenny spoke about taking action against Dr Biagi but I talked him out of it, saying he was mad and pointing out to him that the damage to his leg had been self-inflicted.

I kept telling him that he needed to rest it properly, allow it time to fully heal, or, if it turned really bad, he could run the risk of having it amputated – as it happens, I still have the metal plates and screws they took out of his leg. This is when he finally started to listen, knowing that for the 1986 season he needed to be in great shape or things could end up in a real mess. He had already practically lost two year's income.

What Kenny and I both needed at the end of '85 was the Australian sunshine and the dream deal came for me when I got a call from ex-racer Barry Smith asking if I'd like to come to Australia and race a new 250cc Honda in the prestigious Swan Insurance Summer Series, a famous competition run over three consecutive weekends in December. They said they had a top mechanic to work on my bike, so the deal was done and I was quickly on my way to Melbourne and the land of Oz.

Well, talk about having your heart broken and your arse ripped out. The bike was shite and guess who the mechanic was? Yeah, right – me. No mechanic was provided for me. Yet another Kenny Carter 'dream deal' had gone tits-up, and you didn't need too many of those to push you over the top.

On inspecting the bike, both the front discs were cracked and looked like they had come off a 1940 tractor – I'd never seen anything like it. I took the head and barrel off and saw that the base gasket wasn't even on the stud holes, plus many other things were clearly wrong.

I managed to get it into running condition but it was still not fit for the road, never mind racing. I turned up at the first meeting, missed most of the practice and wobbled around the track more concerned about staying alive than racing well. I finished last – and I was no Howard Gregory, that's for sure. I could do all the basics but no more.

The second meeting was at Oran Park Raceway, in Narallen, near Sydney, a very dangerous track and not the place to be putting my neck on the line on a bike that was so badly put together. The basics were there but I had no back-up – no wheels or spares – and I was just about to quit when it all changed. Honda Australia had a fantastic team but due to my embarrassing situation I'd deliberately kept a low profile, which was very unlike me. Then the team boss, Clyde Wolfenden, came up to me and said: "Do you know Mal Carter?"

I shit myself, because usually when this happened, you either received a verbal blasting or a hero's welcome. I hesitated slightly and then replied: "Yeah, he's me dad."

Much to my relief, Clyde smiled at me and said: "Wow! Me and Mal were great friends on his trips to Australia with Ron Haslam."

Clyde asked me what the problems were and I told him everything that was wrong. He took the bike off me and completely re-built it to a standard Honda RS 250cc. When I got it back it looked like it had just come out of the crate brand new.

Also, one of Clyde's best mates, Dennis Neal, was the boss of Dunlop Tyres. Dennis was another top bloke who liked Dad, and he sorted out the best rubber they had for me. I went from being a struggling no-hoper to the top of the tree in a week.

There was Niall Mackenzie, on his semi-factory Armstrong, making me look stupid, along with some gobby Australian called Vaughan Coburn who was telling me how his rider, Geoff McNaughton, the new Aussie golden boy, was going to kick my ass. They were baiting me all week about it, even taking bets on who would win out of the two of us.

And I was thinking, 'like f*** he is. The party's over, now yer going to see a master class rider kick some ass big-time.'

The icing on the cake was King Kenny flying in with Pam and their two young kids, Kelly-Marie and Malcolm, to watch me.

The last race of the series was on Queensland's Gold Coast at a race track called Surfer's Paradise, and it was fantastic. The bike was brilliant, too. Honda Australia took me under their wing and partnered me with their number one rider Malcolm 'Wally' Campbell – him on the 500cc Honda triple and me on the 250cc. Me and Wally got on very well – this was one of the best weeks I ever had in racing.

We stayed at the Pink Poodle Motel. One night I got so drunk that I fell in my room and left the door open. This was the cue for the Aussies to give me and my room a right blasting with a hose pipe. I was too pissed to move or even care about what they were doing and just disappeared into the covers and went into a coma. But I was almost eaten alive by mosquitoes in the night and my face was a real mess the next morning.

But like any proud Yorkshireman, I wasn't going to be outdone by any Crocodile Dundee hillbillies. The following morning I managed to nick the master bedroom key from the maid's trolley and sneaked into the room where the lads who had stitched me up were staying. Once inside, I turned on the giant ceiling fan and threw all their clothes into it. And just for good measure, I turned on all the taps and flooded their room. The water dripped down into the restaurant and bar areas and the motel management went crazy.

Light in the Darkness

As far as I was concerned, I was now the man and no-one messed with a Carter – certainly not these Aussie upstarts.

I went to bed the night before race day feeling as happy as can be. I realised in the morning that no matter what you did, you could never beat the Australians, and I had to back off. After a great night's sleep I awoke ready to rip . . . only to open my motel room door and see what they'd done to my pick-up truck. The bastards had taken the wheels off it, so I put my bike on the back of Niall Mackenzie's truck and went with him to the meeting.

They were great times, though. Life was just so much fun for me in those days.

There was always something going on. One night Kenny and Pam went out for a meal and left me babysitting for them. I'd been reading Kelly-Marie and Malcolm a story from a book when this giant spider appeared from nowhere and ran across the floor – it was a huntsman, which is bigger than a tarantula. It found its way to the bathroom, where I grabbed the shower hose and tried to kill it, only that did no good because it was like a single raindrop falling on you or me.

So I went outside and saw lots more spiders on the stone wall surrounding our motel room. I can't stand spiders at any time, let alone a bird-eating one the size of this huntsman. I was shitting myself.

At Surfer's Paradise I started on pole position and gave one of the best performances of my career to win the race from start to finish, setting a new track record in the process. But it was really all down to the boss of Honda just taking me in and showing me that one good deed leads to another. Thank you, Clyde.

To complete a memorable day, my team-mate Wally Campbell rode his Honda triple to first place ahead of Wayne Gardner, who crashed out on the much faster factory V4 Honda.

I'd just beaten Australian's finest and all in front of our Kenny. Not only had I won, but I'd done it in fine style, winning by a country mile. This was when Kenny began to realise I was world class, and it was great to see him so excited by his little brother. He was chuffed for me.

I know I'd finished in the top 10 in the world for the previous three three years but Kenny had been so busy himself, he'd never really watched me race during that period. So that momentous day in Australia marked the point where he knew I'd become just as good at my chosen sport as he was in his.

There was a great buzz around the race paddock that late afternoon. Apart from Wally and me winning impressive trophies and a pile of cash, I also received a lovely offer. Dennis Neal, the Dunlop boss, said: "Well done, Alan, you were pure magic to watch today. How would you like to come on my boat for a week on the Great Barrier Reef and chill out with us?" I was taken aback by his kind gesture and accepted immediately.

That night we all had the most amazing party out in Surfer's Paradise, where the drinks were flowing among great company. We were all like-minded people and while we racing people were serious at the track, we often acted like complete crazy buggers when it came to partying and could terrorise any town.

ALAN CARTER

One girl caught my eye. She was beautiful but already taken, married to one of the team bosses, and therefore forbidden fruit. We flirted all week and it was great fun.

The next morning I told Kenny I was going to the Barrier Reef and he practically begged me not to go, saying: "Come on, Nipper, I need you to come to Perth with me and spend some time together there." Kenny only ever called me Nipper or sometimes Nip.

Perth was the other side of the country but he made me feel so guilty that I agreed to go with him after he suggested that I fly my girlfriend Nicola out to meet up with us. So that's what I did. To keep him happy, I cancelled a trip of a lifetime with Dennis on the Barrier Reef.

I felt gutted as we flew west to Perth and my mood didn't improve when we arrived there and it became clear that Kenny had basically set himself up with accommodation with friends and arranged his own transport, but there had been nothing organised for me. I just couldn't believe how selfish he could be.

There I was, in a strange city with no friends, scouring a newspaper trying to rent a flat for four weeks, with my girlfriend about to fly in from the UK. Talk about being pissed off. But that was our Kenny, only interested in one thing – himself.

We only got together a few times in the four weeks we were there – once to visit the Honda headquarters in Perth, where they loaned us a superbike and a scooter to run around on. You can guess who had what to ride. Again, this was typical Kenny – always the best for him and the crumbs for me.

Well, it still never mattered to me. I loved him, he remained my hero. In my eyes, he was a great, gifted kid who could race a motorbike better than anyone in the world.

One day we decided to go to the beach, where the local guys were wearing cool-looking long surfing shorts and we looked a right pair of poofs in our tight-fitting British Speedos. Then Kenny said: "F*** it, let's put a big banana down them and walk past all the girls on the beach."

We did and it was so funny watching all the babes nudging each other as we walked by trying to look as cool as the Aussies in our sunglasses and with a huge bulge in the front of our trunks.

I collected Nicola from the airport and we spent all of December and half of January in sunny Perth, Western Australia.

Kenny had arranged to have Christmas dinner in the middle of nowhere, at a friend's house in the bush. There was Kenny and Pam and their two little bambinos, Kelly-Marie and baby Malcolm, plus Nicola and me. We had a great time in the soaring heat on Christmas Day, having a barbeque and swimming away. I can see us now as plain as day, just chatting and having drinks. We didn't seem to have a care in the world. It's so hard now to look back at that point and think, unbeknown to us all, this was our last Christmas together.

Many times I've been unable to let the past go, thinking if only I could have done this or that for Mum and Kenny, things may have turned out right for all of us.

One night we were coming to the end of our stay in Perth and me and Nicola were

Light in the Darkness

Having fun away from the race track in Perth, on a Honda Spacy 250 scooter.

planning to have a quiet night in. Suddenly, there was a knock on the door. It was Kenny: "Can you come out, we're having a last lads night out before we go back to England?"

I told him I was staying in with Nicola but then he asked her if she minded me going out. She didn't object and so he talked me into coming out with him. I put on my best clothes and came down about four flights of steps to a waiting car. What a shock I got when I opened the door to find two stunning girls sat in the back of our car. Kenny had a big cheeky grin on his face.

We rocked up at a top nightclub, got the drinks in and things were looking good. He was having the time of his life while I was thinking, 'how the f*** have I got myself in this situation?'

It wasn't long before some big Aussie came up to me and asked: "What the f*** are you doing with my bird?" Before I had the chance to explain, the guy decked me and broke my nose. I got up and we had a right fight. By this time I didn't give a shit who his bird was or how our Kenny had got me into yet another mess. I got stuck in and whacked the bastard as hard as I could. Obviously, we were kicked out of the club and then it was time to assess the damage.

My clothes were ripped and covered in blood and to top it off I had to go back and explain to Nicola that some lunatic Aussie had attacked me in a bar.

Aussie star Geoff McNaughton sips from a can while I make my winner's speech.

Nightclub fights aside, the trip to Australia was just what Kenny needed and it was nice to see him relax and enjoy himself in the sun, surrounded by friends and family. It allowed him to put the nightmare of his twice broken leg fully behind him. To show just how well he'd recovered, he was in great form in his comeback speedway meetings he rode in at Perth's huge Claremont track.

There was absolutely no sign of any problems in Kenny and Pam's marriage on that trip to Australia. Pam was a lovely woman – very quiet, but a great mother and she looked after Kenny as well as any woman could have.

Kenny had a good bunch of people around him in Australia, where he'd made a lot of proper friends, including Dave Cheshire, his dad 'Foxy' and Nigel Flatman. There were others he knew from England there, too – old friends 'Dunny' and 'Gaz' went on one trip with Kenny and his former Dukes team-mate Mick McKeon lived there, so he was never short of good company or somewhere to stay.

It was the start of February when we left the Aussie sunshine refreshed and returned to Yorkshire for what we expected to be an important season ahead.

But before we knew, everything in Kenny's life was about to unravel fast.

25 BEGINNING OF THE END

Joining JJ Cobas ... Kenny Carter Promotions ... the Lotus and the fanbelt ... Dukes on the move ... Kenny's troubled mind ... our last conversation.

IT was very soon after we returned from Australia, to be greeted by unseasonably snowy spring weather, that my brother decided to start Kenny Carter Promotions – and I think he'd lost the plot at this point. It was a great idea but the timing was pure madness.

Let's face it, he'd just had two bad years wrecked by serious leg injuries and he really should have been putting everything into his racing, getting himself 100 per cent back on track and re-establishing himself as England's number one and a serious world title contender. But no, not Kenny, he was starting a new business venture.

So where was his mind?

I thought he had so much still to do in speedway but, then again, I was 21, three years younger than him, and still had the spark of youthful ambition in me. Perhaps I'd misjudged his situation. Maybe, privately, he thought he'd pretty much gone as far as he could in speedway – even though I reckon he could have gone on as Bradford's top rider for another 10 years if he'd wanted to. He'd still only have been 35-years-old, and many speedway riders raced successfully beyond that age.

Was Kenny getting bored with racing? After all, the years fly by so quickly when you're young but the fact is he had been racing for eight full seasons by then, and your competitive edge tends to go a bit after all that amount of time, especially if you'd also suffered the kind of serious injuries Kenny had.

Were there bigger fish out there for Kenny Carter, or was he just sick of getting hurt? No-one will ever know.

All I knew, and could see for myself, was him getting involved with other sports stars and leaving me behind, and I sure wasn't going to let that happen. It was as if he'd launched Team Carter at the start of 1985, declaring to the world that we were the most successful brothers in motorcycle racing, as a stepping stone to this bigger idea he had to promote other, more famous sporting names.

Kenny hadn't mentioned a word to me about starting a promotions company while we were in Aussie and it all seemed to happen so fast. He'd started mixing in different circles, with wealthy businessmen like Ron Oldham, John Whitworth and Peter Garside, so maybe they influenced him more around this time.

He rented an office unit in the newly-refurbished and trendy Dean Clough business estate in Halifax, which was built on the site of an old mill. Kenny's office was small, with room for just one desk, a table, a filing cabinet and a secretary.

I remember the day we were at his house to interview secretaries for the job. A lady in her fifties turned up and Kenny's Alsatian 'Gyp', who he kept tied up on a long leash outside, bit a chunk out of her leg.

To look the part, he treated himself to a brand new Renault 5 GT Turbo in white that did 140mph with the words: 'Remember My Name – Kenny Carter' splashed all over it. I bought myself a new Metro Turbo to do the season in and felt great driving it until I pulled up outside his office one day and saw he'd gone one better than me again with the Renault. I didn't know he'd bought it, so I went inside and said to him: "Jesus Christ! Have you seen that white turbo out there? It's the best looking car I've ever seen?"

He didn't bother to respond with words, he just threw his keys at me. 'You bastard!' I thought, feeling gutted that he'd outdone me again. He did let me take the turbo out for a blast, though, so I drove fast towards the first roundabout, flattened it and the car did a full pirouette.

I don't have a clue how much he paid for it but they cost about seven grand at the time. Within a month or so he was driving around in a brand new £31,000 Lotus Esprit, white with red leather seats and personalised number plate of 'KC W1N'. Someone told me the repayments on it were £400 a month.

When it came to getting it, he rang me up and said: "Nipper, fancy coming down to Lotus Cars in Norfolk? I'm picking up a brand new Lotus and you can drive the 5 Turbo back home. I was like, 'yeah, no kidding, I'm going to blow you away in

Kenny Carter Promotions is off and running – and I'm about to be robbed blind by my own brother, bless him.

Light in the Darkness

the Renault on our way home.'

We got to the Lotus factory and Kenny's car wasn't quite ready or there was some paper-work to sort out, so one of the bosses asked if we'd like to go for a spin around their famous Hethel test track with their chief test driver, Alastair McQueen.

It proved a memorable and thrilling experience. I could drive fast and our Kenny was a demon, too, but McQueen was in a different league to us. We came down a long straight and into a hairpin bend doing more than 150mph. In those days there was a fence at the side of the track and as we headed towards it at warp speed, inside me I was screaming 'brake, brake, brake!' and in the end I just closed my eyes thinking I was going to die. But the demon driver McQueen made it round safely every lap, he was brilliant.

With Kenny's new car now ready, we began our long journey back to Yorkshire but didn't get far. The fan belt on the Renault 5 broke, so we had to tow it behind the brand new Lotus. How embarrassing, we must have looked a right pair of idiots.

We travelled this way for about 50 miles, calling at every garage en route to try and buy one to fit, but with no joy until we eventually did find a replacement. I fitted the fan belt but by this time we were both so pissed off at having to tow the car at 50mph that, once the problem was fixed, I zoomed off in the turbo and did the rest of the journey at around 140 while he had to drive slowly because he was still running in his Lotus.

The start of the '86 season would see changes for both of us. We had both negotiated a very good contract for me to race for the Spanish JJ Cobas team in the world championships, and we went down to Spain to finalise the deal together. The company, formed by Antonio Cobas in 1983, agreed that everything would be paid for – all I had to do was turn up and race, much as I had in 1983-84, and I was happy with a monthly wage of £1,000 – even after Kenny's 25 per cent rake off. As it turned out, they were always late in paying and we often had to chase them.

But this was surely going to be a massive improvement for me compared to the struggle I'd had running my own team on peanuts in '85. Antonio Cobas had friends in high places and on one visit to Barcelona he took me to the famous Camp Nou football stadium and introduced me to Barca's head coach, Terry Venables, who later went on to manage England.

Kenny also had a change of scenery in March '86. Due to costly changes to The Shay's track and set-up imposed by the local council, the Dukes moved from Halifax, which had been their home for the past 20 years, to take advantage of a much cheaper stadium rental agreement at the newly-refurbished Odsal, just five miles up the road in Bradford. Kenny rode there a few times in 1985, both for England and in world championship qualifiers, so the fast, banked bowl held no fears for him. And with it being just five miles from where he lived, it really was home from home.

As I said, Kenny didn't show any outward signs of major problems looming at this time, only that he was looking forward to building a great future for himself and his

A warm welcome for me in Barcelona from the senior management of JJ Cobas at the start of 1986.

family. The only thing I noticed was that he was becoming very controlling over Pam and everyone around him, although I dismissed it and took it as normal behaviour for him. He was a natural leader and, like Dad, a bit of a dictator.

In the early months of '86 Kenny started to generate huge media interest in his new sports promotions business by signing-up several stars, the best known being the former Olympic gold medallist Tessa Sanderson. I'm absolutely certain Kenny would have run one of the biggest sports management companies in the world if he was alive today, because he had the gift of the gab and knew the right people in the right places, plus he had good contacts in the TV world and could get maximum exposure out of nothing.

Before the tragic events in Bradshaw on that grave day in May Kenny really did believe that '86 was going to be his lucky year when everything was finally going to go right for him. It was nice to see such great optimism from him again after two injury-hit years.

One of the things where we both went wrong in life, though, was in not managing to find contentment and complete satisfaction. We were never happy no matter how

Light in the Darkness

Wearing the colours of JJ Cobas.

well we did. We couldn't pat ourselves on the back because we always wanted more. If we won 10 races, we wanted to win 12, and couldn't rest until we were world champions, or the best at whatever we did.

Many people over the years have told me: 'If I was half as good as you were on a bike, I would've been happy,' while others would say: 'Just focus on the amazing career you had – you're a legend.' Easier said than done, though.

Me and Kenny couldn't stop wanting it so badly. After all, that's what Dad wanted for us both – to become the greatest riders of our time.

The personal problems that Kenny kept very well hidden simply didn't exist to me at the time. He very rarely confided in anyone, not even me, so I can only speculate now on a number of different problems that could well have been playing on his mind in the weeks, days and hours leading up to the tragedy that unfolded in the early evening of Wednesday, May 21, 1986 . . .

One

Kenny and Pam's farmhouse had recently been burgled. A gang had been watching their movement patterns and when Pam went to the supermarket one day they struck, breaking down a massive, solid oak door and nicking items including the TV, video recorder and microwave – they practically cleaned him out.

They couldn't get all the gear in their van, so they returned for a second fill-up – and that's when Kenny caught them in the act. He hid at the top of the road, watched them load their van and followed them up the road. He phoned the police from his car, and they told him to log the robbers' van registration plate.

He did and they were busted.

Two

He was up before the Speedway Control Board on an assault charge following his attack on his England team-mate Peter Collins, after they had clashed during an early-season match at Belle Vue. The hearing was scheduled at ACU headquarters for Thursday, May 22 – a date he was destined never to make. It was something he felt sure he wouldn't get away with and he expected a riding ban, which would have hit him in the pocket.

I couldn't understand why Kenny disliked PC. They had won the World Pairs title together, Peter was the 1976 World Champion and widely regarded as a great ambassador for the sport. He won the title in an era of legends like Ivan Mauger and Ole Olsen, so I've nothing but respect for him.

For a family of brothers to have all ridden speedway to the high level that the five Collins' did, enjoying amazing success for club and country over such a long period, is testimony to how good they all were.

Three

Kenny had a troubled mind and became paranoid that Pam was seeing somebody else. I don't think this was true – she *did* love him, she just wasn't happy the way she had been treated and fair play to her.

I'd stuck up for her a few times when he'd been a bit heavy-handed with her. I don't think he beat her as such but he would poke her on the arms and I didn't like it, and I told him so. Not that Pam ever complained or made anything of it.

Besides, I thought it was a bit hypocritical of Kenny to accuse Pam of having an affair. It was only a few months earlier that he'd turned up at my flat in Perth with two girls in his car. What's good for the goose is good for the gander.

The marriage had broken down but he just wouldn't accept it was over. I don't think it was the case that he couldn't cope with being a single parent, as much as he didn't want to be left in that position.

I was out of the country when Pam moved out of the house and took the two kids with her to her parents' place up the road, so I wasn't aware of the break-up at the time it was happening.

Things unravelled very quickly while I was in Spain and then Italy for the first two GPs of the season.

Four

Maybe he had bitten off more than he could chew with the new business and fancy car and he was in financial difficulty. We all know how debts and a lack of money can paralyse you, making you feel very nervous and ill. But this theory was dispelled when I recently went to see Kenny's accountant who told me that my brother's finances were in order and that, as far as he was aware, he had no money problems whatsoever. This chap has also been my accountant since I was 16, so I fully believe him. Kenny never worried about money and he always seemed to have enough. He was like Dad – everything he touched turned to gold.

Five

He was upset at the sad loss of his best friend, Ron Oldham's son Richard, who had died, aged 18, just a few weeks earlier in America in tragic circumstances. Kenny wasn't in the best of health either, feeling exhausted and run down with the flu but still working too hard on distractions away from the track.

Six

He expected his business to fly and it wasn't going as well as planned. We all know it takes time, sometimes a very long time, for something to grow. He was under pressure, his own self-inflicted pressure, for it to grow faster than it realistically could.

Seven

And finally there was our father, Mal, and his big mouth telling him: "Yes, she is having an affair, so just f*** her off." That's just what you need when you have a troubled mind.

Kenny was soul-searching and he told me that he'd been down to see Dad and how he'd told him that he thought Pam was having an affair. I said Mal was talking a load of bollocks – I still don't believe Pam was seeing anybody else – but Mal did nothing to put Kenny's tortured mind at rest.

Being the very opinionated person he was, Dad would have said what he did to Kenny without thinking of the possible consequences – and obviously no-one could have foreseen what was about to happen.

But I honestly believe now that if Dad had kept his opinions to himself and just been there for his eldest son in his hour of need, there's a good chance none of this would have happened and both Kenny and Pam would maybe still be alive today.

If you put all of the above seven possible factors into the melting pot, the reason for what happened on that fateful day 25 years ago probably lies somewhere within a combination of all these problems. But none of us will ever know the full truth.

And then there were the things that were going wrong in his racing career, too. The reason Kenny made a poor start to the '86 season, by his high standards, was down to him. He refused to employ a full-time mechanic and his bikes were poorly put together. He was switching engine manufacturers from one meeting to the next and as Kelvin Tatum so rightly said, Kenny did better on his bikes than his own.

How can a world class speedway rider not have a world class mechanic working for him? Well, let me tell you, he can't. Through the best periods of his career 1980 World Champion Michael Lee had his father Andy Lee, a renowned moto-cross rider in his day, by his side to handle most of his tuning and engine preparation.

But all Kenny had was a nice bunch of guys willing to be there and give as much as they could for him but, in engineering terms, they weren't up to it. Sorry, but that's the truth. If Kenny had kept Richard Pickering as his main mechanic or got a world class team around him, I'm sure he would have won five or six World Finals.

My racing year began at Mallory Park on the new JJ Cobas. All the team had come over from Spain but the early signs were far from good. After practice the frame was about as rigid as my great, great granny's body and it handled like a bag of shit. And I was soon going to be racing this in the world championships – in Spain, at the team's home track, on May 4.

The Spanish GP was at Jarama, just north of Madrid, but the JJ Cobas bike was always a pig for me to start. In those days we were still push-starting the bikes and the best I could manage that afternoon was 10th place, which was a good result on a tight, tricky track where we were struggling with bottom end power coming off slow corners.

I was never a big fan of road-racing in February or even March, when it was too cold and you had much more chance of killing yourself on cold tyres that simply weren't designed for freezing temperatures. I'd take it a bit easier. In those days we didn't have the luxury of going to warm, far away countries for testing before the season started, to get yourself dialled in, as they do today.

After the meeting in Spain I flew back to England, where I took a short break before round two in Italy on May 18.

Back home, there were still no signs that our Kenny had any problems, let alone major ones. He seemed fine, so next I was off to Monza for the Italian GP. With the help of a German friend, I managed to lease a motorhome for the year, which meant I first had to go to Germany to pick it up before continuing on to Italy.

The mental and physical pain is showing on Kenny's face after crashing in his last ever meeting, the British semi-final at Bradford on Sunday, May 18, 1986.

This time practice went great and I was looking forward to race day. Somehow, Granddad Willie always used to tune into a radio station and listen to commentary of my races. As all the engines fired up for the race, he heard a delay of 20 seconds before one of the bikes fired up in stone last place on the grid. Yes, as you've guessed, I'd just given the world's best a 20-second lead. I was never going to make up that amount of ground, although I still managed to finish 11th, just one place outside the points.

That Sunday night, just three days before the fatal shootings, I rang Kenny and told him I'd ridden well at Monza but had been unable to start the bike. Kenny had more mechanical problems himself that afternoon and only just managed to scrape through the British semi-final of the world championship on his home track at Bradford. But I don't recall him mentioning any of that, he just asked how it had gone for me in the Italian GP.

Before finishing the call, I told Kenny I was going out for dinner to a traditional Italian restaurant and said I would ring him once I'd arrived in Germany, where the third round of the GP series was due to be staged at the new Nurburgring on the following Sunday, May 25.

I put down the phone and had no idea that would be our last conversation.

26 NURBURGRING NIGHTMARE

*The lonely road ... missing my mates ... Black Wednesday ...
Pam and Kenny both dead ... Ron Haslam's sad face.*

I TRAVELLED all alone from Germany to Italy in my new rented motorhome. It was a very lonely time for me because I loved being around people but suddenly I found myself doing the GPs on my own. My close team members from Halifax, who had been with me from the very first world championship round in 1983, were frozen out of the picture.

JJ Cobas would transport all the team members and my bike in a converted coach while I travelled throughout Europe on my own in the mini motorhome. Nicola was working full time for an insurance company, so she couldn't come with me on these trips, and Cobas said there was no room in my new set-up for Howard, my loyal and long-serving mechanic, or my old school mate Eggis. They had been with me since my first GP three years earlier and I missed them badly.

I rocked up at Nurburgring, got myself a good place in the paddock next to the team and didn't have a care in the world. I was racing for a bunch of crazy Spaniards who loved their Rioja more than racing. Life was ace, I had plenty of cash and a few girls chasing after me and I thought I'd arrived at the pinnacle of racing's elite. Well, that's how I saw it anyway.

On that Wednesday, the day before practice was due to start for the German GP, calls were received by the race officials informing them that Kenny had killed Pam and himself. The people who took those calls were in total shock and didn't know how they could break this tragic news to me. Remember, in those days there were no mobile phones and getting calls through to different countries could be difficult.

This part is largely a blur to me but I'm pretty sure it was not until the next morning, the day after the killings, that I was approached by Ron Haslam, one of the first racers Dad sponsored in the 70s, or maybe Ron and his wife Ann approached me together, I don't know. The organisers probably decided that they could handle it better than anyone because of our close past connections.

A racing legend in his own right, Ron had been a great help and support in guiding me in the first few years of racing and was always a guy you could count on when you were struggling with things at the GPs. He was a very experienced racer and, being British, we all stuck together in those days.

All I can remember is how sad Ron looked. He didn't look like the 'Rocket' Ron I knew, the man who was the life and soul of every paddock.

He came up to me at the Nurburgring and said something like: "Look, I've got to tell you, your Kenny's killed himself and Pam."

My motorhome for 1986 – but it was a lonely road without mates like Paul 'Eggis' Haigh (below).

I just went completely numb, in total shock. I'd only spoken to Kenny a few days earlier and everything seemed fine. I was devastated, unable to believe it.

Ron put his arms around me and, to be honest, I can't remember anything else, apart from one thing. I was told by Mal – via Ron – not to return to England under any circumstances, because the press were having a field day making up all sorts of rubbish about Kenny and Pam.

With Kenny being such a high profile sports star at the time, the story was all over ITV's ten o'clock news and on the front page of the national daily papers.

It was unbelievable, like a bad dream, and I just didn't want to accept this had happened. I still find it very hard to come to terms with 25 years on.

After a very long and hard deliberation, I had three choices:

Light in the Darkness

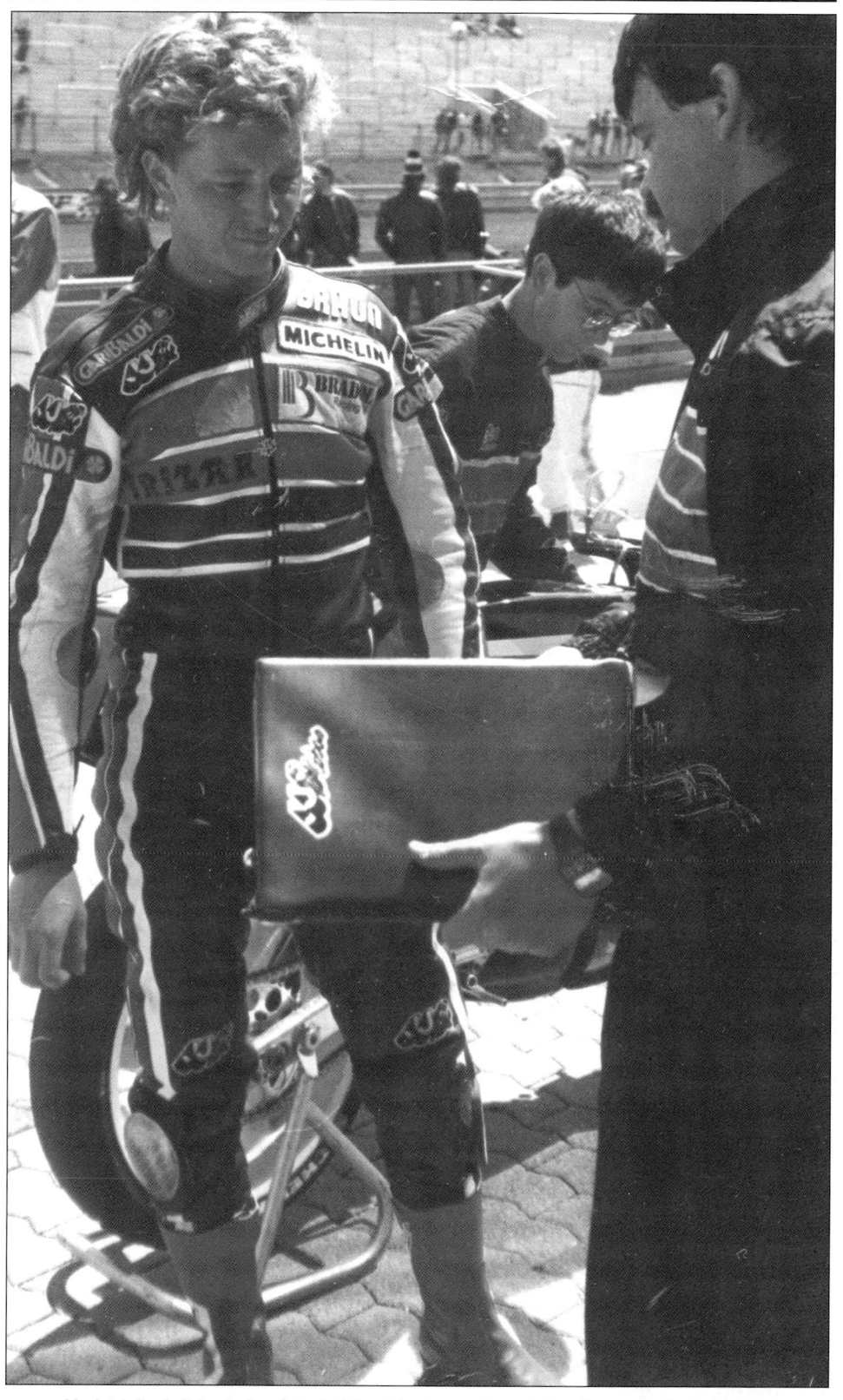

I look totally shellshocked as Antonio Cobas tries to console me before the race at the Nurburgring.

1. Ignore Dad's advice and go home, which would have given the press a great opportunity to get at me. I wasn't going to do that.

2. Pack up and drive off somewhere to get some space and time to think. My team were very understanding and were prepared to pack up and go back to Spain and leave me in peace to cope as best I could. But I couldn't do this either, even though my brain felt as if it was about to burst.

3. This is the choice I made . . . I took the crazy decision to race on, thinking this is what Kenny would have wanted me to do.

I practiced on the Friday with the full support of everyone in that GP paddock. By now they all knew what had happened to Kenny and Pam. I focused the best I could while everybody around me kept a close eye on me. I don't know how, but I qualified in the top 15 for the German GP.

On race day I didn't really have the heart to race. It was like I was in after-shock. The enormity of what Kenny had done was really starting to sink in. I kept thinking, my hero and my brother has died and I'll never see him again. I started to panic and then went into a period of denial, lying to myself and saying 'no, it's not true, he's really OK.'

I did line up for the race at Nurburgring and actually rode well to finish 10th in the race but I have no recollection of it whatsoever. It was all a complete blur.

After the race we all packed up and started to head off in different directions. I drove myself all the way from the track, through Germany, into Holland and to the Europort at Rotterdam but, like the race, the whole journey was another total blur.

As I boarded the ferry bound for Hull, I felt completely petrified. What was I going to be facing when I got home? It was a nightmare.

27 WHY?

Why did Kenny do it? ... Gran and Granddad, the two people I trusted most, try to explain the unthinkable ... the suicide note ... Mal's share of the blame ... double funeral ... racing again.

SO there I was, just a kid of 21, about to get off a ship and drive down the motorway to hell. My body and brain kept telling me to turn around and go back the other way, to run and keep running, and hide away somewhere. I was scared but, as usual, I somehow found the courage to keep going forward.

This was a nightmare beyond belief but little did I know then that by the time I reached 37, I would bury four generations of my closest family, including my own daughter.

When I arrived back from Germany on that Sunday night, the family members I saw were in complete shock. They could say very little but all their faces said one thing and one thing only: WHY?

What had gone so horribly wrong? Nobody knew.

Nicola was a tower of strength but, to be honest, I only fully trusted two people in my life and they would be my rocks until the day they both passed away – my ever-loving grandparents Willie and Gladys. They were the first people I can remember going to see when I got back to Halifax. When I arrived at their house – 11 Reins Road, Rastrick, Brighouse – Granddad was heartbroken and inconsolable, while Gran just burst into tears.

They started to explain to me the last few days of Kenny's life. Gran said that they had both talked to Kenny and, although he said his marriage was over, he was fine and bearing up to things. Due to our unfortunate, tragic upbringing, both Kenny and myself found it impossible to trust anyone apart from our grandparents. I don't know why, that's just how it was. We didn't really confide in each other either, we always bottled things up. If only Kenny could have talked and opened up to someone I believe he would still be here today.

My only advice I can give to people is don't bottle things up, as Kenny and me did, let it all out. When you're very worried about something, have a sleep – you might just feel that little bit better in the morning.

Don't take life too seriously and enjoy what you have – it may be all you're going to get. Tough times never last but tough people do.

Believe in yourself and blow your own trumpet, because no-one else is going to blow it for you.

Enjoy the small, simple things in life ... having coffee with friends, or reading a book or magazine. Whatever it is you like doing, do it more often. Why rush? I did

ALAN CARTER

The note Kenny left Gran the night before the double tragedy.

for over 30 years and you know where it's got me? Nowhere.

At Kenny's request, Granddad had been to his house and secured a few of my brother's personal possessions, which he and Gran were asked to look after because Kenny was afraid they'd go missing while he was out. His suspicions were also expressed in the last note he left for Gran at his house the day before he died, which is reproduced on the facing page.

Kenny also explained to our grandparents that he was going to buy a new house across the road from my place – they were building a second phase development there at the time. Outwardly, Kenny seemed to be handling the break-up of his marriage as any other man would – probably feeling totally devastated but still going through the motions, as many of us have done at certain times in our lives.

On the day Kenny died Gran had cooked tea for him. It was a family tradition that, if we weren't racing somewhere, we always went to Gran's house at Rastrick for tea on a Wednesday, no matter what. Mum, her second husband Dave Wood, Kenny and me would always visit for our Wednesday night ritual.

Gladys cooked the best food I've ever eaten. Fish and chips was Kenny's biggest favourite if he was buying food from a shop but we both loved Gran's cooking. Her speciality was her home-made stew and dumplings, or home-made shepherd's pie, followed by rice pudding.

But Kenny was late arriving on this particular Wednesday night, so Gran rang him at home and asked if he was still coming for his tea as usual. "Yes," he replied – but he never did. He had just murdered his wife and was about to kill himself.

Kenny gets a cuddle from Gran. They loved each other so much.

ALAN CARTER

Many times when I scrape uneaten leftovers from my dinner plate into the bin, I think about Gran doing the same with the food she'd prepared for Kenny on that fateful night. And I imagine that throughout the next 20 years she lived beyond Kenny's death, she probably had the same thoughts as I occasionally still do today.

I have no idea what happened in the last few hours of their lives, other than Kenny had apparently had a massive row with Pam in the yard of their home, and basically told her to "stop and come back, or I'll shoot you."

Kenny usually did what Kenny said he was going to do, and he carried out his threat. He shot Pam in the back with a 12-bore shotgun he'd borrowed from a mate and killed her.

He then went into the house and wrote a suicide note, which I still have to this day, or at least a copy of it, before making the last call of his life, to his businessman friend Ron Oldham. And that was it. He shot himself in his bedroom, a broken man.

I think it was Gran who gave me Kenny's note, which read something like:
"I can't live without her.
I know she loved me.
Bury us together.
I want Ron Oldham to look after the kids.
And tell my brother I love him."

I remember Dad asking me if I wanted to go and see both Kenny and Pam's bodies in the funeral parlour but I declined without a moment's hesitation. The horrific vision of Mum, lying there in her coffin with gritted teeth, came flooding back.

Mal and I only spoke to each other on and off after he was no longer involved in my racing career and we certainly didn't become any closer after he'd lost his eldest son either. I was now the only surviving son he had left after two family tragedies but he would still continue to treat me like a leper.

Kenny and Pam's joint funeral took place a week later at the church in their small village of Bradshaw, near Halifax. Again, most of this is a complete blur to me. All I clearly remember was seeing a massive turnout of mourners.

By and large the press had given me space and left me to grieve alone – and it was a good job, too, because I would've given them nothing but a mouthful of abuse, or maybe even attacked them.

The day after the funeral I was pictured by the local press crying my eyes out. I was a lonely figure at the graveside. All I kept thinking and asking was: Why?

Another thing I recall from the funeral was a guy singing. I thought, 'who the f*** is he to be singing at my brother's funeral?' There were people there I didn't even know.

Kenny had changed in the last few years of his life, losing touch with his roots and friends and moving on at a rapid pace. I didn't like this person – it wasn't the Kenny I knew and loved. And to be honest, I didn't give a shit about all his new millionaire friends either. They all seemed to me like a bunch of hangers-on, only interested in a piece of Kenny Carter.

Light in the Darkness

A mass turn-out for the joint funeral of Pam and Kenny in the village of Bradshaw.

But you couldn't tell him anything. All he wanted was for you to jump on his bandwagon. It was more like a ship without a rudder. And sooner or later it was bound to hit the rocks.

Like me, Kenny could be very vulnerable at times and naively believe anything people told him. The four times speedway World Champion Barry Briggs summed him up to a tee when he once told his fellow Kiwi Ivan Mauger: "Be careful what you say to that kid, because he will do whatever you tell him."

Why was Kenny Carter so pig-headed? For me, there is only one answer: Mal Carter, our Dad, and what a bastard of a father he was. Mal's answer to everything was "f*** 'em off" or "hit the bastards". Now this wasn't the best fatherly advice you could ever give your sons.

There were many sides to Dad, though. He was a fantastic coach and knew more about racing than probably anyone. He could analyse things immediately and knew how to turn everything to our advantage. So, yes, on that front I loved working with him. I was the pupil and he was the master in my eyes. It was a great team.

On the other hand, he was the most callous, mean person I ever met. The words he said to me you wouldn't use on a dying pig. After the loss of his youngest baby son, who died in his arms, and then the tragic end to our Kenny's life, you would have thought he'd have treated me like I was the next coming of Christ. But all I got from him was more verbal abuse until the day he died.

Both Kenny and me had more falling-outs with Mal than you can ever believe. It usually started when we'd call at his place to say 'hello' and see how he was doing, only to be verbally attacked and humiliated in front of his crony hangers-on – and he sure had lots of them.

Sometimes Dad and me would go for periods of up to three years and not speak to each other. It always followed the same pattern . . . me giving in and calling in to see him. Often I'd receive a friendly welcome and we'd spend an enjoyable night talking and eating together. It would end by me saying: 'Goodbye, I'll see you soon'.

Maybe a week, or even only a few days, would pass and I'd call him back, only to be on the end of yet another verbal assault. This always confused me, as the previous time we'd said our goodbyes, he'd seemed happy to see me.

Whenever Mal verbally abused Kenny and me, we had to stand there and say nothing, or I'm sure he would've beaten us physically, too, if we'd said or done anything back to him. I remained scared and nervous in his presence until the day he died.

Kenny was 25-years-old when he ended his life, still relatively a kid in a man's world. He had everything going for him – a great future, a wife and two kids, a dream house and he was still Bradford Dukes and England number one. How did it all go so badly wrong?

I have had the past 25 years to reflect on what he did on that senseless evening in May 1986. Many people have said their own piece but I stand by what I believe: it was first degree murder.

We have all fallen out with a loved one at some point in our lives. And many of us have found ourselves in a serious situation, whether it be with a stranger or a family member, and lost our heads in a moment of anger. But I can't say or even begin to think what was going through Kenny's head. All I know is, he was a very calculating, cunning, cold blooded murderer.

Not only had he driven more than 20 miles to get the gun he used to kill his wife and mother of their two children, he also hid his car and himself out of Pam's sight before confronting her with the gun. This was not a spur of the moment act, it was a very well planned job indeed. Kenny was driven by his own demons and no-one was going to stop him.

I also believe it's a huge, huge blessing that the kids were being cared for at the home of Pam's parents and were not with their mother at the time of the killings. Would Kenny have ended their lives as well as Pam's? Who knows – and I thank God they were not there.

Many journalists said the death of Kenny was also the finish of me as a rider and that I was never the same racer I was before my brother's death. I did struggle on for many years and also showed flashes of the old me. I don't want to blame our kid on my own failure to become world champion. All my fans know that no guy ever gave more on the track than me every time I went out to race. It just wasn't meant to be, so Kenny and I became the nearly guys of British racing.

The spring of May '86 was a terrible time for me for another reason. Within a month of the death of Kenny and Pam, I also lost my mate Gary Padgett, one of the best TT racers and a very sad loss to the racing world. He put his neck on the line on some of the most dangerous race tracks in the world but was killed in an accident when, I believe, he was riding his bike and crashed into the back of a car parked on

Light in the Darkness

The press had a field day. Kenny loved publicity but could never have imagined headlines like these.

the roadside.

Gary was a playboy through and through and we had some great times together. He didn't have a care in the world. I've been a passenger with some very fast car drivers in my time but going from Cadwell Park to Louth with Gary was the only time I thought I really had shit my pants – he was mental.

Kenny was still my manager at the time of his death and I had a contract with JJ Cobas to finish the world championships. I didn't know how I would be able to go on because my life felt like quicksand and I was drifting along in my own little world for a while.

It was only 18 days after the double tragedy that I left the deep gloom of West Yorkshire behind again and was in Austria for the next round of the world championship and, not surprisingly, I didn't do at all well at Salzburgring. After qualifying in mid-pack, on race day I was stone last off the grid and despite working hard to get through the field, the engine broke and I was out of yet another GP. To be honest, my form was the least of my problems.

All I could think about was poor Pam. Nobody deserves what she suffered. How could Kenny have done this to her? He had ruined the lives of two families and left his kids orphaned.

It made me feel ill to think about it.

28 KELLY-MARIE AND MALCOLM

Custody battle . . . Lunds get the kids . . . Odsal let-down . . . seeing red at Assen . . .
Dad returns . . . more heartbreak at Spa.

THE bickering back home over Kenny and Pam's kids escalated to near fighting point as the two families argued over who was going to bring up three-year-old Kelly-Marie and two-year-old Malcolm after Ron Oldham said that it was best that they remained with their closest family.

Dad wanted the two children to come and live with him and his wife Janet and their daughters on his farm, while for Pam's parents Bob and Veronica it was like, 'over our dead bodies will you be getting these kids'.

I was praying that Bob and Veronica would end up with them both. They had been great, loving grandparents and had played an active part in their short lives. OK, maybe they lived in a ramshackle farm – it was only about 200 yards from Pam and Kenny's place – but they were a very close, loving family and had brought up four children of their own.

And besides, why the hell did Mal want them anyway? He'd had nothing to do with them whatsoever – he was a complete joke as a grandfather.

At one point there was even talk of Dad gaining custody of Malcolm and the Lunds having Kelly-Marie but that was a stupid idea, too. The kids would need each other as they grew up together.

What a total mess Kenny had left behind, it was heartbreaking.

In the end, thankfully a court ruled that both children would go to live with Pam's family.

After Pam and Kenny died I went up to the Lunds' farm a few times to see the two kids and considering I'm their uncle I suppose I should have visited them more often.

But I just couldn't get my head around what had happened and it wasn't a nice situation to be in. The Lunds would talk to me but I wasn't made to feel very welcome at their place and I can fully understand why.

I felt so sorry for Pam's brother Adrian and her three sisters, Heather, Diane and Wendy. They had lost someone they loved so dearly – and for why we'll never know.

One of the immediate things that needed to be sorted out was what would happen to all of Kenny and Pam's assets and their personal possessions, including the racing bikes, cars, farmhouse, the lot.

I know that many items did go missing and to this day I've no idea what happened to everything. There was some kind of sale or auction of Kenny's speedway bikes

ALAN CARTER

and equipment but I was travelling around Europe competing in the world championships while all this was going on back home.

One thing I do know is that all the tools I'd lent Kenny after his mechanic had crashed his van in Poland the previous year disappeared and I would never see them again.

The only things I personally salvaged from our Kenny's belongings were a few books and some of his designer clothes, which to be honest were about as trendy as a tramp's vest – he sure had no fashion sense.

Kenny's last season in speedway at Odsal, which included just a handful of home matches between March and his final meeting on May 18, was a let-down. From a fan's point of view, you seemed relatively miles from both the track and the pits, unlike at Halifax where there was a much better atmosphere and you could get up close to the action and almost hear the riders talking as they went about their business in The Shay pits.

Odsal, where the track was built inside a concrete bowl, always seemed to be blowing a gale, too. After four or five races I was so cold I'd go home and have a hot bath and a nice glass of wine. Kenny would ring me and say: "Where the f*** are you?" I'd say: "I'm at home, I'm not wasting my time freezing my bollocks off watching you." And he'd go: "You cheeky little c***, get up to mine later on and we'll have a few drinks."

Sometimes I look back and think how fantastic it would've been if he'd switched sports and got into road-racing. Then I would've been the one with years of knowledge and track-craft behind me, the daddy, and I would've taken great pleasure in blowing him into the weeds, although I don't think he would of handled that too well from his kid brother. Yes, I would've loved it, taking the piss out of our Kenny every week, saying: "What's wrong, you got the choke on?" That would have fired him up.

Around 1985-86 he did once talk about possibly trying road-racing, he fancied it, but it never materialised. He would've had to work his way up through the ranks, though, he couldn't have gone straight in at grand prix level.

Probably just as well, too. I don't think Kenny would have survived two minutes in road-racing – he was too brittle. Every time he crashed on shale doing 40-50mph he seemed to get badly hurt. When I crashed on tarmac doing 150mph I rarely got injured and I'd bounce back up as right as rain most of the time. Mind you, some of my toes and fingers are a bit mangled now and I've got a lump on one of my collarbones.

To be honest, I just loved our Kenny, and what a great rider, too. If only he could've handled people a bit differently, I'm sure he would've had an even bigger fan following and made some good friendships among his fellow riders.

My next big race was the Dutch GP at Assen, where I got embroiled in a right war with an Italian nutcase called Maurizio Vitali. He was somebody I'd never really

Light in the Darkness

Pam, Kenny, Kelly-Marie and Malcolm . . . how could this happy family scene turn to such horror?

encountered on track before, I was far better than him, but because my head was all over the place, my confidence and concentration was just not there, so I was at the back of the pack.

Well, this idiot decided to run into me on the track and then kept trying to kick me clean off the bike. I'd done six years of racing, three at the very highest level, and had never come up against anything like him before. I was raging and tried my best to kick him off his bike. It was mental and I was going to punch his lights out when the race was over.

After the race I went straight over to sort the prick out but his team members and others jumped in and pulled us apart, and that was the end of that. I never had a problem with Vitali ever again, although God knows what happened to him after that.

Arriving back home, I had a break in the GP calendar and things seemed to have settled down a bit regarding Kenny. I was talking to Dad and said: "How do you fancy coming to the next GP, it's only over the water in Belgium at Spa?"

"OK," he replied, "and do you mind if I bring my mate John too?"

This would've been a great trip but for one thing, I hated smoking. But these old-timers never stopped from the moment we left Halifax until we reached the port at Hull. I wanted to cancel the GP and go direct to hospital in Hull for a lung transplant – I felt like I'd smoked 500 Woodbines.

I qualified well at Spa but on race day it pissed it down. The start was on a giant downhill and I was last away from the start in every GP that year except this one. Dad was here to watch me for the first time in two years. All he'd done in that time was tell people, because we'd split, that I was done with and rubbish since we parted. So I was more determined than ever to win the '86 Belgium GP to prove to him that I was still up there with the best.

I was one of the best GP racers in the world in wet conditions or dry, given the right bike, and now I sensed my moment of glory. I hadn't won a GP in three years but I was going to either win or die trying on this occasion.

I'd worked my way up to second place without even trying, I was on tickover. Having crashed out while leading the British GP the year before, yet another win I had on a plate, I told myself 'f*** it, just stay here, work the laps down and then two laps from the end just wind it on and f*** off'.

Everything was going great until the engine started to misfire. There was water in the electrics, the bike started to splutter and it was down to about half the power. My heart sank. 'No, no, this can't be happening!' I felt I was about to explode in my helmet as people started coming past me. Although I managed to finish the race, I'd dropped down to fifth place.

I was world class but I just needed someone to step in and nurture me, show me some love and give me a works bike. Then I would've been pure magic to watch on the right gear.

Packing up that night in Belgium was such a low point. I'd had my best result of the year but fifth place was no consolation for missing out on a grand prix win because they were hard to come by. As usual, all I got from Mal was him telling me what I should and shouldn't have done in the race at Spa – and all I wanted to tell him was "shut the f*** up, get out and walk home." Just a few compassionate words like "hard luck, son, there's always the next race" would have been nice.

Instead, there I was taking the long trip back to England with a pair of chain-smoking whingers for company.

29 DOWN BUT NOT OUT

**Haslam helps me to start . . . on a mission at Silverstone . . .
seconds from second . . . the British GP haymaker.**

WE had three weeks off before the British GP and I made a solemn vow leaving Belgium that day: I would win at Silverstone. I trained harder in this short summer break than I'd ever done in all my life, so I was fit and ready to win my next GP and erase the bad memories of the previous year's disaster there.

Racing for the JJ Cobas team was difficult because they were all Spanish and spoke little English, although to be honest I made no effort to learn Spanish. The same bike problems would re-surface at every GP, we never seemed to move on. There was even a cock-up over my racing leathers, which were made in Spain. One set wouldn't have fitted Pee-wee Herman while the next pair were more suited to Hulk Hogan. They were poor to say the least.

The JJ Cobas bike was, though, made for Silverstone's fast, flowing corners and I just couldn't see how I could lose if I got it off the start line. And thanks to the help of Ron Haslam, I became better at starting the JJ Cobas bike. What I'd been doing was pulling in the clutch too soon, before the bike had a chance to fire – I was applying the same technique I'd used to start the Honda in '85, but with the Cobas you had to push it much further to get it started and leave the clutch out longer.

I was going to be winning Silverstone not only for me, but our Kenny too. My crew got the bike warmed up for untimed practice on the Thursday and after we'd finished, for the very first time in my world championship career I was in first place. Well, the buzz around Silverstone that evening was electric. It may have been the first day of practice and still a long way to go before Sunday's race but, trust me, all the riders rode every GP practice like a GP race, so I knew I was up there on merit.

The next morning – Friday – was the first timed session and I was on a roll. 'Now watch this, I'm going to really let fly now'. I rode the first lap nice and steady and then coming out of the final corner – Woodcote, a flat-out 140mph, fifth gear bend – I tucked in tight and this was it, my first flying lap. I came past the pit lane and hard into the first corner but as I was coming down the gears, the bike seized solid and spat me down the road like a rag doll.

I was badly shook up and, luckily for me, just badly bruised with nothing broken. I missed the full practice session, though, and had gone from first to last place overnight – that's how tough racing was back then.

I managed to pull things together by the end of the two days' practice but by then my confidence in the bike was very low. As any two-stroke rider will tell you, it's no fun riding around with your hand on the clutch, fearing the engine might seize at any time.

We hadn't seen a drop of rain all week but on Sunday morning – race day – it just rained and rained all day long. I was rubbing my hands together, thinking this was my best shot of winning the GP.

There were over 70,000 fans all waiting, probably even more nervous than me at the time because they knew, just like me, that Alan Carter would be winning the British GP or crashing out.

I made a good start, was in mid-pack and gradually making my way towards the front, then bang! I hit the front. But even I was shitting it by now, thinking 'for f*** sake, just stay on'. That was the point when my rev-counter packed in – another disaster, which meant I had to run over half the race without it. This made it harder to hit top power before changing into the next gear and I was struggling to do this well. I had to concentrate much harder to listen to the engine note, as this was all I had to go by before changing gear.

My good mate Dominique Sarron came past me to take the lead, although I'd stay in second place, albeit sometimes drifting back a few seconds per lap before catching him again. I had second place in the bag as we started the last lap and could see I was closing the gap on him. I started to think maybe he was in trouble or just slowing down too much, just as Thierry Rapicault did in the French GP in 1983.

Now I was on a mission . . . I was going to try and catch Dominique and maybe beat him over the finish line and win the British GP in front of my home fans on the very last corner.

But heartbreak and disaster were rarely ever far away from me. Just two corners from the finish line, I crashed out in the big one at Silverstone for the second year running.

I tried to get up on my feet even before I'd stopped sliding, such was my desperation to get back on the bike and still finish second. I had more than a 10-second lead on the next guy but as I picked the bike up to get back on track, I saw that the clutch lever was broken. I needed to jam it into place only the once in order to get going again and I managed to fix it, too.

But that's when my race well and truly ended. A marshal knocked against my hand and, unbeknown to him, knocked the clutch lever back out.

In sheer anger and frustration at my failed attempt to re-mount and rejoin the race and grab second place, I totally lost control and tried to punch the marshal with a giant haymaker.

By this time my brain was in meltdown.

I shoved the bike for more than 50 yards but it would not fire up. In all the confusion and panic I'd put it into sixth gear instead of first. At this point I had nothing left, so I dropped the bike and laid by the track-side, having collapsed in a heap of sheer exhaustion.

30 LIKE A BLACK SHEEP

From seventh to 17th in the world . . . helmet lifesaver . . . I couldn't blame Kenny's death . . . thrown a lifeline by Japanese team . . . then more agony at Suzuka on a pogo stick.

SO there I was again travelling home a broken man. Not only had I crashed out, but I was only two corners away from picking up a few grand for finishing second. That vanished, too, and I'd be going home with nothing.

Little did I know this would be my last British GP and I would soon be out of grand prix racing altogether at the tender age of 22.

Yet again the season was coming to a close and the penultimate round of the world championship was in Sweden.

I had no-one to go with me. All my mates were working full-time, so I asked my Granddad if he fancied a trip to Sweden. He was in his late sixties at the time but he was always there for me and he said 'sure, I'll come'.

So Granddad and me set off for the next round and we had a great time together travelling through Holland, Germany, Denmark and Sweden.

It was so hard to get fired up at Anderstorp. I'd just lost the last two GPs and I also had a gut feeling that me and the JJ Cobas team would be going our separate ways at the end of the season. They were Spanish, I was English and it just didn't gel.

Under the circumstances I put on the best performance I could in Sweden and I rode well to a fine 10th place finish.

I set off from Yorkshire and travelled to Italy on my own for the final round of the championship and, I'll tell you this for nothing, it was a sad, long journey.

We were racing at Misano, which was an anti-clockwise track where I never did any good for some reason. I just hated it. In the race I went flat out down the back straight and shut the throttle off. Just as I was coming down the gears the bike seized solid and threw me down onto the road so hard that it split my helmet. I'm sure to this day that my Arai helmet saved my life. I was a lucky boy that day – someone was watching over me.

By the end of the season I'd gone from seventh in the world to 17th. If only I'd have come first in the Belgian GP and second at Silverstone, I'd have finished the season in the top six in the world. But there we go, again if only...

But what could I say? I couldn't blame it on our Kenny because I was the rider and it was me to blame, not him. I know Kenny's tragic death affected me but what could I do? What I did do was turn up for every race whether I liked it or not and I never let the team down. They believed in me and I had respect for them, so I always gave JJ Cobas all that I could.

During my four years in the world championship I changed teams every season, and that was the last thing you wanted as a rider because you just never got a chance to settle. First there was Mitsui Yamaha. They decided to pull out after one year, leaving me high and dry. After that Kenny Roberts came in for a year then quit, which meant I was looking for a ride again but nothing came up so I had to run my own team.

I finished seventh in the world when I went it alone and after that we managed to get the JJ Cobas deal but, to be honest, if they had continued for another year I'd have had to say 'no thanks, it just didn't work', although I must say what a lovely bunch of guys they were.

I spent that winter of 1986-87 looking for a team but I never received a single call. I was like a black sheep and didn't have a ride for the '87 season.

My head was in bits – I was a world class rider, wasn't I? Other countries and companies were pumping large amounts of money into road-racing and riders who were crap. Not the British, though. Oh no, you just couldn't even get a spark plug out of those bastards.

I spent thousands on flights all over the place to try and get someone to sponsor me because, after making endless telephone calls, the only vision people had of me was a greasy yob, not a clean-cut guy who had a dream of becoming World Champion.

In early 1987 it was looking like I was not only out of the world championship but that I'd also be quitting racing altogether. It was only a few weeks before the first round of the championship when I got a call from Moriwaki, a Japanese company specialising in tuning and performance motorcycle parts.

They made me a one-race offer to ride in the Japanese GP, which would be the curtain-raiser to the championship. I said 'yes, that would be great' – so one minute it was all over, the next I was on a jumbo jet to Japan.

When I arrived in Japan they gave me a hero's welcome and threw a big party for me. This, I thought, was amazing and, on top of that, they gave me a flat in Suzuka city, close to the factory and near the grand prix race circuit, for the duration of my stay in Japan.

But I nearly died when I saw the bike. It had twin rear shock absorbers and it looked like something maybe Phil Read or Mike Hailwood would have raced in the early 70s.

But, not wanting to upset anyone, I said nothing. I just thought maybe it worked and that they must know a thing or two because they were a big engineering tuning company. That was the bad side – the good side was it had a full works HRC factory Honda engine and the last time I rode one of those I finished fourth in back-to-back GPs in 1985, so I was very optimistic and excited as the Suzuka race track was a very fast one.

Well, after the first practice session it was clear to see that the bike was a rocket in a straight line but like a pogo stick on wheels around the corners. It must've been the worst thing I ever raced in my life.

What happened was this – I'd go out and practice on the bike, then come in and

Light in the Darkness

tell the team all the problems. They would say they couldn't change things there and then but back at the factory they'd sort it all out.

So back at the factory I'd tell them all the changes I wanted and they made them, so I was happy. But by the morning they'd changed all the settings back, saying what I'd told them to do just wouldn't work. Now this baffled me as I'd had over four years' experience in the GPs.

In the end I just gave up – I was pissing in the wind. I qualified mid-pack and to be honest, because I was racing around on a pogo stick, I felt like I'd won the world championship just by getting on the grid for the race.

Have a guess what happened on race day. Yes, it pissed it down. I was flying – I made it up to third place in the race and all was looking fantastic because I knew that if that's where I finished, I was bound to get a ride somewhere for the rest of the season.

Then my world fell apart. Not only did I crash at the famous Spoon Curve, but so did the race leader and the rider in second place too, so some guy who was miles behind us at the time ended up winning the GP. Talk about being pissed off.

But, just like they say, it's not over 'til the fat lady sings.

ALAN CARTER

After touching down in the USA for the first time in 1987, Bob MacLean picked me up in his sleek black Merc. His large house (below) in Connecticut was even more impressive.

Light in the Darkness

31 THE AMERICAN DREAM

Latest setback made me hate myself . . . it felt like Kenny was telling me to go for it . . . Stateside opportunity meant turning down Ago . . . Bob MacLean and Kork Ballington . . . flying start to my USA adventure.

HAVING just crashed out of the first round of the world championship, I was now on my way back from Japan to England without a ride for the rest of the year.

Life was hard and I was even harder on myself. But you know what it's like – the inner-man inside starts talking to you, and in my case he said something like: "Alan, you dumb prick – what the f*** did you do, crashing out like that and missing out on another top place?"

To be honest, all I could think of was that one minute I was just cruising and everything was going great, then the next I just lost all grip and I was down on my arse again. The race was over all in the blink of an eye.

"So," I asked myself, "what are you going to do now? If only you'd stayed on, you'd be in a great position now, you wanker." I hated myself because by this time I'd f***** up so many times it was a joke.

Getting back to Yorkshire after the long trip from Japan was dreadful. I was out of a job again and I wasn't getting on with Dad, so I didn't really have anywhere to turn for support. It was a strange feeling – as if Kenny was saying: "You're on your own now kid. You're the one who needs to make it happen, so be brave and go for it. You can do it."

That was all fine and dandy but where was I going to get a ride? But talk about a stroke of luck – I had two offers in a week. My life was more up and down than Blackpool's dig dipper.

The first call was from a wealthy team owner in the USA, a great guy called Bob MacLean. Bob introduced himself to me and asked if I'd like to go and race in America for the rest of the season and team up with four-times World Champion Kork Ballington.

He said they were running RS250cc Hondas and that they'd pay all my expenses for the year plus the full running costs of the team. All I had to do was race the bike and I could keep all the prize money, too. I liked the sound of the guy – he seemed genuine and the dream of going to the USA to race really got my juices flowing, so I was sold on this one big-time.

I started negotiating with Bob and the deal was more or less done when I had a call from 15-times World Champion Giacomo Agostini saying that his number one rider Martin Wimmer had broken his leg and he wanted to know if I'd fill in for him for

ALAN CARTER

two or three GPs.

I told him I needed to think about it and asked if I could get back to him. 'Ago' must have thought I was a cheeky little bleeder for having to think about riding for him, but I'd made so many mistakes in the past that this time I froze and I just didn't know what to do.

I had two choices: I could do a few GPs on the factory Yamaha that they were struggling with at the time, which meant I could be on my bum again, or I could have the rest of the season in the USA.

Looking back now, there was only one choice and that was to get back into the world championship on the factory 250cc Marlboro Yamaha for the legendary Italian. It was my chance to show the world I was the best.

So what did I do? I rang Agostini and told him 'thanks, but no thanks' because I'd decided to race in America for the rest of the year.

My '87 team-mate Kork Ballington.

That's right, Yorkshire's finest with the brain the size of a f****** pin prick got his race kit together and jumped on a jumbo jet bound for New York's JFK Airport to spend the rest of the 1987 season in the States.

Bob MacLean, my new team boss, was there to greet me at JFK and whisked me off in his car – the most amazing black Mercedes I'd ever seen. Now Dad had some fantastic Mercs in his day but this thing was a beauty.

I took one look at it then opened my big Yorkshire gob and said: "You could've picked me up in something decent." Bob just looked me straight in the eyes with a steely expression and said: "I was going to come in the Ferrari but I didn't think we'd get your kit in it."

Obviously I assumed he was just joking after what I'd said to him but, as we approached Bob's vast house in a multi-million pound complex in the middle of a Connecticut forest, there, covered up in one of his garages, was a Ferrari. I thought: "This guy is well rich . . ."

Bob made me more than welcome. He explained that we'd stay only in the best hotels and that everything would be paid for. He promised me they'd really look after me and, I'll tell you what, they did.

He got me a great mechanic called John Lassak who was a bit inexperienced at the time but, like me, was a fast learner. He was a fantastic guy and I got on really well with him.

Light in the Darkness

The Honda I rode in '87 looked awesome with its red, white and blue fairings and red wheel rims.

Our first race was the second round of the Castrol Oils AMA 250cc Championship at Brainerd International Raceway in Minnesota which, after checking out on our arrival, I discovered was a fast track with a lot of late-braking corners. I knew I'd be fast there once I'd learned my way around it.

It was my first attempt to qualify for a race in the USA but, after a few days' practice, I was on pole position. That wasn't a bad start to my American adventure and I sure impressed my new boss as well as everyone else in the paddock, including my old team-mate Wayne Rainey and Kevin Schwartz.

Yes, I soon made lots of friends and they were all impressed with the way I could ride a motorbike. The only problem was that I was in the team to support Kork Ballington and help him win the championship ahead of a young kid called John Kocinski.

Help him? I'd just out-qualified everyone. It was fantastic and Bob was so excited that he had two riders who both could win the race.

On race day I was like the new kid on the block and I was loving every minute of it. Now I was where I belonged, on the front row, not like in the GPs where I was riding a bag of shit with no money and feeling worthless. Come race day I was sure going to be kicking some Yankee ass.

As the flag dropped for the race and we all shot off down a massive drag strip of a straight, I soon moved into second place behind Kocinski who was a great rider and very fast.

I was having a right tussle with Ballington, Randy Renfrew and Kocinski. I had it all planned out that on the last lap I would outbrake Kocinski into the final corner and win it on the line.

But just as I was pulling out of Kocinski's slipstream to outbrake him as planned, Ballington and Renfrow came flying past both of us. They ran wide on the last corner but just managed to beat me.

So I finished fourth in my first race in the USA and was less than half-a-second from winning it, too. It was one of the best races I had in the three years I would spend over there.

Bob was so happy that both his riders had finished in the top four, and we had a fantastic party later that evening. He was a lovely man and knew how to do things right.

32 FEELING THE HEAT IN MEMPHIS

My rivalry with Kocinski . . . mooning in a limo . . . queuing for The King . . . how I ended my team-mate's season.

BY now I had arrived on the American racing scene with some serious intentions of winning and getting back into the swing of things.

It was nice to get my first race out of the way and see who I'd be up against, and I soon figured out that I had everyone covered apart from John Kocinski. He may have been a skinny, freckle-faced redneck with a limited personality from the Deep South of America, but this kid could ride a 250cc two-stroke racing bike better than anyone I ever came across – even me.

On the real scratcher-type tracks like Loudon or Laguna Seca I could match him for pace, but on the technical circuits he was in a class of his own – sheer magic.

I never gave in and I pushed harder at every meeting. And the more John raised the bar, the more I tried to match him which sometimes ended with me getting hurt.

He was a protégé of Kenny Roberts who, as you would expect, had a great set-up in the USA. They were running Yamahas and we were running Hondas but there wasn't a lot in it.

What I loved about Kocinski was that he never seemed to make any mistakes. Was he human or was he an android? I just couldn't figure it out, so I just got on with my own thing, trying to be the best I could be.

Bob MacLean, my new team boss, loved everything first class and even had his own limousine service. He used to send the limos to JFK Airport to collect me and my team-mate Kork Ballington – which was all very posh, but little did he know we were mooning at people from the moving car. We thought it was hilarious, passing people going about their daily business with our arses sticking out of a giant stretch limo. The things you do when you're young.

Inevitably word got back to Bob before long and he asked to have a word with us. He explained how it had taken him 10 years to find the best limousine service in New York and now we'd basically gone and f***** it up for him, so that was the end of that. We'd been idiots.

The next race was in Loudon, New Hampshire, and nothing could have prepared me for the type of fans I would be facing there. Dad had told me all about this track because he'd been there in the late 70s and reckoned I'd love it.

But it was more like a Hell's Angels convention there. The fans were nothing like your average British supporter, that's for sure. Whereas we might be worried about getting hold of a ticket over here, the main deal for these guys was how much dynamite, booze and drugs they could get.

ALAN CARTER

Luckily we were segregated from these big-time heavies. I sure wasn't going to be punching one of these guys because if I'd tried, they'd have ripped my head off, shoved a stick of dynamite down my neck and blown me up. I knew my limits.

One of the first things I always did on arriving at a new track was to have a walk around it, just to get a feel for the place. Loudon looked a bit bumpy but I didn't give a shit because I'd soon be out there learning my way around.

Dad was right, I liked it. I got down to business and was soon up to speed in practice, putting my number 97 Honda on the front row of the grid. I was riding as good as ever and going to the States had been just the tonic I needed. Everyone made me feel so welcome and riding for the second biggest team in the country was a real bonus.

When the big day came we had a 32-lap race ahead of us – a long, hard race around a tight, twisty track. After a fantastic start I was soon in front and for 28 laps I battled it out with Kocinski as we passed each other over and over again. Every lap he would try to outbrake me, then I would try to get away from him, but it just wasn't happening.

Then the red flags came out. There was a big crash on lap 28 and the race was stopped. Over here you'd have expected that to be the end of it, but not in the USA. They told us we had to be back on the grid to complete the four remaining laps so, after a discussion with Michelin, we decided to put a new soft rear tyre on for the restart since we were only doing a short distance.

I made a fantastic start and soon me and John were at it again. But as the race neared its climax I went into the slowest corner on the track and lost the front end. I crashed out and after 32 laps of hard racing I had nothing to show for it.

Only the night before the team were treating me like a hero, but after crashing out Bob was so disgusted that he just took off and didn't even say goodbye or ask if I was OK. I was already pissed off but that really upset me because it was heart-breaking for me too. He certainly spat his dummy out that day.

Our next adventure was at a new race track in Memphis, Tennessee. I was so excited about this trip because I was going to be staying in the best hotel in town – the Hyatt Regency – and it was 1987, the 10th anniversary of Elvis Presley's death. I was a big fan of Elvis and I have happy memories of listening to his records and watching his films with Mum and my stepdad Dave.

On arriving in Memphis I booked a ticket to visit Elvis's house, Graceland, but to be honest I hadn't put much thought into it. I expected to just turn up, breeze around and have a look – but when I arrived there must have been 10,000 people queuing up to get in.

Now we racers are not known for our patience, but I joined the queue and I was genuinely shocked at how Elvis had influenced the lives of some of the people waiting to get in.

Some of them were hysterical and others had tears streaming down their face and it was all a bit unnerving. After listening to them, I started wondering whether Elvis had killed himself or had been murdered – there were even stories that he was still alive and all I could think about was why he or our Kenny would do that because

Light in the Darkness

My biggest rival in America John Kocinski.

they had everything to live for. I know that Kenny left a big hole in my life and the lives of many others too – the devastation that people leave behind is indescribable.

The queue gradually inched towards the house and when the tour began the first place we were taken was to Elvis's grave. We all got a chance to have a moment next to him and I felt a bit numb as I said a few words to The King.

Next we went into his house and it was amazing – I mean, one minute I was on the racing scrapheap and the next I was in Graceland.

Back at the hotel, Kork, myself and our team mechanics decided to order a Domino's pizza. They had a fantastic deal on that year which guaranteed they would deliver your order within 30 minutes and, if they didn't, you could have it for free. This was more like a game than a meal to us.

We would order about £50 worth of food, then all set our stopwatches. The race was now well and truly on because they had to get all that food to us on the 15th floor of our hotel inside half-an-hour or they'd be giving it to us for nothing.

As you can imagine, we were all pissing ourselves laughing when the knock on the door came no more than 40 seconds too late. But late it was, so we just shrugged and said "sorry mate" as we all showed the poor delivery lad our watches. He must have felt like kicking the shit out of us. We were awful but the pizza was lovely and I'm surprised Domino's didn't ban us from ever ordering from them again because we pulled this trick in every town we went to.

Arriving at the new track in Memphis was like a breath of fresh air. Instead of the rundown old dumps I'd been going to, this one was brand new, although there was one problem. It had Armco barrier all the way around it so, if you came off, you were definitely going to be visiting Jesus and I didn't fancy that at the age of only 22. It had obviously been designed for car racing and not for bikes.

The reason I was in America in the first place was to help my team-mate Kork Ballington beat Kocinski. I was going to be the fly in the ointment and steal points from Kenny Roberts' team riders to help Kork win the championship.

But what I agreed to do and what I actually did weren't the same thing. I always rode for myself – I just couldn't go along with that team-riding crap because the way I saw it was that it was everyone for himself once the flag dropped.

Practice at Memphis went great. I took to the track instantly and I was the fastest guy out there. I was over two seconds a lap faster than nearly everyone else, but then it all went pear-shaped.

I was still tucked behind the screen as I approached a group of riders in front of me when they all jumped on their brakes early. This took me by surprise and I just managed to avoid hitting anyone before clipping the last rider who, of all people, turned out to be Kork.

It was the first time I'd ever knocked anyone off and it had to be the rider I'd been flown out to American to help win the title. He broke his wrist in the fall and that was it, his season was over. I felt terrible.

The race itself could have gone so much better, too, because with sweltering temperatures of 110 degrees and 100 per cent humidity, the conditions were almost impossible.

I led the way for a long time but I was sweating so much that the inside of my helmet was like a river. I couldn't see a thing, so I had to keep opening my visor and, although I got another great finish, I was still waiting for a win.

33 LOVING IT IN THE STATES

Well looked after by the Leisner family ... explosive revenge for pushing my pal into the pool ... a track with shrines on the corners ... how I earned money from my mechanic's party trick.

I SOON made friends in the USA and one racer who really looked after me was Andy Leisner who lived in Pasadena with his mum Sue, dad John and sister Jayne. They were the nicest people you could ever wish to meet.

They lived in a lovely house on a fantastic street and we all just hit it off. I was a lucky boy because I was thousands of miles from home and until I met them I didn't really have a base to stay at.

John and Sue treated me like I was their own son. They had a tennis court in the back garden where Andy and I would play for hours, neither of us giving the other an inch because we both wanted to win as much as we did when we were out on the track.

These were very special times and the memories I have are just beautiful. The occasions we sat out in their back yard just shooting the breeze were priceless.

One night my great buddy Chris Knight was there spinning some yarns as he chatted up some girls. It was all going well for him until I decided to push him in the pool with his best clothes on, thinking it would make me look cool.

Unfortunately it backfired as far as I was concerned. Chris's soggy dollars came floating to the top as he surfaced which, of course, made the girls he'd been chatting up feel sorry for him.

As he emerged from the pool dripping wet Chris gave me the eye as if to say "you bastard, I'll have you for this," but that's what I loved about him – he never got aggressive but his cunning mind would always devise a plan better than mine. And get me back he did, after patiently biding his time until the next party.

There we were by the pool, chatting away to a group of girls, when Chris seized his moment. Unbeknown to me he'd managed to pick up some very strong fireworks on a trip to Texas and suddenly he pounced with better accuracy than an American Navy Seal.

He dropped some type of explosive between my legs and it just about blew my knackers clean off, singeing my legs in the process. It was sweet revenge for him and he was laughing his head off as he told me: "That's what you get for being a prick – I said I'd get you back."

We were soon back on the racetrack and our next port of call was across country near Chicago, at Elkhart Lake, another new track. As usual the first thing we did

ALAN CARTER

when we got there was walk the track and my immediate impression was that it was a very dangerous circuit. For a start, on two of the corners were mini-shrines to people who had been killed there and that's not something to build your confidence on your arrival.

Believe it or not it rained during our first practice session – the only time in my three years in America that I experienced wet weather at a race meeting. Because of the rain not many riders bothered to go out but I gave it a shot, only to crash out, although luckily with minimal damage to my bike and none to myself apart from my pride.

The rest of practice went OK, although the track was lined with Armco with not much run-off, so it wasn't on my list of favourite racetracks around the world. That said, it was in one of the nicest settings I've ever seen.

I qualified on the front row and finished about fifth, which was rubbish really, but, like I said, I wasn't taking any chances at this place. The best part of the trip was the after-race party in Siebkens Bar, which was on a beautiful lake setting. The Yanks had been partying at this place for years after race meetings and usually ending up getting completely drunk and skinny dipping in the lake. It was great fun.

The second year I went they all got stripped off and did the can-can through the bar. Being a smart arse, I locked the exit door. So when they came in at one end and danced through the pub either completely or semi-naked, they got to the door and had no way out. I brought the house down that night.

My mechanic, Yank, told me his party trick was to do a hand stand and drink a pint of beer upside-down in one go. My mind was working overtime, so I asked him to show me how he did it. He did, and I was amazed.

When I got back into the bar I told several team members about it and naturally they reckoned it was bullshit. So I took some bets, got Yank a pint and the show was on. Everyone just stood back in sheer amazement as he performed the feat perfectly. Afterwards we split the cash we'd made, which was brilliant – we must have made more money scamming people than racing motorbikes.

My time in America was a funny old mixed bag of allsorts. I met some fantastic people and they just couldn't believe how many states I'd been to, as most of them hadn't been outside their own back yard.

I was having the time of my life and tried not to think too much about what our Kenny had done, even to the point that I didn't believe it had really happened. I just wanted him to jump out from behind a bush and say "boo".

I tried to make my time in the States a mixture of business and pleasure, and I made a point of seeing as many of the amazing places as possible.

I went to places like Long Beach to see the Spruce Goose flying boat and the Queen Mary ship docked there. And we went to Carmel in Monterey County, where Clint Eastwood had his own bar – he was actually there when our team owner Bob MacLean called in but I'd missed him by 24 hours when I visited. It would have been great to have met him but, never mind, I was loving the States.

34 FOCUSED ON KOCINSKI

New team for the new year . . . Treated like a VIP at Universal Studios . . . second place on Daytona debut.

TRAVELLING all over the United States was heaven. Flying in, collecting the keys to my hire car then breezing down to the hotel – I'd arrived. To me, this was the pinnacle of racing.

It felt like something Dad had planned out for me and Kenny when he was alive – either that or we were just plain lucky. We had the talent and Dad jumped straight onto it. Mal certainly had great vision and gave me and my brother everything we needed to succeed.

By now I'd done some serious miles up and down highways all over the world, and one journey I must recommend is the drive from Los Angeles to San Francisco. It's just amazing coming up that coast road, passing the famous Pebble Beach golf course, then hitting the beautiful town of Monterey.

Getting to the Laguna Seca racetrack was a task in itself. As we were winding up a mountainside I was thinking, 'you're having a right laugh here.' Surely there couldn't be a racetrack up there? Well, there was, and it was an absolute beauty.

It all looked great as I walked the track but then I got to the famous Corkscrew corner and I was like, 'holy shit, how are we going to get round there?' You see there was a massive difference between standing there looking at it – and even then it was very intimidating – and actually riding round it on a racing bike. It looked almost impossible but once you got out there on the bike it was a piece of cake. The main thing was getting the braking right before it, as there was no run-off whatsoever in those days, so if you crashed you were going to really hurt yourself.

This was the last year of the old track before they made the changes to accommodate the 1988 USA GP and I was given a great tip before I rode out on it for the first time. "Just be careful into turn one," I was told, "there's no run-off and a guy got killed there last year." I was really grateful and, as it turned out, it was a proper fast corner and I loved it.

Kenny Roberts didn't attend many of the races with his team because he was far too busy chasing world titles in Europe, but this was his home track and he was there to watch his young riders John Kocinski and Cal Rayborn Junior.

Carl never really cut the mustard in top flight American racing, to be truthful, but John made up for his team-mate's poor performances and the kid just couldn't put a foot wrong.

In Laguna Seca I'd found a track I loved as much as Cadwell Park. I was flying in practice and the added incentive of my ex-boss Roberts being present gave me that

Left: With my mechanic and sponsor John Lassak and (right) visiting Alcatraz prison.

little edge and I qualified in pole position again.

Talk about being on top of the world – finally there was a real buzz in the air and I felt I had the beating of John. I hadn't just done one fast lap in practice, I'd done a load of them.

I was fit, hungry and desperate and I only had to turn up on Sunday morning to show everyone what I could really do.

The adrenaline was pumping as I waited on the start line with Kocinski next to me. His boss Kenny Roberts, my hero and the three-times world champion, came over to him to wish him good luck and said: "Stay on, kid."

I was thinking: 'Stay on, kid? I'm going to skin the bastard today – just you watch.' I was so excited. This was *my* day – I was gunning for my first win on American soil.

The race started and I was right there at the front pack, just about to pounce to take the lead and try to put some distance between me and the rest when the bike started to lose power.

My heart sank. 'Oh no, not again,' I thought. It turned out the piston pin had come out and damaged the barrel. That in turn made the engine lose about a third of its power, so I crawled around the track for 20 laps before limping home in about fifth place.

Just how much could a man take? That season most, if not all, the teams running RS Hondas had a problem with the piston pins. We'd been OK until then but it all went wrong on the day I had the best chance to win a Castrol AMA 250cc Championship race. Once again it had all gone up in smoke.

We moved on up north for the final race of 1987 to Sears Point Raceway, just

Light in the Darkness

above San Francisco in the Napa Valley wine region, and it was a great trip.

In San Francisco I did the tourist thing – had a look at Chinatown, went down the famous twisty Lombard Street and booked a visit to Alcatraz. Now Alcatraz is a must-see attraction and how anyone ever escaped from there, I'll never know. It certainly gives you the creeps looking in the cells where the famous Bird Man and the rest were all locked up. Leaving Frisco and going over the Golden Gate Bridge was another high point.

Yes, I was a lucky boy in many ways. I'd spent three years racing in the UK where I became the best British racer and supposedly the next Barry Sheene, then four years in the world championship and now I was on the next leg of my racing adventure with three years in the United States.

It was all thanks to Dad's love of motorbike racing. I owed him a lot but I could never give him the gratitude he deserved because he would slag me off before I could ever say the words "thank you, Dad."

Sears Point was a disappointment – yet another racetrack in poor condition and very dangerous. The Yanks just put up with it, though, and their attitude was 'get on with it or piss off', so I fell in line with them.

I'd ridden on the greatest tracks in the world so what I experienced in the USA was a right shock for me. At best the tracks there were OK and some were quite simply dangerous and you could tell by my performances when I was happy or not. If I was happy with the track I'd be on pole and if I wasn't, I'd be fifth or thereabouts.

So going into my final race of the year in America I just wanted to stay on and get a result, which is what I did.

Once the meeting was over I had a meeting with Bob MacLean. We had champagne and oysters in a San Francisco restaurant where he told me he thought the season had been OK but didn't know what his plans were for the following year. We shook hands, waved goodbye and I flew back to the UK.

During the year I'd built a very strong relationship with my new mechanic John Lassak. He'd only started working for Bob as my main man a few short months earlier when he had no idea who I was and vice-versa. He seemed a bit inexperienced at first but he made up for it in dedication and a keenness to learn quickly. He was a very clever man.

We kept in touch over the next few months regarding the 1988 season, although I never heard from Bob MacLean again – he was out of racing for the time being.

Back in England, I worked hard trying to get a ride in the world championship but nothing came up and I was now completely out of the world picture. I didn't want to race in England either, because it would have been a backward step.

It was looking like I had nowhere to go for 1988 when John Lassak rang to say he was putting a two-rider team together and wanted me as his number one. He had a few sponsors on board and the first race was at Daytona in March. Well, that was brilliant. I now had the chance of a full season's racing working with John for a second year, which could only be good for both of us.

We agreed that he'd sort everything out and pay for it while I'd race the bikes and keep my prize money, plus any sponsorship I could bring in.

All winter I focused on my fitness and sorted a few deals out so that I was ready to fly out to the USA at the end of February. I worked hard in the gym I had at my house and I also did lots of running, imagining as I did so that Kocinski was catching me as I pounded the roads. That, of course, made me run faster and harder.

I also put a picture of Kocinski on my dart board and hit it with the precision of Phil Taylor getting a double top. I was on a mission to try and beat this kid. We would also be running Yamaha race bikes, just like Kocinski's, and we'd be on Dunlop rubber, so we were on the most level playing field I would ever see. It was now down to me – no excuses.

I flew into Los Angeles in late February to a hero's welcome. Through John's new sponsor, an LA lawyer called Bob Pave, I was supplied with a lovely new Cadillac to use and he also told me to get down to Palm Springs for a week to relax before the first race as Bob had a condominium there. I was on a real high straight off the bat here.

I had a great time in Palm Springs with my first wife Nicola who I'd married after the tragedy of our Kenny and Pam – it seemed like the right thing to do at the time. It put a bit of a feelgood factor back into the family, although that would be short-lived because I was about as good at relationships as I was at staying on a race bike. Very unpredictable.

My mate Andy Leisner arranged some VIP treatment at Universal Studios for me and Nicola. His dad, John, worked there, so we did a tour and were pulled out of the crowd to do a scene in one of the ET sets – it was a right shock at the time.

My team-mate was a guy called Rich Oliver who was a nice kid but I didn't fear him because he wasn't in my league, or so I thought.

I'd talked to Dad about Daytona and he told me it was so important to get straight to the top of the banking , which was something I'd been thinking about all winter. I'd heard it was very steep and I worried that if I crashed, I'd fly through the air over the top and probably die.

But all my fears were put to one side after I went under the tunnel and looked back at the track. I realised I'd blown it all completely out of proportion and that it didn't

Light in the Darkness

Getting down to business at the fabulous Laguna Seca.

look anything like the mental monster Mal and my mind had made it out to be.

It was at Daytona where I first met Jimmy Filice. I'd heard about him in the early 80s when, apparently, he was the greatest kid in the world but he never made it to the GPs in Europe and by the time I had got to America he'd maybe lost his edge.

He didn't do especially well in the AMA series in 1988 either – he just couldn't seem to get his RS Honda to work for him and we kicked his ass every weekend.

Even so, he was one of the nicest guys you could ever wish to meet and if everyone gets a break in life, then Jimmy got his a few months down the line in the first American GP on a factory NSR Honda. That day he rode the race of his life and won it in fine style. He sure showed the world that day and, just like me, he could have been a great world champion given the right backing

Anyway back to Daytona and round one of the 1988 AMA Championship. Practice was going great and there were two races to qualify for the Daytona 100 Miler. I won my heat and I was on the front row for the main event. It was my first time at Daytona and this was another track I just took to – I liked it and I was on the gas.

Come race day, it was looking like I'd have my work cut out because Kocinski was also flying on the Roberts Yamaha. When the flag dropped the pair of us shot straight to the front and started battling it out.

In the early stages I was losing too much time on the infield through the fast left-hander. We were so fast but I just couldn't seem to get it right – I made time up on the banking but I kept losing out on this one corner. What the f*** was wrong with me? I just couldn't get it at all.

When we hit the back markers I lost about five seconds and it was game over. I gave it everything but, to be honest, I don't think I could have beaten him because he was a better rider than anyone else in the world at that point. I finished second in my first Daytona race meeting and that was about as good as it was ever going to get.

The team were over the moon with my performance but I sure wasn't. Winning was everything and second didn't matter to me.

35 FADING DREAMS

*Long hours on the road to meetings ... back to the UK for treatment ...
concern at the state of tracks ... right hook for the weirdo ... brushes with the law.*

FINISHING second in the opening round of the American 250cc Championship was about as good as it got. So there I was moaning about coming second to a guy who would go on to fulfil all the hopes and dreams I once had.

For not only did John Kocinski win three back-to-back American Championships, but he also won the world title at his first attempt on a bike that was no more than average and with no track knowledge at all, as he'd never even been to Europe before.

Every now and then along comes a guy who is a bit special – it was me in the early 80s and John just a few short years later. My career had lots of flaws, like Dad pushing me to breaking point, crashing too often and the whole thing of our Kenny completely losing his mind and killing himself. In the end it just wore me down and I was only half the man I could have been.

The next few rounds of the American Championship were a complete disaster. I crashed out in the next race just as I was about to start the last lap, which was so disappointing because it meant the hard graft I'd put in all week had been for nothing.

The meetings were weeks or sometimes even months apart and on top of that it wasn't like travelling an hour or so to Cadwell or Donington – in America you had to travel for days to get to the track where you were racing.

We set off for one trip in Andy Leisner's vintage motorhome. Andy was driving while I was in the back with my new mate Chris Knight, who I'd only met a few weeks before at Daytona. Chris was always fun to be around and I really liked him.

It wasn't long before a pack of cards came out. Now I don't remember how much cash Chris had left home with, but I do know that after only a few miles he had none. I'd won the lot off him and he wasn't a happy kid. I told him I'd buy him a McDonald's to make him feel better but he must have been thinking: 'You cheeky bastard, that's my cash.'

We travelled all the way from California to Loudon in New Hampshire, which took us about three days non-stop. Driving in Europe was nothing to getting around in the USA.

But here I was on my favourite track again, which was a blessing as most of the others badly needed re-surfacing.

On a typical American track you would come down a black tarmac straight, then find yourself on strips of concrete on the inside of a turn and after that on different colours of tarmac. It would look more like a patchwork quilt than a racetrack and it used to f*** my head up because I just couldn't get to grips with all the surface changes.

So on a track with a great surface I'd be fast and loving my time in the States but then I could be no more than a top 10 guy riding on a track I considered wasn't fit for motocross racing.

But boy did I want to win at Loudon. Not only was I still looking for my first national victory, but also our team sponsor Bob Pave said he'd buy me any racing pushbike I wanted as a reward for the win and I had my eye on a beauty – a white carbon fibre Kestrel that would have cost about three grand.

I'd been living at Bob's house in between races with his wife and their two great kids, Sacha and Bjorn, who were mad keen on racing and I was there also to attend club races at Willow Springs to show them the ropes.

On the Saturday there was a six-hour endurance race at Loudon and I was in the paddock when a very excited Chris Knight came back and said he'd got a ride in it. Chris was a few years younger than me and I'd never seen him race a bike, or even ride one, but he assured me he was the real deal and could mix it with anybody given a fair crack of the whip.

Watching Chris out there on track was brilliant. He was aggressive and really giving it a right go on what looked like a bag of shit at best, but it wasn't long before he pitted, saying: "It's f*****."

Chris took his helmet off and peeled his leathers down to his waist – he looked absolutely knackered and glad to be out of the race. I soon found out that the gear lever had bent under the engine casing, so I quickly grabbed a ring spanner, fixed it and said: "Come on, we're back in the race." He just looked at me as if to say: 'You bastard, I'm f***** and now I've got to get back out there.'

For my own race I was on the front row again and I knew that if I couldn't win here, I was never going to win a National.

Unusually I didn't make the best of starts while Kocinski got a flier. I was expecting him to just disappear and leave me for dead, so I had the bit between my teeth but, as it turned out, I was too eager to catch him.

I was on cold tyres and on the third corner, a tight right, I lost the back end and got thrown over the bars. I was lying beside the bike with the throttle wide open and that shot me off the side of the track. At that point I abandoned the bike, which flew down a steep bank and into the lake in the middle of the track.

I followed it down the bank like Eddie the Eagle doing the Olympic ski-jump with all the marshals running around trying to find me. "Bob, are you OK," they were shouting – I had my sponsor's name on my leathers and they assumed my name was Bob Pave. That pissed me off even more because I'd just thrown away a genuine chance of winning a big race and really banged myself up in the process.

As I climbed out of this cross between a swamp and a lake I had all sorts of shit all over me and the crowd were going ballistic, screaming and chanting at me. I responded by throwing my gloves into the crowd but they wanted more, so I lobbed them my boots. Even that wasn't enough, so I started to get my leathers off before suddenly realising I only had some skimpy underwear on. I changed my mind and walked away.

That night my leg stiffened up. I could hardly walk and my hand was like a football.

To try and cheer me up Chris suggested a few drinks and a game of pool. I was a decent player but Chris was like Ronnie O'Sullivan, so we accepted the challenge when some local pool hustlers asked us if we fancied five dollars on a few games. We were always up for winning some money but this time we were skinned alive and lost just about everything we had, so now we were both down and out. I certainly wasn't looking forward to driving thousands of miles back to our base after not even completing a single lap on race day. Racing could be a very cruel world indeed.

It was a few thousand miles to our next race, too, and along the way we hit a small town just north of Chicago where a friend of a friend was going to be putting us up for the night.

Chris and I decided to hit the local town, grab a bite to eat and shoot some pool – and everything was going great. At the bar I got talking to this really friendly guy, although, being a bit slow, I didn't realise he was gay. The chap made a bee-line for Chris and, not holding back, proceeded to tell him that he was the most amazing guy he had ever met. Chris was totally taken aback and, to be honest, so was I.

We had a bit of a reputation for flirting with the girls but this guy really wanted Chris, so much so that I thought he was going to get a smack for his troubles. Sensing what could happen, I moved in and smoothed things over for him.

Chris said he needed the toilet and, while he was gone, the guy asked me what his chances were of getting together with him. I told the guy that Chris really liked him but that he was very shy – I said he just needed to take it easy, back off a little and if he did that they'd make a great couple. If Chris had known what I'd said at the time, he'd have killed the pair of us.

We moved on to another bar to play pool and just as I bent down to take my shot I heard this American voice say: "Hit me with the pool cue."

I thought I was hearing things but he looked me straight in the eyes and said: "Hit me with the Goddam pool cue." I told him I didn't need this, but then turned round, handed Chris my cue and gave this weirdo the biggest right hook I'd ever produced.

This guy was out cold on the floor when the bar manager and his staff all told us to go upstairs. Chris and I looked at each other expecting to be given a good pasting in return with our bodies dumped in Lake Michigan, never to be seen again.

We got upstairs fearing the worst when, to our surprise, these guys congratulated me on knocking out the town idiot, saying he'd had it coming to him for years. They shook our hands and threw a party on our behalf – we were local legends and we'd only been in town a few hours.

I couldn't even bend my leg to get it on the footrest for the next round at Elkhart Lake. I struggled all week and in the end just gave it up as a bad job.

ALAN CARTER

I rang Dad in England trying to sort out someone to fix my leg and the best option was to go private, so that's what I did. I had keyhole surgery in a private hospital followed by very intense therapy at Leon's clinic in Yorkshire, where they had been looking after me for the last eight years with all my racing injuries.

I returned to the States after rehab feeling like a new man, and the fact the next round was at my favourite track, Laguna Seca, made me feel even better. Practice went great – both my team-mate Rich Oliver and I were going well and there wasn't anything between us and Tom Stevens and John Kocinski, the two Kenny Roberts team riders. We were all in with a great chance of winning this one.

The four of us all started the race at a rapid pace but once again there was a painful early end for me. Coming out of the Corkscrew corner and down the hill to the very fast left-hander, my vision was poor. I got in a bit tight and ran over the inside line which no-one ever did. F*** knows what I was doing on it because you went about a foot wide, it was so bumpy.

As a result I lost the front end and had one of the biggest crashes of my life. God only knows how, but yet again I walked away from it without a scratch although I was battered and bruised.

By this time there were only two races left and I didn't really like either of the tracks they were on because they were too dangerous, so I went for a finish rather than giving it 100 per cent and risk hurting myself.

I loved the time I spent in America, the people always treated me fairly and honestly plus they were a pleasure to deal with. The weather was fantastic and I felt like it was my new home. If only they could have resurfaced the tracks to make them a lot safer, I would have been much happier. But the Americans were into their car racing and we were just more of a hindrance than anything.

I did a track inspection before the American GP at Laguna Seca and told them to make some changes before the cream of Europe turned up but they did very little and all the riders refused to race until all their requests were met. What they didn't know was that it was one of the safest tracks in the USA and I thought: 'You should come to some of the places I have to race at.'

I was always highly motivated to win races in America, although after doing the GPs in front of crowds of over 100,000 fans, racing in the States was small fry.

They couldn't even get 5,000 fans at some tracks, which was a bit deflating, but I was still a happy chappie in the paddock wherever I was in the world and I always had a positive outlook. It wasn't going to get me everything in life but, as my Gran always told me, no-one likes a sour face. Whether I had the best bike or the worst one, I always gave everything I had and more.

I never drank before races and I can honestly say that neither myself nor our Kenny took drugs at any time during our racing careers. But we were larger than life characters, rubbing people up the wrong way for fun and banter, saying what we were going to do – and pulling it off more times than not.

Every sport needs a rebel and Kenny and I sure ruffled a few feathers along our racing journeys across the world. It's a shame we never both became individual world champions – Kenny's gone and I have to live with that for the rest of my life.

Light in the Darkness

I really enjoyed my three years in the States. This was taken by Derek on our way to Laguna Seca in 1990.

My first year in America was my best because with Bob MacLean everything was paid for and done first class. Don't get me wrong, John Lassak did a great job in 1988 but just didn't really have the budget to be mixing it up there with the likes of Kenny Roberts' team, although we gave it a great try with very limited resources.

I finished my second season fifth in the American Championship after crashing out of three of the seven rounds. If only I'd stayed on the bike more often.

Despite all the tricks we got up to I only had a few brushes with the law in America and the first time was when Doug Holtom and I went to the Willow Springs Raceway in California.

We got out of Los Angeles on the highway heading north and decided to see how fast the Cadillac I'd been provided with could go, and we got her up to 120mph.

We were in the middle of nowhere near Edwards Air Force base, where the Space Shuttle used to land, when all of a sudden there was a big police chase. Doug was driving and, because of the speed he was going, the state troopers were gunning for him. They pulled us over and I heard the officer say to Doug: "You do know this is jail?" I was absolutely wetting my pants in the car expecting him to be dragged off to the nick. I have no idea how Doug talked his way out of this one but he did, the jammy bugger. If it had been me, I'd have been locked up.

The second time I got into in trouble was after visiting our local nightclub in a local hotel near Woodland Hills, California, called Tickets.

We were all half-cut and I was driving home along the same back road we'd used all year. Ahead of us we spotted an accident, so some smart arse ripped the handbrake on and the car screamed to a halt right next to a police officer.

ALAN CARTER

The officer promptly dragged me out of the car and when he told my gang I'd be spending the night behind bars if no-one gave him 600 dollars bail, they all said "sorry mate, we're skint," and, to their amusement, I was carted off to the local nick for the night.

On the way to the police station the officer told me he wanted me to walk the line, which was a test they used to gauge if someone had been drinking too much. Well, my balance was always crap even without a drink, but the officer said it was real close and that I could be done for drink-driving.

We stopped at a local hospital to collect another convict and then finally got to the station well over an hour after I'd been hauled out of the car. The officer handcuffed me to a bench and asked if I wanted to take a blood, urine or breath test. I didn't know what to say because it wasn't done like that in England, so he said he'd give me time to think and come back in five minutes.

It was about an hour later when he did return and offered me the same choices, so I acted confused and opted for the breath test. I was really crapping myself but I blew it up and the officer said: "You're not going to believe this, Alan, but you're just under the limit – that's fine, you can go home."

The problem was I lived about 10 miles away, so I asked the officer if there was any chance of a ride home. As luck would have it, he said he was finishing his shift in five minutes and he took me home. What a result that was.

Relaxing on the beach with Doug Holtom.

36 FROZEN OUT

**Another winter searching for a deal . . . a disappointing season but great fun . . . .
how the Bible helped me . . . end of the American dream.**

WAS I in for a shock when I came back from the States in October – I'd spent all year in the warm American sun and the British winter of 1988-89 was bloody freezing.

I was still living in the bungalow I'd purchased with some of the money from my Kenny Roberts deal in '84. Being in a wheelchair, Mum's dream was to have a bungalow and although it never came true for her, it was something that was always on my mind. Friends could never understand why a young kid like me wanted to live in a bungalow but my only answer was that I was fulfilling one of Mum's dreams and that way maybe I'd feel a little closer to her. I was missing my mum.

The winter of 1988-89 was just the same as any other close season in that I spent all my time on the phone trying to chase either a ride or sponsorship for the following year. I found this the hardest part of being a motorcycle racer. It was a shit job – nobody ever rang you back and I had more chance of getting the money from robbing a bank than from a serious sponsor in England. Talk about being a taboo subject.

In America, on the other hand, people were very positive. They were happy to know you were doing well, wanted to be involved with you and would call you back to arrange a deal – what a breath of fresh air compared to the negative British society we live in here.

Over the years so many people made me so many promises that it made me realise they were just a load of bullshitters, and that was hard to take. My dad, however, always did what he said he was going to and was straight to the point. I was missing him and I wanted him to be part of my team but the damage had been done and there was too much water under the bridge. Mal had lost interest and wasn't making the big money he used to.

Dad would throw thousands away just buying drinks, wasting as much cash on trivial crap as he spent on the racing bikes themselves.

Negotiations for a ride for the 1989 season were non-existent and I had basically nothing in the bag except for a handful of loyal personal backers. Apart from a helmet sponsor and a leathers deal I was up shit creek without a paddle.

I tried getting back into GP racing but nothing came off. I spent thousands on letters and phone calls but pissing in the wind was a major understatement and I was getting nowhere fast. As a last resort I spoke to John Lassak in California who said he wanted to run again but didn't have much of a budget, so he suggested I rang Bob

ALAN CARTER

Pave, our main sponsor.

As luck would have it, my mate Andy Leisner was coming over to Europe for a crack at the world championship and hadn't found a buyer for the Aprilia race bike he used in the '88 season, so Bob and I arranged to buy it. We agreed to give him $9,000 each so we'd be joint owners of the bike with John paying the running costs for the year. We also agreed we'd run the bike in the same colours as the '88 Yamaha under the Lassak Racing Team banner.

So we were back in business. Talk about scraping a deal together at the eleventh hour.

Setting off to Daytona at the back end of February was brilliant. On paper the Aprilia was just the right bike because Daytona was all about top speed, and I had bucket loads of optimism too, so maybe I could win this one. But on arriving at the track I soon realised that things were not going to turn out as I'd pictured them.

John had found another two riders from somewhere, namely my old mate Robbie Peterson and a new kid called Miguel Duhamel who I'd never even heard of.

Miguel seemed a nice guy, even if he was a bit scary, and I found out that his dad was Yvon Duhamel, a famous Canadian racer from the 70s and a real hard-looking guy.

I can't remember much about Daytona except that I finished fifth in the race and wasn't happy.

Doug Holtom had flown out with me to oversee the bike and he was a great mechanic who was always there for me. After Daytona we brought the bikes back to the UK and took the front forks off so Doug could get them modified by a top guy in England.

Doug wasn't able to go back to America with me but suggested I took his mate David Watton, who everyone on the UK racing circuit knew as Yank.

Yank was a scary f***** to say the least and he'd done more time in prison than Ronnie Biggs. But without Doug I was in Shit Street and anyone was better than no-one, so I struck a deal with Yank. He said he'd work for me for nothing all year and all I had to do was buy his plane tickets and give him some fags and beer money. He'd always wanted to go to America, so the deal was struck and I had England's number one pikie working for me.

Unfortunately Doug never told me that Yank was both an alcoholic and mentally unstable. I was in for both a shock and the best year of my life.

Things didn't get off to a great start because, looking to save some money and reckoning I could worry about it later, I only bought him a one-way ticket to the USA. I didn't think he'd be any the wiser.

But when we arrived at Manchester Airport I was promptly advised at check-in that the ticket was invalid due to the fact you needed a visa if you were only going one way. I froze as I wondered what the hell I was going to do while Yank reacted by threatening to chuck himself off the top of the terminal building if he wasn't allowed on the plane. And, trust me, he was more than capable of doing that and taking a few other people along with him, too.

I'd only just hooked up with him and it was already starting to go pear-shaped, but

Alan Carter

International Grand Prix Motor Cycle Racer
6 BADGER HILL, RASTRICK, BRIGHOUSE
WEST YORKSHIRE, HD6 3UE, ENGLAND
Telephone: (0484) 400219
Fax: (0422) 347256

MARLBORO YAMAHA TEAM AGOSTINI

FAX NO. (39) 35 693268

Dear Mr. Agostini,

I would like you to consider myself as a possible rider in your team next year in the 250cc World Championships. I have had the best results this year with 10 wins, two second places and three new track records, riding Honda RS 250 and am still only 25 years of age. I believe I have a lot to offer your team.

Last year at one U.S.A. Championship round Brainard, I qualified pole position in front of John Kocinski only to break down on the first lap of the race.

I look forward to your reply.

Yours sincerely,

Alan Carter.

This letter I sent to the great Giacomo Agostini was typical of my desperation to get a ride.

I managed to calm him down and purchased another ticket, this time an open return. So now I was skint as well as pissed off.

Feeling stressed out after the ordeal, I decided to have a drink at the departure lounge bar, where I saw the father of one of my best mates who was about to jet off on holiday. What was strange, though, was that I didn't recognise the woman he was with – it certainly wasn't my mate's mum. But the guy just winked at me knowingly and I nodded in return. I knew what he was up to but I had enough problems of my own to say anything to him about his shenanigans.

Yank and I flew out to California and stayed at Bob Pave's house, where we were made more than welcome – but it didn't take long for Bob to get fed up with us just messing around too much. He certainly didn't take too kindly to us throwing his cat into the swimming pool and suggested he got us a nice apartment.

Sure enough, he sorted out a three-bedroomed apartment in a place called Simi Valley which had a tennis court, a swimming pool and also came with membership of the local Gold's gym. Life was great.

Yank visited the local bike dealers in the town and they offered him a part-time job which worked out great for both of us. His only problem was that he didn't have a work permit, so I told the guys at the shop he could use mine. That way they paid the money to me and every Friday I charged Yank $50 to cash his cheque, so everyone was happy.

ALAN CARTER

Yank had a great personality and was always smiling – well, in between thinking about killing himself – and he never did his drinking in front of anyone, so I began to think he wasn't an alcoholic at all. It was only one morning at about 8.00am when I thought he was drinking a glass of water that I realised it was actually neat vodka.

Yank would come out of work on a Friday and go down to the local strip bar where he'd blow a few hundred dollars. Then I'd pick him up and we'd go to the famous Elephant Bar, which was a great place to eat, drink and meet new people.

One afternoon I was in there I could see this big black guy staring at me. I was thinking of ways I was going to chin him when he came over and asked where I'd got my jacket from. I was wearing a fantastic leather jacket with a massive boxer motif on the back, which I'd bought in Miami.

I told him I was a big boxing fan and he told me his name was James Toney. He said he was a boxer and that he was going to be world champion one day. He did go on to win several world titles as well, so I think our Kenny must have been watching over me that day because can you imagine me giving James Toney a crack? It would have been like hitting him with a sponge.

While I was in the USA I'd kept in contact with a girl in England called Julie and I asked her if she fancied coming over. She did, so I told her to sell her Jeep, get a flight over and we'd pick her up at the airport.

She came over and I talked her into going halfs on a new Mazda pick-up. It was red with massive wheels and we set off in it to the next round of the American Championships about 2,000 miles away in Georgia.

But we racers are a funny breed and one thing I learned from our Kenny was that we only stop for a piss or some grub if we need fuel.

Yank was in the back with a sleeping bag and a ghetto blaster while Julie and I were in the cab with all the comforts, laughing at the dimwit in the back when, after about 300 miles, Yank tapped on the window saying he needed the toilet.

I told him he was having a laugh – we still had half a tank of fuel. A few miles further on and he tapped again but I just pointed to the fuel gauge. It happened again a few miles later but I really took notice this time because he had my racing helmet out of the bag and said he was going to shit in it if I didn't stop. I pulled over immediately.

Yank sprinted behind some bushes and came back about five minutes later like Clint Eastwood, the gun fighter. He put his face right up to mine and said: "Next time if you don't stop, I'm going to kill you." I was like, 'No problem buddy,' and we moved on. I've no idea what he wiped his arse on but he had no socks on when he came back to the van. We continued our journey right across the USA from out west to near the east coast – it was a fantastic drive and I truly recommend at some part of your life that you make this incredible journey.

There might have been three of us but we became something like Bonnie and Clyde – we were the Dick Turpins of England. We had very little money, I had about $10,000 on credit cards – I was paying one with the other – and I juggled things around better than any circus act could. We did some crazy stuff but we had no choice. The dream days of riding for Bob MacLean were a distant, fading memory

Light in the Darkness

– the top hotels and limousines were well gone and we were lucky to be getting a motel for the night

Many times Julie and I would wait for Yank to fall asleep, then dive into a pit stop to grab a bite to eat. Then we'd carry on the journey without him even knowing and if he said he was hungry when he woke up we'd say: "You greedy bastard, we're not stopping yet," and carry on the road trip. He did the same to us, though. Many a time at a racetrack he'd say he was off to the toilet and then I'd catch him lining up at a burger stall. It made me laugh, as we were all playing the same game.

This would be one of my poorest years in racing but the fun we had was priceless. Yank was brilliant, he just had something about him. He'd lived with Colin Appleyard and Peggy for a time in the UK, working for my mate Robin.

People just took him in and once his boss at the bike dealers got to know him, he moved in there. It was a fantastic home and I was happy for him because he hadn't had the best start in life, coming from a very poor background, but that never held him back. In fact he was very inspiring and in a funny way I learned a lot from him – he'd help keep me balanced and my feet firmly on the ground.

Arriving at the Road Atlanta race track was great. We'd travelled thousands of miles knowing the national speed limit was 55mph. I could never understand why these intelligent Americans had such a crazy speed limit.

The problem with speeding in the States was that one minute there was no-one on the highway so you'd get your foot down, and the next you'd be pulled over by Mr Invincible, because PC Plod had appeared out of nowhere. Then he'd get his gun out and you'd shit yourself and do exactly what he said. We picked up speeding tickets in just about every state.

At Road Atlanta the great John Kocinski crashed out and hurt himself in practice for the first time in over two years. He broke his wrist and was out of the meeting on a track where nobody could even get close to his track times. A year before I'd flown Dad out to this meeting and he said the kid was brilliant and that I'd have my work cut out beating him on any track. Yes, Dad was right again.

It's funny how many times fathers are right, only for their kids not to take any notice, and that's something I'd soon learn with three boys of my own.

So with Kocinski crashing out I was second fastest in practice. The Aprilia could be a temperamental thing but it was flying. The straight was massive and it was looking like I could win on a track I didn't even like. All I had to do was finish in the top three in my heat, get the bike dialled in a bit more and we were laughing all the way to the bank.

So what did I do? I crashed out coming onto the back straight, that's what. I came out of the corner, got hard on the gas and then hit one of those pieces of track that had been patched up with a 10-foot square of new tarmac. I lost rear grip and got catapulted down the track, hitting the ground like the Hiroshima bomb.

I was badly shaken up but I was as hard as nails and crashes never bothered me. You'd have had to cut my legs off to stop me racing.

Going back to the pits in the back of a breakdown truck was always a sad, lonely trip as not only was the bike trashed but so were you. Then I had to face a mechanic

ALAN CARTER

Above left: With my team-mate Robbie Peterson, a top South African racer, at Daytona in 1989.
Above right: With my friend, mechanic and sponsor John Lassak in 1989.
Below: Back at Donington in 1988.

who would be pissed.

I was lucky in that all the people I ever worked with never complained. They just rolled their sleeves up, got on with the job and made sure the bike was ready for the next practice session no matter what.

We had no spares but Yank now had to fix the bike while I went to see the organisers and try to charm them into letting me race in the final from the back of the grid. Fortunately they were a great bunch of people and they said yes, that would be no problem.

I started the race stone last but worked hard through the pack, eventually finishing sixth. To enable me to race, my fairing brackets had been made out of a rear brake arm and it was held together by two rolls of Gaffa Tape. The engine casing was leaking oil onto my footrests which caused my foot to slip off on every corner, but I'd never stop unless the bike ground to a halt.

We had another long drive to the next meeting and we needed some bearings for the engine leak. We'd been told about a place to get them in Cleveland, Ohio. I parked the car and went to look for the place that did the bearings when I was confronted by this huge, black American guy brandishing a big stick with a knife coming out of the bottom.

He demanded money but my plan was to give him the biggest right hook in history, as Dad had always told me to bang them first and talk later. I was just about to belt him when Yank came around the corner, so I told the guy that he had all the money. Our new friend then turned on Yank who picked him up off the ground by the throat and nearly choked him to death. After a few polite words from Yank, the guy ran off faster than Ben Johnson. Nobody was messing with the Blues Brothers.

After getting the bearings we needed to find a place to heat the casings to get the old ones out and the new ones in, and we soon found somewhere. The American people were just so helpful and nothing was too much trouble for them.

We had some time to kill before the next race so we decided to travel up and see Niagara Falls. This was one of the greatest things I'd ever seen and until you actually get there in person you just can't comprehend the sheer size of them.

In the early days after our Kenny's death I started to read a lot of books by the great writer Dr Norman Vincent Peale. This was a very low point in my life but Norman's books, especially *The Power of Positive Thinking*, were a huge support to me. It was also at this point that I got my first Bible. Was I cracking up, too? I must've been the first Carter ever to own a Bible.

It gave me some comfort at the time and, after reading it several times, I could relate how the Devil said to God that Job only followed him because he made his life so fruitful, so God started to punish Job and take everything away. That's how I felt, because it seemed like everything bad in the world was happening to me.

Yank, Julie and I went through some right hillbilly towns on our travels and on one occasion we stopped in an eerie place that looked a bit like the Bates Motel from Psycho. Julie was tired, so Yank and I left her in this dump of a place and found the

ALAN CARTER

Don't mess with the Blues Brothers – me and Yank with some trophies we collected along the way.

most rundown bar I'd ever seen. We sat with our drinks and started to play cards when I noticed a good-looking girl at the bar and I couldn't help wondering what she was doing in such a shithole. Maybe it was the only place in town to go?

That's when I experienced the most shocking thing I've ever seen. This old granny, who looked like a witch, came through the front door and walked straight up to this young girl on the bar stool. She dragged her to the ground by her long hair and started beating the crap out of her. It was one serious fight and it left me and Yank in shock. Were we really seeing this or were we hallucinating?

It all happened in a blink of an eye before some guy dived in and separated them. Apparently this young girl had split the old granny's son's marriage up and she wanted to kill her – we were just innocent bystanders having a quiet beer.

Light in the Darkness

Our next destination was Loudon, one of my favourite tracks. I loved it – the crack was good, it was a racer's track and I was hoping the Aprilia would be OK as it was more suited to the big race tracks.

Well, the bike did struggle on the small Loudon circuit. There was no bottom end and the Yamahas were killing me off on the slow corners and by then my engine had started to get tired.

I came home fifth but that was like finishing last to me on one of my best tracks. Nothing was working out – we had no money, the team had none either and things had started to crumble.

Back in California, I rang the engine tuner and asked if he would rebuild the engine as we needed a complete overhaul. He told me I had to be kidding and I was shocked to discover that the team hadn't paid him for the parts he'd supplied or the work he'd already carried out. I told him I was sorry, that it was nothing to do with me and after a long talk he told me to bring him the engine along with $600 and he'd do it. He was as good as his word and at least we could get to the next round.

Little did I know that the journey to Elkhart Lake in the middle of America would be my last road trip and my last race in the USA. Things had been getting worse for John Lassak and when I saw him next, I could see a big difference in him. He had a lovely wife and a young family and he was spending too much time and money away from them, plus we weren't really getting any results on the race track.

The Aprilia suited the long, fast-flowing circuit and I finished third. Being on the rostrum was brilliant and it had been a long time since I was last on it.

But the American dream was over. We'd run out of money and after the race I told John I would be going back to England. He told me he would be keeping the bike and he'd send me the money when it was sold, but I wasn't having that. I was keeping the bike until I'd been paid for it, as I had over $9,000 invested in it.

We were both very angry and a scuffle broke out in the back of our race trailer but

ALAN CARTER

Yank and I managed to get the bike on the back of our pick-up and we headed off on the long journey back to California.

Word quickly got around the paddock that I'd stolen a race bike but that was a complete joke because I owned half of it and I wasn't going to be done out of my last $9000. So we hid the bike for safe keeping until I had chance to talk to its co-owner Bob Pave.

I told Bob what had happened and he was a true gent. I told him it had been blown out of all proportion and he invited me out for dinner so we could sort the cash out.

I turned up with the bike as promised and Bob paid me. We had a lovely meal out and a great evening and we were all sorry it had come to the end of the road. We shook hands and went our own ways.

Reflecting on the three years I spent in the States, all I can say is that I had a fantastic time. People treated me very well, I fitted in, I gave everything I could and I saw some of the greatest places in the world.

I'd recommend America to anyone – you only get one life, so live it. Take a chance because, you never know, things might just work out for you. Be positive and always remember that even when you're down ,you're not out. There are lots of sceptics and critics out there but don't let them steal your dream – they never built monuments and statues of them, only of people who did things in life.

37 HOMECOMING

Homeless and penniless ... a dream ride in the British GP ... a U-turn from the new boss that cost me my best mate and thousands of pounds.

ARRIVING back in the UK was a new low for me. Earlier in the year I'd got divorced from Nicola and we sold the house and split the proceeds, so I was wifeless, homeless and rideless. I had absolutely nothing.

Me and Nicola didn't last together because we were living separate lives. God knows what I was thinking by going off to America for three years and not taking her with me.

We split at a time when my head was all over the place. I'd come back from the USA and we decided to go our own ways, although she did try to make things work out. One day we met in a pizza restaurant for a meal to try and resolve our differences but ended up arguing again and I walked off. I still had a lot to learn about life, that's for sure.

I moved in with Doug and his dad Owen, a Spitfire pilot in the war and a really nice guy, just to get settled in. But what was I going to do now? All I'd ever done since leaving school was race motorbikes. Dad sorted me a car out, so I had some wheels to move around and I was ducking and diving all over the place trying to get any ride possible in July and for the rest of the season.

Doug suggested riding Simon Beck's RS500 Honda Triple in the British GP and said he thought he could sort it, so we got on to Shell Oils and they sponsored me to race at Donington Park with the kind support of Simon and Stan Beck, who was a lovely chap.

After racing in the USA for three years I'd put a bit of weight on and had a mullet to rival Peter Stringfellow's. I'd come back with nothing and the next thing I was racing in the biggest bike race in the world, the British GP in the premier class. What a result this would be.

Getting down to the business end of things I out-qualified Simon Buckmaster on the same bike and he'd done all the GPs. I was on an out-dated bike as well, so I really wasn't doing at all badly.

I finished in the top 20 which gave me some great exposure. One thing led to another and before I knew it I was having a meeting with Honda UK's team manager Neil Tuxworth with a view to riding Honda RS250s in the British and world championships.

I didn't really know anything about Neil, only that as a kid I had watched him race many times at Cadwell Park and he was a very good rider, but I saw this as a way back into the big time.

ALAN CARTER

Above: Playing cards with Matt Wroot (right) and Nigel Binns. Honda Britain's insistence on Silkolene as our oil sponsor ruined my friendship with big Matt.
Below: My great friend and spanner man Derek Rhodes.

He offered me two bikes and a spares budget for the year while I'd be running the team and paying all the costs, as in 1985 when I finished seventh in the world. I also arranged with Neil to purchase a factory kit – the best Honda did at the time – for £10,000.

I secured backing from the best sponsor I ever had thanks to a-long standing relationship with Shell Oils which Dad had set up in the early 70s. It was all agreed with Tuxworth and Honda UK.

The main Honda UK team would have red livery and run under the Silkolene banner while I'd basically be running a private team supported by Honda and Shell Oils. We'd be running under the Shell Gemini colours of blue and gold, they'd be paying me £25,000 and everything was looking sweet. This was going to give me the best start to a racing season since riding for the great Kenny Roberts.

I managed to negotiate with my long-standing friend Derek Rhodes to work for me and he was as excited about this as I was. We did a deal and I told him there was no problem with the money as we would be backed by Shell and that if everything went well we could build on it in the years to come.

True to Neil's word, the bikes and all the kit arrived and we based ourselves at Derek's mum's place in Hornsea, where she had a large garage which Derek converted into his own private workshop.

We painted the bikes in Shell colours and, thanks to sponsorship from Mirage who did the best paint jobs in the UK, they looked amazing. Jumping the gun, Neil wanted the £10,000 up front for the race kit but I didn't have that kind of cash so I borrowed it from my mate Matt Wroot.

I was waiting to receive my cheque from Shell when the bombshell dropped. I received a phone call from Neil Tuxworth to say that Silkolene were going to pull the plug on the Honda UK Racing team if I wasn't part of it. He told me there and then that if I wasn't going to be involved, I had to return all the race bikes and spares immediately and the deal was off.

This would become the start of a nightmare three years which should have at least seen me win the British championship three times before maybe retiring after a distinguished career.

To me this was blackmail and now I had nowhere to go. How could he even think about doing this to me? My life was now totally shattered. I had to let down Shell Oils, which would finish our relationship forever, and I also owed £10,000 which ended up costing me my friendship with my closest mate at the time, something which has not been rectified to this day. On top of that I had a mechanic who had given up a great job to come and work for me but now I was left penniless with no money to pay him and we hadn't even done a race.

I'd quickly taken a disliking to this guy but this was just the start of things to come.

I now had no budget, hated the team manager and still no van to get to the races. Happily Dad stepped in and bought a van for me because I think, deep down, he still loved racing and wanted to be involved in it.

If it wasn't for my sheer love of racing I think I'd have quit right there and then. I'd jumped out of the frying pan in America straight into the fire here in the UK. What was going to be my big comeback from the brink of obscurity was about to fizzle out before we'd even turned a wheel.

When we turned up for a shakedown meeting at Cadwell Park the bike was still painted in Shell colours but with Silkolene stickers now all over it, and that made me feel sick. No offence to the Silkolene people, they were lovely, but to be shafted in such a manner was beyond belief.

I won with ease at Cadwell and after that we had to get the bike crated up and shipped to the Japanese GP for round one of the world championship.

The aim was to do the first two rounds, then see where we stood before making plans for the rest of the GP series. But there wasn't much point in going to either the Japanese or American GPs after Tuxworth had completely ruined the whole year in one stupid move. We were technically broke, and we only went because we had made agreements with the FIM and IRTA (International Race Teams Association).

We'd won at Cadwell on supposedly the best rubber available at the time but by the time we arrived in Japan the 4.5 inch rear rims we'd used back home were obsolete. All the tyres were meant to be run on 5 inch wide rear wheels. They designed all the latest tyres around the magnificent-looking NSR works 250cc Hondas, which made my machine look like it had come out of Steptoe's yard. They were 15kg lighter and 20 bhp faster, so I was on a hiding to nothing.

Every Japanese rider and his great granny had some kind of factory bike or engine and they passed me like I was out on a Sunday afternoon cruise.

Many of the Japanese top brass of the Honda Racing Corporation were coming over and asking why we were last in practice. I said that in horse racing terms my rivals were riding pure thoroughbreds and I was on a two-legged donkey. On top of that, it had taken us until the morning warm-up before the race to get a five-inch rear wheel which alone would enable me to knock two seconds a lap off my times, technically putting me 15th on the grid for the race.

During practice I also asked Derek to change the gearbox settings, although first we had to beg Moriwaki for a first gear. Derek asked the team next to us – Lucky Strike Suzuki – if we could have some of their paper roll to lay our internal gears on but they declined so we had to put them on the floor. Cheers guys. That night back at the hotel I found the store room and took about 50 bed sheets and cut them up into lovely rags. Next day the Lucky Strike boss asked where I'd got them from, so I said: "Can you keep a secret?" He said he could, so I replied "Well so can I – f*** off."

I just managed to qualify and finished about 15th in the race, which was a miracle considering how many factory bikes were there.

We'd set off with only 200 quid and that was Derek's. I was doing fantastically well on the machine I was riding and Derek was doing his best. At least we'd made some money and could afford to go to the USA for the next round.

Light in the Darkness

38 ENVY OF THE PADDOCK

From Japan to America with just £200 . . . broken bones no barrier to a quick return . . . leading the British Championship . . . a hero's welcome at the British GP.

AFTER leaving America mid-season in 1989 with just $9,000 to my name, I couldn't in my wildest dreams imagine that so soon I would be back as England's number one and racing in the first two rounds of the world championship the following year. It was fairytale stuff.

If only Neil Tuxworth and Honda had let me go ahead with Shell Oil's support it would have made such a big difference and taken away all the pressure and worry of having no budget and a huge debt hanging over my head. To make matters worse, the guy I owed the money wasn't just a good friend, he was also a massive body builder who knew the right people in the right places to sort me out if he wanted to, although luckily Matt was fully aware that I'd been well and truly shafted.

Derek was crating the bike up before we moved on from Japan to the next round in America when the guys from Moriwaki came around for the rear wheel and gearbox part they'd let us borrow for the race. He had to take the bike back out and give them the wheel but they told Del not to worry about the engine part. They weren't going to make him strip the engine, which was good of them.

As we prepared for our next trip I found myself looking back to 1985 when the Honda Racing Corporation's top man Mr Oguma wanted to give me a test on one of their full factory 500s but I'd missed my chance. The mental tortures I put myself through are as fresh today as the day he offered me the ride all those years ago.

Derek and I arrived back on American soil for the 1990 GP at Laguna Seca which was one of my best tracks. If only I'd been riding Honda's flagship bike, the factory NSR 250, then I would have been fighting for the win instead of just being a grid-filler and a spent force.

We were back to the 4.5 inch rear rim and I nearly crashed on every corner – running off the side of the rim was a lot worse on the tight Californian track. I knew I'd be practically last, watching Kocinski and the rest fly past me.

We managed to beg a rear wheel from Little George, Freddie Spencer's former right-hand man, and that instantly pushed me up to ninth on the grid. I was riding great but, as always, there was no substitute for the sheer straight line speed of the factory bikes.

During the race I worked my butt off and slowly climbed through the field. I managed to get into the top 10 but the piston broke and the bike ground to a halt. The race was over.

When you have a dream and a desire it's amazing what you'll do. To do two grands

ALAN CARTER

Winning on my first visit to Pembrey in 1990.

prix in faraway countries with only £200 we must have been raving mad – I wouldn't even leave the house with less than that. What a joke. I was being talked about as the next Barry Sheene but didn't even have the cash to treat myself to a McDonald's.

I was like cheap pop – plenty of fizz for a few seconds, then flat as a pancake. Next Barry Sheene? I was on my way to becoming one of England's greatest wasted sporting talents due to a combination of mis-management, an ability to self-destruct and just pure bad luck.

Roll in all the family tragedies and not only did I miss out on being world champion, I didn't even become British champion either.

But Derek Rhodes was my rock. He had more belief in me than I had in myself and many a time he could have just walked away, especially as paying him was starting to become a problem too.

Dad had supplied the van for the year and it was great to see Pharaoh Racing on the side of my fairing again. Derek insured it as I had no money to do it, plus I was banned from driving for a year – the second time I received that punishment – for doing over 140mph on a dual carriageway.

I started dating June-Ann, who was the best mate of Derek's girlfriend Carol, and, like them, lived in Derek's home seaside town of Hornsea on Yorkshire's east coast. Things were starting to look a bit brighter and it turned into one of the happiest years I'd had for a long time.

I had to put my differences with Neil Tuxworth, the boss of Honda Britain, aside because I didn't want to ruffle anybody's feathers, least of all his.

After one UK race and two GPs in Shell colours, the bikes were taken away and painted red for the rest of the year.

My first outing with the new livery was a national meeting at Donington in April,

Light in the Darkness

which I won by a country mile. Compared to America this was easy. I had a great bike, a top drawer mechanic and I was racing on some of the best tracks in the world. Winning and being on pole position was my life and now I had a fair chance to do both every weekend.

After winning at Donington we decided to go to the Spanish GP at Jerez. Derek and I travelled all the way to southern Spain with a few drums of red diesel courtesy of Dad and avoided the motorways with their toll charges. There was no other way we could have afforded to get there.

After practice I was wondering what I could do to go that little bit faster, so I decided to go out for a couple more laps. Derek warned me the front tyre was just about shagged but I just wanted two more laps, so he pushed me down the pit lane and the bike fired up. I was off like a rocket but going into the very last corner, a slow left-hander, I lost the front end and crashed. My foot got caught and twisted by the back wheel and chain, badly breaking my left ankle and foot in several places.

I went to the mobile clinic run by Dr Claudio Costa who told me I'd be out for at least 56 days. I was gutted. Ron Haslam had also crashed badly, injuring his hand, and we flew home on the same plane.

I rang Dad and straight away he made some phone calls. He bunged a surgeon £500 and the next thing I knew I was laid in a Manchester hospital bed having just woken up from an operation with my foot throbbing like mad. The pain was horrendous.

We were only two weeks away from round one of the British Championship and I had to stay in the hospital for nearly a week.

The first thing I did on leaving the hospital in Manchester was go to my sports injuries specialist Mrs Puckas, a big Polish lady who had fixed me up no end of times.

I was in so much pain that I could hardly get up her steps on my crutches and the first thing she noticed on inspecting my ankle was that it had started to go sceptic where the surgeons had cut into me. She called in her husband, who was an absolute genius, and he went off to fetch some potent cream he'd just made. I put some on and within a few days I'd been amazingly cured. I had magnetic field treatment, too, so in less than two weeks I'd crashed, had an operation, recovered and was at Snetterton racetrack for round one of the British Championship.

I was limping badly but ready to give it a go. It was like the glory days of our Kenny winning his British title at Coventry in '84 – you can't keep a top man down.

I was fastest all weekend and put my machine on pole position for Sunday's big race, which I knew would be one of the hardest of my life given the condition I was in.

On the Saturday night Derek and I took the two girls out for a meal. Pole position and two of the most beautiful girls in the paddock – we were on cloud nine and the envy of everyone.

My team-mate at the time was Steve Hislop who I didn't know much and didn't really see as a threat to someone of my calibre.

ALAN CARTER

In the morning practice before the main event Hislop blew his engine to pieces. I knew nothing about it at the time because my sole focus was winning the race and getting on with the job. We may have been in the Honda team but we pretty much kept ourselves to ourselves, doing our own thing.

The team manager, or whatever you wanted to call him, came over to see me and asked if I could lend Steve my spare engine so he could race, and of course we said that was no problem. As a result of our kindness he was in the race and I was always a big believer that a good deed like that could perhaps be returned one day if I ever needed some help myself.

Being catapulted straight into the Honda team after being out of the country for three years must have rubbed a lot of riders up the wrong way, but I was just doing my job and getting myself sorted out. If you wanted a top ride, you had to do it on the track.

For the race I not only had a great package and a great bike, I also had the best rubber in the country. Tuxworth had done a deal with Michelin but although the rear tyres were great, the front ones were dreadful. You only had to see what they were doing for the likes of James Whitham – who was crashing his brains out every weekend – and Steve Hislop.

I told Honda I was losing two seconds a lap to the likes of Nigel Bosworth because of the crap they'd put on my wheel, so I bought some new soft tyres from Dunlop to put on the front and used a Michelin on the back. It worked a treat – no-one ever knew what I'd done because the Dunlop tyre was all stickered up with Michelin decals.

When the flag dropped I shot straight to the front but as I accelerated down the long back straight, 'Bozzy' shot past like he was racing a 500. At the end of every straight I'd take 50 yards out of him but the Aprilia was a ballistic missile. Boy did I have my work cut out with my badly broken ankle and knowing I couldn't afford to crash or I'd have been in deep trouble because I shouldn't have been racing for at least another four weeks.

I couldn't believe my luck when Bosworth crashed out near the end – had I done a Kocinski and pressurised him into making a mistake or was he just pushing it too far, as I'd done for the previous three years? Either way he was out and, with no disrespect to Nigel, I had a grin from ear to ear. I had it on a plate and won the first round of the British Championship in fine style.

The luckiest rider of the day was Steve Hislop because not only did Nigel crash out but so did Martin Jupp and on the final lap Ian McConnachie ran out of petrol, gifting my team-mate second place – something which would come back to haunt me in the final round of the championship.

There was now a four-week break in the calendar, so I concentrated on getting even fitter and started to train harder, running and riding my bikes all over the Yorkshire hillsides.

John Kocinski was never out of my mind and I figured that if I used him as my benchmark, no-one would even get a sniff. I was leading the British Championship and had my sights set on overall victory.

Light in the Darkness

The Honda Britain team's next outing was at the famous Isle of Man TT races but I wasn't there. It was something Dad never wanted me to do because he'd seen way too many riders killed on the road circuits, so I never did it out of respect to him.

My next race was at Donington in mid-June where I received a pleasant surprise – my official Honda Team Racing jacket from Neil Tuxworth, all wrapped up in cling film. At last I had it and I was so excited. But on removing the wrapping I discovered oil stains all over it. He'd given me one of the mechanics' jackets he'd had dry cleaned after the TT. I was disgusted – just how low could you go? This guy was unbelievable and it was just the start of my three-year nightmare working with him.

I had many conversations with Bob McMillan, one of Honda's top brass, about how this guy was treating me but all to no avail. He'd employed him in the first place, so his hands were tied.

I don't think Neil particularly had it in for me personally, it was just the way he was with everyone. I've always been very wary of people who can't look you in the eyes when they're talking to you.

Many times Derek would ask Neil for a new chain or some spark plugs or something, only to be told 'no', so he took a dislike to him, too.

Still, I won at Donington as well and we were on a roll, I was enjoying my best results for years. I was totally confident nobody could beat me at Cadwell Park the following weekend, especially as it's my favourite track of all I've ever ridden and I'd so many great memories of the place. But as it turned out, I didn't even make the race, let alone win it.

I had a massive crash going into the Gooseneck during practice and knocked myself out. I remember as I came round I was shouting at Derek, asking who the f*** had been riding my bike and smashing it up. He swiftly got me into my car and explained I'd had a big crash and knocked myself out.

He left me for an hour while he went to sort the bike out and when he came back I was talking sense. I seemed fine, so I went out for the next practice, only to crash in the same place and this time I was clean out, lying on the track like a rag doll. All I remember was waking up in Louth Hospital with no recollection of ever going out on the track. Never take anything for granted, you just never know what might happen.

Fortunately I could take the big knocks that came with racing and I knew I'd be more than prepared for the next race at a new track in Wales I'd never heard of called Pembrey. It was a magic little place and I won the race in style from pole position.

I was riding well and Derek's bike preparation was second to none. We never broke down and I was staying on like I was glued to the seat.

You could've eaten your dinner off my swinging arm, the bikes were so clean and we even got one of our Kenny's best mates, Craig Myers, to polish the alloy frames and they shone brighter than a diamond. I always loved to turn out looking a million dollars regardless of how much money we had.

Our next race was at Knockhill in Scotland, which wasn't one of my favourite tracks due to the weather more than anything else. It was always either blowing a

ALAN CARTER

gale or pissing down there.

Come race day the stupid bastard of a starter kept us on the line for ages and my engine was over-heating, so I was waving like mad to get the race underway. I took both hands off the bars as I raged at the starter and, of course, that was when he dropped the flag. I stalled my bike on the line, so I was stone last with an engine at about 110 degrees.

I managed to get up to seventh place by the finish but it had been a complete disaster and, to be honest, I was just glad to be getting out of there and travelling back home.

Before the next round of the championship we managed to squeeze in the British GP at Donington, where I received a hero's welcome from the fans who always appreciated my aggressive riding style.

We couldn't get the bike running right at all in practice and it was only in the warm-up on the morning of the race that we started to get it dialled in. I was about 10th quickest and very optimistic for the race in front of my home fans.

I was up against the world's best riders who had far better machinery than me but I finished 13th. When I crossed the line you should have heard the crowd roar. They knew I'd ridden my heart out and was still one of the best in the world but against the factory Yamahas and Hondas I was just wasting my time.

The top level had changed beyond belief and if you didn't have a few million pounds in your budget you were just a nobody in the GP world.

I know in my heart that had I ridden the factory NSR Honda, I could have won the world title for many years but it was not to be.

My next taste of domestic action was at Thruxton, where I'd only been once before, and won. This time it coincided with my 26th birthday and I had one of the closest races I'd ever been involved in.

Usually you could count on me winning a one-to-one scrap on the final lap but this time I was beaten by Ian McConnachie who was riding brilliantly and was, in my opinion, another rider who should have gone on to be a world champion.

I was stuck in fifth gear, unable to select sixth, when he came flying past me on the back straight, going into the final corner. I tried to have a final stab at getting back past him but I came down the gearbox so fast that he locked the rear wheel and it came full sideways on me. I looked more like a speedway rider than a road racer and I don't know how I stayed on.

But that was it, I'd been well and truly scalped by a better man on the day and I lost out by a bike's length.

39 PIPPED AT THE POST

*Last race agony in bid to be champion . . . left to rue a pre-season deal . . .
missing my right-hand man . . . an eligible bachelor, but not for long.*

MONDELLO Park in the Republic of Ireland was the venue for a big international meeting and we were invited to take part. It was a great track and if you had your bike set up well, you could more than give the bigger machines a run for their money.

The Irish knew exactly how to look after you and make you feel special, so Derek and I were looking forward to our adventure. Ten years had now passed since I stormed to my first national win there but we still received a fantastic reception.

Derek and I took our racing very seriously and believed what Dad had always told us – that you win the race in practice. If you can post track record times in practice, you can do them in the race as well.

Dad had been a genius in his day and I now had all the weapons to replicate his wise teachings – and disregard some of the bullshit he came out with, too.

On this occasion at Mondello we entered three 750cc unlimited races as well as the two 250cc races and did a complete clean sweep – we won the lot and split the cash between us. We were the stars of Mondello yet again.

When I had a great right-hand man I was pretty much unstoppable but the problem was that I changed teams all too often and worked with less than competent people. That was OK if you were pissing around playing at club racing, but I wasn't.

A lot of it was completely out of my control but it was only after time that I realised what I'd got myself into and by then it was too late.

Mallory Park was our next destination. It was Bozzy's home track, so I wanted to beat him here to prove I could beat him anywhere. Beat him I did and that meant I'd now won six races on the bounce, which was more than I'd won in the last five years, so I was on top of the world.

Going into the penultimate round of the championship at Oulton Park it was starting to look like Steve Hislop could be a problem and I'd need all my wits about me to outfox him. I could see he was a devious, slimy bugger and could wrap Tuxworth around his finger. He seemed to be an arse-kisser and Neil loved it but I'd be having none of this and I told them what I thought.

For whatever reason I found it very hard to get a feel for my bikes at Oulton while Steve, on the other hand, was a genius around the place and I was struggling to get anywhere near his times.

To make it worse, we were having a load of hassle with Tuxworth. Derek had asked for some basic parts, like plugs and a chain, but he wouldn't give them to us.

ALAN CARTER

Racing alongside my team-mate Steve Hislop. I did him a big favour that backfired on me.

Left: Interviewed by Fred Clarke at Cadwell Park and (right) by Dave Fern at Donington in 1990.

Chasing hard after Ian McConnachie at Mallory Park in 1990.

Light in the Darkness

Talk about running on a shoestring, and this was Honda Great Britain.

Derek was so pissed off that he went to the Padgetts' race support vehicle and bought the things we needed with his own money. He also ended up making a chain for the main race out of bits and bobs – it had two rivet links in it – what a joke that was.

It was very windy on race day and it had started blowing in the opposite direction, which made gearing the bike very difficult. One small mistake at this level and you'd be out of the running.

On the warm-up lap the bike started to misfire so when I pulled up on the start line Derek ran over and pulled the fairing off to get some more plugs in. The organisers didn't really give a shit about me and wanted us off the track so they could get the race underway, but one of our main rivals had his mechanic messing around with his bike too, so we got the extra few minutes we needed.

Derek sorted the bike and I managed to finish fourth on my worst track, so at least I got a result and not a DNF.

It meant the title race went down to the wire. The final round was at Donington Park, where it would be either me or my team-mate Steve Hislop crowned British champion. If I hadn't screwed up on my best track, Cadwell, or lent Hislop my spare engine, I would've still been leading the race for the championship, but that's racing.

We'd figured out that to win the title I had to win the race with Hislop fifth or lower, which wasn't out of the question but was going to be a tall order.

I put my Honda on pole position and I knew the rest was in the hands of the gods. With his golden boy Steve Hislop on the verge of winning the title, I sure wasn't going to get any help from Neil Tuxworth. A proper team manager would have said something like: "Steve, you wouldn't even be in this position if it wasn't for Alan being so kind and giving you his spare engine in round one, so I want you to finish fifth."

But that was never going to happen because racing was full of selfish people and it was dog eat dog. I personally would have never thrown a race for anybody but if I could genuinely help somebody, I would.

It was pouring with rain on race day but that probably gave me a better chance as I was fantastic in the wet and Steve was poor. Plus he had only qualified sixth anyway, so I was in with a real chance of my first British title – something I wanted to do to emulate our Kenny's speedway success in 1984 and '85.

By the end of the first lap I was leading and Hislop was down in ninth but there was nothing I could do about him so I just got my head down and concentrated on winning the race. Roger Burnett was the commentator as the race was live on TV and he told the nation exactly what I'd always thought – 'if only Alan Carter was riding the best bike in one of the big teams, we'd have a world champion in the making'.

Over the next eight laps I was four seconds faster than any other rider and Hislop still wasn't in the top four although, due to others crashing, he had made his way up to fifth, which was a bit close for comfort.

Many of the riders who had come to grief had crashed on the entry into Coppice

ALAN CARTER

Corner and their bikes were all lined up at the side of the track. I could see a large group of riders all sat there watching the action when, and I don't know why, I started to show off, running it deeper and deeper into the turn.

One of the guys told me later that they'd all kept saying: "He's going down this time," and eventually they were right and I crashed right in front of them.

I dragged the bike out of the gravel trap and got back in the saddle. To my amazement, I was so far in front that I was still leading when I got going again. I crashed, got back on and still won the race – the fans were going crazy.

If there was one guy who could have helped me beat Hislop it was my mate Kevin Mitchell, but he went out right at the end which allowed my big rival to finish fourth and win the British title from me by a single point.

The commentary that Fred Clarke gave me over the years was absolutely amazing, billing me as a proper racing star who always gave his fans everything he had.

To top off a fantastic year's racing, the ladies' magazine *Company* voted me one of the top 10 most eligible bachelors in the UK, which was a shock at the time but I was loving the fame I'd found since my three years in the wilderness in America.

It was great to be back on English soil and I'd enjoyed what would be my best year, winning 12 races. It was like going back to the early 80s – the best fun of any racer's career is the beginning when you're a bit naive but keen as mustard and soaking everything up like a sponge.

Unbeknown to me, during the close season Honda approached Derek and asked him to work for them the following season. He asked if it would entail working with me again but Tuxworth told him they wouldn't be keeping me on. Being loyal to me, Derek turned down the offer, which was nice.

Due to the usual bullshit in between seasons there was little on the table for 1991 even though I'd only missed out on the championship by a solitary point.

Derek was having a hernia operation in the winter and I had no firm plans so when he was offered a full-time job, he took it which was great news for him but I'd lost my right-hand man after my best year in racing.

Two guys who'd given me some small measure of support during the year were interested in doing something for 1991, so I did a deal with Tuxworth to run my own team with Padgbury Motor Company

The company's co-owners, Dave and Keith, had been quite successful in the lower leagues of racing and they seemed like great guys and talked big, so I was impressed.

Tuxworth said he'd give us a bike to keep along with the racing spares for the year, subject to us purchasing a bike from them. Dave and Keith said they had a sponsor, so it was no problem – they'd pay Honda for the machine.

Only they didn't pay Honda for it. I rang Neil and told him we needed to get all the stuff back but he responded by telling them under no circumstances should they let me anywhere near the bikes. I was livid – was he completely stupid? They were the people messing him around, not me. All I was guilty of was getting involved with some people who were completely out of their league.

It turned into a complete disaster and there was no winner here. Eventually I did

Light in the Darkness

Ready for action in 1990 but I wish I'd been allowed to to retain the backing I had from Shell Oils.

get everything back and once again Dad came to the rescue and we were working back in my old workshop on his farm.

That was also when Doug Holtom came back in to help out for free as much as he could. If only he could have put more time and effort into it I could have had a great year, but he had other commitments.

By now I was sick of Neil Tuxworth and he must have been sick of me, too.

Being vulnerable and having limited amounts of money simply opened a large can of worms. If I could have turned the clock back and have my dad taking control of everything so that I could just concentrate on winning, I would have done because it could have all turned out so different. Those two words again – if only.

The 1991 season turned out to be a mixed bag of wins and poor results. Before the Padgbury split we entered a bike in the European championship race at Donington

ALAN CARTER

with a full race kit on, but due to the team being unable to set it up it was just about the slowest thing on the track and I refused to ride it in the next race at Pembrey.

Instead, we got another brand new bike out of a box, put some tyres on it, fuelled it up and it flew. I won the race no problem on a standard bike that anyone could buy.

This was the year I met Nick Jeffries who was racing for Honda UK in the Isle of Man TT. He was a nice bloke and one day he bet me I couldn't get a meeting date with his wife by pretending to be male model. Kate owned a model agency called Catwalk in Bradford at the time, so I rang her and told her I was a bronzed god with a body like Rambo and that I'd just flown in from California. She said: "You'd better get around here," so that was it.

On arriving at the model agency there was a good looking girl on reception, so I turned on the old Carter charm and before I knew it Sherry Masters became my new girlfriend.

We spent the next seven years together, mainly fighting each other over a load of rubbish because we were both as bad as each other.

I had limited racing success in 1991 and one race that really hurt was the Donington round of the British Championship. Doug knew that the bike needed new pistons for the race as the mileage was up but decided not to bother changing them for one reason or another, so I just had to go along with it.

I qualified on pole and was winning the race with ease when, with just a lap-and-a-half to go, the engine seized and I was thrown down the road fast and hard. The piston had cracked and seized the engine – I was so mad it's indescribable.

Hislop was now officially Honda UK's number one 250cc rider, which was a joke and partly due to my generosity.

Obviously I was hoping he could return the favour, and I thought it might be forthcoming when HRC flew in two sets of factory magnesium carburettors from Japan. Hislop didn't know which ones he wanted but said I could have the other pair. Cheers, mate.

So indecisive was he about which set to have that two months down the line he still

Light in the Darkness

hadn't made his mind up, so I never did get any. Tuxworth faxed Japan to find out what the difference was and discovered they were identical, and that one pair had been bought for me and the other for Hislop.

Some team-mate he was, and Tuxworth admitted that Hislop had caused so many problems that after the TT they'd be getting rid of him and giving me all his equipment. Obviously I took it with a pinch of salt and, of course, it never happened.

I raced against some great British riders such as Nigel Bosworth, Ian Newton, Woolsey Coulter, Phillip McCallen, Steve Sawford and a guy called Paul Brown who was the new kid on the block and a very fast rider indeed. There was also Iain Challinor who was pure magic around Oulton Park, while Martin Jupp was also in there along with Ian McConnachie.

But my favourite was Kevin Mitchell, from Preston. Kev and his brothers were a great bunch of guys to be around. They were sponsored by the Medd brothers who loved their racing and we had some great banter winding each other up before races.

Another race that comes to mind was at Mallory Park. Sherry sure picked her times to row with me and just before practice or a race was certainly not a good time, as that was exactly when you needed a clear head. On this occasion I survived

ALAN CARTER

a crash at the Bus Stop, only to have a row with her and proceed to crash again next time I went out, this time at the Esses.

The two marshals looked at each other as if to say: "F*** that, do you know who he is? I'm not picking him up." So I crawled to the edge of the track where they handed me a can of coke – at arm's length, looking scared to death.

Everyone in the paddock was gossiping and saying I'd ground my toes off, which I pretty much had. I turned up the next day for the race with Jesus sandals on and my feet still bleeding but, amazingly, I won the race from the second row of the grid. I was made of hard stuff but with Mal Carter as my dad I needed to be.

My relationship with Tuxworth got off to the worst start imaginable and one problem followed another all the time I rode for him. But I have to be honest and say that, in a certain way, I actually liked him.

I was certain we'd be parting company at the end of '91 but, to my surprise, Neil told me he wanted me in the team for 1992. He said they'd have full control but they'd give me Ray Hughes, who'd been Steve Hislop's right-hand man. They were running everything from their headquarters in Louth and all I had to do was ride the bikes. Ray was probably the best mechanic in the UK at the time, so this was a great offer, even if it was the only offer.

They also gave me a brand new top-of-the-range Honda Civic car in blue, and paid me the miserly sum of £2,000, which I just laughed at. As I explained to them, you could earn £15,000 stacking shelves at Morrison's. They wanted me to be England's number one road-racing superstar for just two grand – that would hardly cover my gym membership.

I told Neil that if I could have half the fairing for my personal sponsorship, the deal was on, and we shook hands on it. It would be the first time I'd started a racing season with Honda with a clear head and with us all knowing what the deal was from day one. Neil and I would start the season friends even though I was still 10 grand out of pocket.

It meant I could train and focus over the winter of 1991-92 and now there was no excuse left in the world. This was it – if I didn't win the British Championship I was going to call it a day. I was in tremendous shape, had the full backing of Honda UK, no team-mate to worry about and Honda were getting full support from Castrol Oils.

On a personal level, I'd agreed the biggest deal I'd ever done in racing with Hein Gericke, a German clothing company, thanks to their UK managing director Tom Walker.

With the input of my personal dietician and sports massage guy Mike Duffield too, I was going to be far too strong for anyone even to get close to me.

40 FINAL COUNTDOWN

One last bid for glory . . . denied the title by injury . . . back in the saddle on a Ducati . . . bowing out on a high at Donington . . . honest words to the Honda boss.

THIS was it – shit or bust. I was determined to be British Champion and I had two bites of the cherry as we had the MRPC series and the ACU British championship.

We had two bikes for 1992 – a brand new RS Honda with upside-down forks and a 1991 bike, too. I soon found out I didn't really like the new bike as to me it was just too stiff on the front end. You got no feel from the bike at all, which in turn gave you no confidence in the machine, so I ended up racing the '91 bike for most of the year.

Ray and I had a strange relationship. He was a much more introverted type of guy and much quieter than Derek. He always seemed to be deep in thought and was hard to get to know on a personal level, although after a short period working together I realised it didn't matter that we weren't really mates – what did matter was what he was fantastic at his job and would put 100 per cent into everything.

I missed Derek and all the fun we had together but maybe this was a good thing for me. With Ray it was all about racing – we would never develop a personal friendship and it was more like turn up, do the business and get out of there. That suited me as I'd turn up for most meetings, bang the bike on pole, win the race, then jump in my new car and head for home.

We started in fantastic form. Not only was I staying on the bike, but I was winning from the word go, too.

My exploits attracted the attention of Peter Smith, the boss of Swift Caravans in Hull, who provided me with a lovely new caravan and also used to loan me his personal motorhome. He said I was the only guy to use it and bring it back cleaner than when it left the factory. Peter was great to me.

I was running late on the day I collected the caravan, so I was in a rush when I called in at Sainsbury's to load it up for the weekend. In my haste I managed to scrape the whole of one side on the ticket barrier. It was badly damaged, so I rang Peter immediately and he just said: "Don't worry, Alan, these things happen – we'll fix it." What a great bloke. His son Guy went on to have a good car racing career and they were a lovely family.

Midway through the season I was leading both championships but it started to go wrong one day when we were testing at Cadwell.

I arrived there with my old mate and GP mechanic Eggis and we got him involved straight away doing the lap times and pit board. I was flying and the times came down further all day and I posted 6.66 around the old club track – a devilishly good time on any bike, let alone a 250.

But as I went into the Hairpin under braking I lost the front end and had a massive crash. Once again I was lucky to be going home with nothing more than serious bruising but I was black from my shoulders to my toes and I couldn't even move, so how Paul even got me into the car was a miracle. They wanted me to go to hospital but I was having none of it – Leon's clinic would sort me out.

I attempted practice for the next round at Silverstone but I was in far too much pain and had to give it up as a bad job.

Honda's Superbike rider Simon Crafar took my place for the weekend and put my '92 Honda on pole position, which was brilliant but also made me look a fool after I'd said I couldn't ride it with any confidence.

But Crafar came a big cropper after losing the front end and he did exactly the same thing after putting the bike on pole at Brands Hatch later that year when I was out with a broken leg. Maybe I was just a little bit more in tune with these bikes than him, all I know is that this particular bike just felt way too stiff on the front. I was a very hard rider and loved to push the front beyond the limit into corners – that was just my all-action riding style.

I was the king of Cadwell in my dreams and that's where we were next. I knew the way things had gone for me I'd be lucky to race but, unlike at Silverstone, there was no keeping me out this time.

But once again I was left to reflect on why I was great in practice when most other people were piss-poor, while it was me who would f*** it all up on race day by trying too hard instead of just letting things flow.

On this occasion I had an early scare when the engine seized on the first lap. I pulled the clutch in, then let it out again – maybe it was just a minor nip up? Luckily for me, it was.

I took it nice and easy for four laps and, seeing the leading group going into the Gooseneck as I approached the end of Park Straight, I figured I could catch them.

I hadn't even been trying, so I got my head down over the next 10 laps and pulled the full length of the straight back on the boys in front and I was right on their tail. All I had to do now was pass them and leave them for dead.

But instead, I came out of the Hairpin and had the biggest high side I'd ever experienced and went down with a right bang. I couldn't believe I'd done all that hard work only to throw it away in a moment of madness.

I was hoping for better at Snetterton next time as it was a lucky track for me and I led from start to finish, just as I did at Knockhill in the following round. Things were looking up and I was now leading both championships even though it had been a bit of an up and down season so far.

But the wind was taken out my sails when Neil Tuxworth announced that Ray would be leaving with immediate effect as he was going to work for Eskil Suter in the world championship.

It was one of the biggest blows of my racing career and I was absolutely speechless. It had taken me two-and-a-half years to get into this position of leading

Light in the Darkness

Main pic: Arch rival Nigel Bosworth stalking me at Cadwell Park in 1991. Top inset: Tackling the Mallory Park Hairpin in 1992. Bottom inset: On the start line at Mallory Park in 1992.

ALAN CARTER

two championships and now I was there, I was told my right-hand man was leaving.

What sort of person could do this to anybody and what kind of manager would stand for this? It was beyond belief. This was meltdown time.

Tuxworth, the Honda Britain racing boss, seemed to have no respect for anyone. He would make disgusting, lewd and crude comments towards not only my girlfriend but also those of the other team riders and mechanics. This I found quite disturbing and he came close to getting a beating on several occasions.

He replaced Ray with a guy called Ian who wasn't even fit to be the team gofer. I knew he didn't have a f****** clue what he was doing after he told me we had new pistons in the bike. I asked him if he'd jetted it up a bit and he answered: "What for?"

In his first race with us the clutch fell off, then something else went wrong, too. It was meltdown.

I got back in touch with Derek Rhodes to see if he could help out and he came back for the next round at Snetterton. Practice went well but on the morning before the race the engine seized.

Derek was given parts to rebuild the bike for the race but they weren't right. The piston was hitting the head and that seized the bike up solid at the end of the straight, throwing me about 30 feet into the air, badly breaking my leg and feet in about 15 places on landing.

My foot was so badly damaged that the hospital told me they were thinking they might have to amputate it and after a few days the doctor told me I should really think long and hard about calling it a day because I'd broken my ankles so many times.

I made a comeback for the final race of the year at Brands Hatch but I was very down and I'd totally lost interest by this point, although I was sparked into life by the sight of my old adversary Niall Mackenzie coming out onto the track on Paul Brown's spare bike for the Rob McElnea team. It was like a red rag to a bull – there was no way this kid was going to beat me.

I couldn't win the title as it was almost certainly going the way of Nigel Bosworth, who was a great rider. We'd had a few comings together over the last three years but nothing serious – some were his fault and once or twice I'd been a little unsporting myself.

I'd run him off the track on purpose at Donington one time when he tried to come around the outside of me, which I apologised for. But he more than got his own back in qualifying at Brands when he deliberately cut straight across me as I was putting my bike on pole position. I was so disgusted that I marched over to confront him in the paddock but he just punched me straight in the face and busted my lip. I was in shock, to be honest, he certainly took me by surprise.

We both respected each other much more after that, so maybe it had been coming to a head over the years. I never hold grudges – it was what it was at the time and they were some of the best days of my life.

All my life I'd dreamed of becoming the 250cc World Champion and I was now

Light in the Darkness

facing my last ever race on a 250cc bike, but at least I won it.

Bosworth's bike broke down, leaving him in despair at the side of the track and putting Paul Brown on course for the title, only for him to crash out in front of me while I was putting him under massive pressure.

That left only Mackenzie in front and it took me a few laps to reel him in but once I had him in my sights, there was no way he was ever going to beat me. He was world class and had an almost perfect career while mine had been a mixed bag of heartache and even more heartache, but I was having my moment of glory.

I dived under him on the very last corner of the very last lap in my very last race on a 250cc racing bike to win the final round of the British Championship. I felt like I'd won a grand prix. In fact, it was better than that as I'd scalped him one last time. I was England's golden boy, the crowd were going crazy and to see Niall's face on the rostrum was brilliant – he wasn't a happy man but for me it was sheer ecstasy.

I had an official engagement to attend for Honda at the end of 1992 and I used the opportunity to tell Bob McMillan, the big boss of Honda UK, what a joke his team manager was. I told him, in front of Tuxworth himself, that if he was in football or rugby instead of motorcycle sport, he'd have been sacked two years ago.

That, of course, sealed my death sentence with Honda UK and shortly afterwards I received an official letter from Tuxworth saying they would not be needing my services for the 1993 season. He thanked me for giving nothing less than 100 per cent on the race track every time.

My main sponsor that year, Hein Gericke, had also suggested I run one of their franchise outlets. They were Europe's biggest seller of motorcycle clothing and accessories, so I took them up on their offer. But the business suffered due to its location – they decided to pick Bradford ahead of Leeds – and I chose the worst position in town, so that turned out to be a disaster and I wasted another two years of my life.

I made a comeback in 1994 after Doug Holtom said he had a great bike for me. I told him I wasn't interested but he brought the bike over for me to look at and I changed my mind. It was an absolutely fantastic Ducati Supermono single and the first two races were in the USA, at Daytona.

We rallied around to get a great group of guys to sponsor us along with Silkolene Oils and set off to the States. Having been out for so long I was rubbish to begin with but by the end of the week I was flying and I won both my races by half-a-lap.

Next up was Daytona and we arrived on a real high. They set the races off in different waves at the time and I was in the second wave, 20 seconds after the first.

I tried to do a deal with the organiser whereby if I won both waves they paid me double, but if I didn't they wouldn't have to pay me at all. But they were having none of that because they'd seen me win the week before.

I carried on the good work, too, winning at Daytona for the first time, which was brilliant. I was buzzing.

Back in England, the good form continued and at Donington Park I lapped faster than the 600 supersport guys on a 600 single. It was such a good bike that it made them look stupid.

But prior to the main race someone flicked the ignition switch on which drained the battery, so I was stood on the track on pole position waiting for Doug to get the bike started. He never did, so I had to walk off the track as the race started without me – another bitter pill to swallow

This was also the year that my hero, the great Ayrton Senna, was killed. I loved this guy, he was my man in formula one racing and his crash at Imola, along with that which paralysed my ex-team mate Wayne Rainey, made me realise it was time to call it a day and finish racing while I was still in one piece.

I finished the season with some success but Doug had been developing a new oil with Silkolene which, unbeknown to me, kept seizing the engine so our dream comeback came to a end.

At least we went out on a high. First we did the support race to the World Superbike round in Italy on the single cylinder where I managed to finish third behind the works Ducati of Pier-Francesco Chili and another works bike. It was great to get close to them but they were just killing me down the straight.

I took Sherry and her parents on this trip. Her dad Phil was a great bloke and he ended up on a piss-up with some American marines. He could hardly walk by the time he got back to the bedroom we were sharing and when he went to the toilet to be sick, his false teeth fell out and went down the toilet, never to be seen again. I pissed myself laughing for the rest of the week.

Virginio Ferrari, the factory Ducati team manager, was riding the team's spare bike at that meeting and while I was watching the race Carl Fogarty's mum came up and said: "That should be you out there, not our Carl." That was quite a shock and a compliment since her own son was Ducati's number one rider.

During the meeting Ferrari crashed the bike and made a right mess of it. We asked him if there was any chance I could ride it at the next round of the world championship at Donington Park and he said he'd first have to talk to Carl.

Now I knew that Carl and Doug were in dispute about something and weren't talking, so I figured Carl would say: "No way, tell him to f*** off," but he didn't and I got the thumbs up to ride in the next round of the world championship in the premier class on a factory Ducati. This would be the final race of my life.

I turned up for this meeting a little nervous as I had little experience on a big bike due to Dad scaring the shit out of me as a 15-year-old on a 750cc Yamaha.

I had a frustrating start because the oil cooler was leaking and I was black flagged in the first practice but in the second I wound it on big-time, figuring it was my big lap. But it spat me over the bars at warp speed and I qualified practically last for Sunday's big races.

Come race day, the heavens opened like you wouldn't believe, and that put me in with a shout.

In race one I worked my way past most of the pack, including the factory Honda boys, and I got up into fourth place. I was the first British rider home, even beating 'Foggy', on a bike with an engine that was way over its mileage. The fans were

Light in the Darkness

going mad and I got a hero's welcome in the pits where once again going past the Honda team was extra special.

I made a bad start to race two as the bike went sideways off the line after I'd got too much power down and lost grip. It took me too long to work through the pack but I eventually finished sixth in my farewell meeting on my best track. I'd done a great job for the team.

After that meeting I never received a single phone call from a racing team, which was quite a disappointment given how well I'd gone at Donington.

So I decided to call it a day and finish on top. I'd done OK for a young kid from Halifax who was proud of coming through a difficult childhood with a less than loving father.

Over the years I worked with some fantastic people. Howard Gregory was a top man and set the benchmark – with him I finished in the top 15 in the world and moved up to world number seven. If only I could have got a proper works ride and had Howard and some of the other top brass guys alongside me, I could have been invincible.

Losing my right hand-man on several occasions was like having my legs cut off as it meant I was on a hiding to nothing. Road-racing isn't a solo sport, it's very much a team sport and without the right team you can be the most talented guy in the world and still be going backwards. You have to have all the key people in the right places and a bit of luck along the way.

Kenny Roberts was my hero – a great rider and a fun guy to be around, so it was a shame I raced for the first team he ever had because the bikes were very poor and it was a learning curve for everyone involved. But to be selected by him from all the riders in the world was very special to me.

Wayne Rainey was a good 250cc rider and almost unbeatable on the 500cc bikes and although he was maybe far too inconsistent in that first year of GPs, this emphasised how poor our bikes really were. Nevertheless, he showed flashes of sheer brilliance at times.

So the fact I was able to give him a hard time and beat him simply proved that I was truly a world class rider who sadly never fulfilled my true potential.

I'd started racing at 16 and spent 13 years in the sport. In that time I worked my way through the British ranks to become the youngest GP winner of all time while my brother became a double British champion on the shale.

Kenny and I both came close to world titles showing the drive and will to win of our dad Mal who had guts by the bucket load.

When I stopped racing it was like being put in solitary confinement. I thought I was going mad and it took me more than 10 years to come to terms with it.

But at 28-years-old I was completely burnt out. I'd been robbed and pushed from pillar to post, and I made too many mistakes both on and off the track. Dad had opened doors for me and closed just as many but, maybe like me and Kenny too, he was too crude. We needed polishing around the edges.

Over the years I had great support from all my sponsors and the fans were

Above: Leading the way from Steve Sawford and Nigel Bosworth at Donington in 1992.
Below: On the Honda in 1991.

fantastic. My family and friends stood by me to the very last day, so I've been lucky to come out of competitive racing with my life and body in one piece. Too many weren't so lucky during my years as a motorcycle racer, some paying the ultimate price, including my team-mate Donny Robinson who I hold dear to my heart – he was a true gentleman.

But everything has a beginning and an end, you just never know how long the bit in the middle will last, be it a career or a relationship. All I can say is, ride the crest of the wave, give it everything you have and walk away with your head held high. Believe in yourself and don't let your own doubts steal your dreams.

41 BAD DREAMS

Struggling to adjust ... Kenny's kids growing up ... Malky's learning curve ... and 'do you have any Fallopian tubes?'

I WOULD often have bad dreams about racing motorbikes. I'd be walking around a race paddock, all confident and cocky, and in my dreams I was the man. Then, just before the race, something would always go wrong. I either had square wheels or none at all.

The bike was always on the front and rear stands as the race was just about to start, so I'd be panicking like mad and worrying that I was going to miss another race. And I was usually always on pole position too.

I'd awake from my dreams in a state of confusion. If I had this dream once, I had it a thousand times.

Life is strange with its twists and turns and can nearly push you over the top on many occasions. Sometimes I think it would've been better for me if I'd never raced at all and gone into a normal job instead. I say this now because after it was all over, I found it almost impossible to adjust to a normal working life. It took me about ten years to adapt to this challenge.

I made too many financial mistakes during my racing days, treating it like an amazing adventure that would never end, so I lived for today and spent what money I made and focused on having the time of my life.

I loved my fans so much that with the exception of my French GP winner's trophy, I gave away all my silverware, pictures, leathers, boots, gloves, the lot. I had nothing left, only the most amazing memories of life's adventures. But I know this much, I've been a lucky man to have travelled all over the world doing what I loved most.

Naturally, thoughts of Kenny and the horrific events of May '86 were never far from my mind. All I wanted was to have him back but he'd broken mine and other people's hearts and our lives would never be the same again.

He left behind a trail of destruction that would never end for me and our grandparents, who were devastated by his callous actions and the loss of their eldest grandson. Sitting at Gran's house on a Wednesday and seeing Kenny and Pam's empty chairs at the dinner table sent chills down my spine. There were times when it was all too much to handle and all I could repeatedly ask myself was 'why?' but I never got an answer.

Poor Malcolm and Kelly-Marie had lost their mum and dad in one of the biggest horror stories ever known in the world of sport, and they were both so young and oblivious to everything. They probably didn't realise it at the time, bless 'em, but their lives had been changed forever.

Pam was robbed of being a great mum to her two kids and denied the simple pleasure of seeing them grow up. She was cut down in her prime, at 25, when she should've had her whole life before her.

Kenny and Pam's son, Malcolm Robert Kenny Carter, was born on May 18, 1984, his second birthday coming only three days before he lost both of his parents. He developed into a deeply withdrawn child but our Malky would become a big part of my life.

When the Hiroshima bomb had finally settled over Halifax, Malcolm and his sister Kelly-Marie would spend all of their childhood lives growing up on Black Horse Farm, the home of Bob and Veronica Lund, in Bradshaw.

Pam's parents became the kids' mum and dad but to say their place was an absolute dump would be overrating it. It soon became evident to me that they were treating little Malcolm like dirt and would appear to take out most of their anger and frustration throughout their grieving process on him. They couldn't hurt our Kenny for his unforgiving actions but they would make his son – their grandson – suffer the consequences instead.

On the other hand, Kelly-Marie, who was three when the Lunds gained custody of the children, would become their little girl, the nearest they had to a replacement for the daughter they so tragically lost. As the two kids grew up, I never saw that much of Kelly-Marie, although I know she is now very much into her horse riding. I'm aware that she has helped to keep Kenny's name alive in speedway by putting up trophies for junior speedway championships held at Scunthorpe in recent years.

Just looking back at photos of Malky when he was a young boy makes me cringe. They sent him to school wearing glasses that were about 20 times too big for him. No wonder he got a beating most days, he looked like a complete nerd.

I found it very hard to visit Kelly-Marie and Malky as their uncle in the early days. Going to see them at the home of the parents whose daughter had been killed by my brother made me feel uneasy, so I tended to stay well clear. I was racing in the world championships at the time they went to live with the Lund family and would then spend the next three years in the USA. Time was flying by.

When Malky entered his early teens he started working with Big Mal, which brought him out of his little shell. Anyone who could withstand Dad's dictatorship was on his way in life.

I'll admit, I gave Malky a few digs myself. I'd bend his arms behind his back, almost making him cry, then t**t him very hard in the ribs, saying: "How do you like this, you little bastard?" Subconsciously, I was getting some of my own back for what our Kenny did to me for many years – and getting some satisfaction doing it to Malky.

One day Malky and I were walking up the road from Black Horse Farm when he found some industrial piping and decided to whack me behind the legs with it as hard as he could before running off. Talk about pain. As he was running away, I grabbed a big builder's brick, threw it and with pinpoint accuracy hit him in the ribs,

Light in the Darkness

Kenny's boy, Malcolm (kneeling right) with the Sheffield Prowlers junior speedway team in 2000.

breaking a few in the process.

This went on for a few years, with me basically getting the better of our play-fights. We were both as bad as each other.

But he was a hard, little bugger. One day in my wife Sherry's Dad's orchard we were having an apple fight, trying to knock each other out by throwing apples at each other. I was winning the battle this day, so he ran off, climbed up an apple tree and started pulling faces at me. Talk about the golden shot. My next one came out of my hand like a cannonball, hitting him right between the eyes.

I think this was the only time I ever saw him cry, so I comforted him saying: "You soft bastard, do you want another one?" I was no better than my Dad. I had been treated badly, so Malky and my kids were having some of it too. But it was all harmless fun really.

I would become great friends with Malky over the years. When he started working he would come up to my house once a week to play cards. To say I was a card shark would be an understatement and 13-Card Crash was my game. I was brilliant at it, whereas poor Malky didn't even know what diamonds, hearts or clubs were back in those innocent days. He was so engrossed in the colours and look of the cards, I could cheat like mad.

Most hands I was playing with about 15 cards to his 13 and I'd take a week's wages off him every Friday night. I was skint at the time and he was an easy touch. He soon picked the game up, though, and figured out his loving uncle Alan was a right cheating bastard. Malky became a very bright kid indeed.

Me and Malky laugh now about the good old days we had together, gambling and

ALAN CARTER

messing around doing stupid things. I once lost a bike race to him that cost me 75 quid.

Another game we used to play a lot was throwing coins to see who could get them to land nearest to the wall. Normally we'd play for a quid and end up winning or losing 10 or 20 pounds to each other.

Until one day we got a bit drunk and decided to have a 45-quider. Me and Malky could regularly land the coin to within 2mm of the wall. This time he went first and I don't know what happened but his coin came down about three feet away from the wall. He looked totally devastated as I rolled on the floor laughing my head off, waiting for him to beat me to a pulp for mocking him.

Then I took my turn. It was going to be the easiest shot ever but, disastrously, the coin just slipped out of my hand about and dropped about two feet in front of me. I was in shock and I've never seen him laugh so much. We didn't like losing to each other at any time, so it was gutting for me to be £45 worse off.

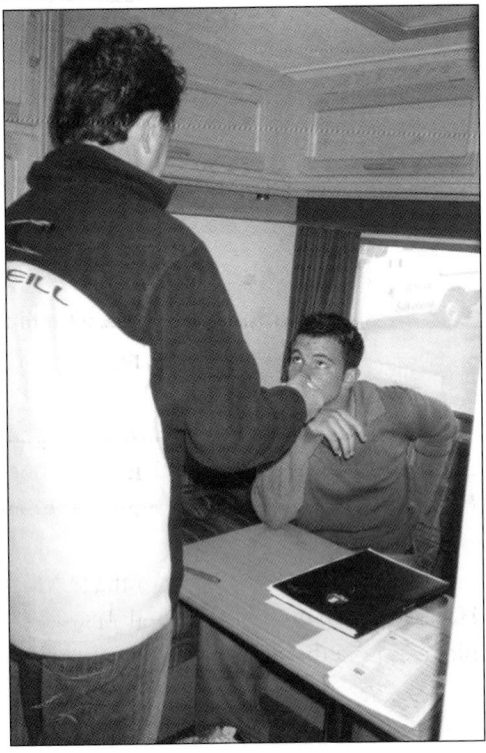

Offering my advice to Malky (seated).

Once he had to work for me for two weeks without pay because I'd won his wages off him.

Me and Malky were driving along in the van one day when I tried to wash the windscreen but found that the washer bottle was empty. I pulled into the petrol station and said to Malky: "The wipers are f*****, go in there and ask that woman for some Fallopian tubes – we need to unblock the washers."

Watching him walk into a petrol station and ask a mature woman for some Fallopian tubes was brilliant. Her face was a picture of total disgust before she gave him a right telling off.

Over the years me and Malky have had some great laughs at each other's expense, with neither of us really coming out on top. We stopped fighting as I was hitting my late-30s/early 40s – he was just too fast and strong by now and I was getting hurt too much, so I accepted defeat gracefully.

Light in the Darkness

42 NOWHERE TO GO

Racing grinds to a halt ... turning to religion ... the vicar's daughter ... miscarriage and then the birth of baby boys ... marriage break-up ... in business as a market trader ... Montego Man and Postman Pat.

RACING ground to a halt for me at the end of 1994. I'd just done a one-off ride on the factory Ducati at the World Superbike round at Donington Park and finished fourth and sixth respectively, beating some of the world's best riders.

There was a massive buzz in the paddock and walking up pit lane past the factory Honda boys managed by Neil Tuxworth gave me great satisfaction. Some of the blokes I beat that day were earning thousands of pounds a year and travelled around in luxury motorhomes that I could only ever dream about. I'd just kicked their ass but, as usual, I hardly had enough money for the petrol to drive home.

After Donington I was shocked that I never even received a phone call regarding a possible ride for the 1995 season. Since the age of 16 all I'd ever done was race motorbikes but now I was lost with nowhere to go. I quit racing a broken man at 30-years-old.

The stories about me chasing all the girls in the world and having been in more beds than Alan Titchmarsh are true. I was a little bugger, with more front than Brighton pier. It all started when our Kenny would have the most amazing girls in Halifax chasing after him – Beverly Crouch, Michelle Marshal, Carol Bins and many others.

One of the very first pair of breasts I managed to grab hold of belonged to a gorgeous lady called Caroline, who was the then girlfriend of the former road-racer and now Sky TV speedway GP commentator Keith Huewen. Caroline was absolutely stunning and I had a massive crush on her. One day we were at this race meeting somewhere and she offered me a ride on the back of her paddock bike. I was hanging on the back when my wandering hands accidentally slipped up and before I knew it I was having a good old feel – shit, Keith's going to kill me when he reads this!

My life consisted of two of the greatest things known to man – motorbikes and girls – and I've had plenty of both. Women used to say I was a cheeky-chappie, small but well-proportioned (I've never had any complaints in that department). But some of the scrapes I got myself into were acts of sheer madness and would have tested the great Houdini to the limit.

One of the most interesting situations I found myself in was when I was about to marry Sherry. She wanted to get married in the parish church at Haworth, the village made famous by the Bronte sisters. The vicar said that if we wanted to get married in his parish, one of us would have to live in the village for two weeks.

Calling in to see the vicar Colin one day, he asked if I'd found anywhere to stay yet. When I replied "no", he said: "No problem, I'm going to Cornwall for two weeks, how would you like to stay at the rectory for two weeks with my daughters?"

On arriving at the start of my two-week stay I banged on the massive front door of the rectory and that's when it swung open and before me was standing a drop-dead gorgeous blonde.

"You must be Alan?" she said with a wink of an eye before inviting me in. I'd only just got through the front door when she offered me a whiskey. I hated whiskey but said: "Yes, I'd love one."

We had a great chat and then she said: "My younger sister will be home soon, and my boyfriend will be coming over later."

When her sister arrived, she was also a stunner. I was laughing to myself about what a great two weeks I was going to be having – and I did, too.

The eldest sister's boyfriend arrived later and he was a real breath of fresh air – a positive, upbeat young man called Paul Hudson. He told me he worked at the met office and his dream was to be on live television doing the weather reports. His dream came true and now Paul is the well-known Yorkshire TV weatherman.

My two weeks spent charming the vicar's daughter was great, just what I needed. But there was only one possible snag I hadn't considered.

On the day of mine and Sherry's wedding, I was walking up to the church and there, standing right in front of me at the entrance with their arms folded, were the vicar's daughters. I now had a lump in my throat and thought 'oh shit'.

I went to the front of the church, the service began and everything went smoothly. I must confess, though, I was sweating like a pig when Colin turned to the congregation and asked: "Does anyone know why these two people may not be married in holy matrimony?" I was a nervous wreck and could hear voices in my head saying 'yes, Dad, he's been screwing me all week!'

Luckily for me, the vicar's daughter kept quiet and the service went through without a hitch.

I married Sherry but God knows why. We were falling out every week and she went back to her mum's more times than I've had hot dinners.

From about 1994 I went through a brief religious phase. To be honest, I just couldn't take any more plus I met a mad vicar called Malcolm Gray Smart who introduced me to some amazing people – or maybe they weren't so amazing and it was simply me feeling lost and vulnerable at the time? I don't know because I was so f***** up in the head, I just needed something else in my life as my racing career was coming towards its end.

All I know is, every time the vicar came to watch me race he'd ask if he could pray for me before each meeting. He'd ask the 'big man upstairs' to keep me safe – but I crashed every time he came to watch me, so soon I was trying to hide from him.

Light in the Darkness

Final laps . . . on the factory Ducati at Mallory Park in 1994.

I was also introduced to a really nice kid called Phil Starbuck, a devout Christian and the captain of Huddersfield Town Football Club, and we both attended a house meeting. This was the time they asked if I wanted coffee and when I explained that I couldn't drink it because it made me ill, the vicar said that God had declared all food clean and that the group would also pray for me.

So here I was in a strange house with a bunch of Bible-bashers all gathered round with their hands on my head. After a few minutes they said I'd been cured and asked 'would I like a coffee?' I loved coffee and, convinced I'd been cured, I must have consumed about two percolators full that night.

But the morning after I was so ill, you have no idea. I don't think I drank coffee again for another two years – and I never attended another religious house meeting either. I could see this was going to be about door-knocking. Imagine me knocking on your door with a Bible in my hand! I'd 'gone' by this point and even had thoughts about joining the French foreign legion.

Phil Starbuck once told me an opponent stamped on his foot and said: "Get God to fix that." I loved football as a kid but I was never really any good at it.

Talking of football, our local church had its own five-a-side team and the league we played in must have been the roughest in the country. One thug doing a good impersonation of Vinnie Jones chopped me down about four times, so I angrily hit him with a crunching tackle that almost broke his leg and would put him out of action for a few weeks.

After the tournament finished we all had dinner and there was a big announcement to introduce the guest speaker – a reverend and Manchester City FC's chaplain. Everyone gave him a big round of applause and as I looked up to see who they were clapping, I saw this guy I half-recognised hobbling into the room. I'd only taken out the guest speaker for the night. I must have been a black belt for getting myself in the shit.

ALAN CARTER

My born-again Christian days didn't last long. Sherry suffered a miscarriage and as two other young couples proudly showed off their new arrivals in the church, while I was pleased for them I couldn't figure out why we'd lost our baby. This was another dark period for me.

A few years on, though, our first son came along on March 6, 1996. I named him Louie, after the famous Aussie motorcycle racer 'Angry Ant' Paul Lewis who, like me, was about as mad as they come. Paul and I just clicked and we were the rebels of racing in a quirky way, so that's the name I wanted.

But Sherry wanted to call him after almost all her family, so he became Louie Philip William Roland Alan Carter. All I could think about was the poor lad, later in life, writing his name on his school books and getting the piss taken out of him, bless him.

My second wife Sherry with our first born son, Louie.

Eighteen months down the road, on August 27, 1997, our next bundle of joy arrived – Jay Alexander.

Both babies were absolutely beautiful but so different. Louie would wake up in the morning all grumpy and wanting his dummy and I must have purchased at least 500 for him. On the hand, his little brother, 'Jay Jay' as I call him, would wake up with the most smiley face in the world.

Me and Sherry would fight about nothing all the time, split up and then get back together. We tried to make things work but it didn't, so in October '97 we parted when Jay was less than a few months old. It was a heart-breaking time for us both I guess.

Our kids were just babies when we sadly split up. We'd become just another UK statistic like many other families having to live through difficult and heart-breaking times. I feel for anyone who has been through this.

I went to live with my half-sister Lindy in Halifax. She was usually working away, so I was on my own in the house most of the time. I'd just started a new business and had a lot on my mind doing this and that, plus having the two boys at weekends.

I had nothing much left to my name and when you think things can't possibly get any worse, they do. One day I came out of my sister's house to take my washing off the line and found that someone had already done it for me. They nicked the last possessions I had in the world – my clothes were gone.

Light in the Darkness

Starting my new business as a market trader, I needed some transport and saw a Montego estate in blue that looked ideal. I knocked on this door and a nice chap called Duncan answered and said: "It's sound kid, that car, I've just been to Cornwall in it and it's got a 2.0 litre engine."

I asked how much he wanted for it and he said: "Three hundred quid to you, kid."

"I've got f*** all," I replied, "so can I give you 50 quid a week?" He said: "No problem, kid" – I couldn't believe my luck.

Next up, I needed some cash to buy stock. I knew Mal had loads of money but I didn't have the balls to say: "Hi Dad, it's yer skint son, any chance of helping me out?" So, instead, I asked his wife Janet for four hundred quid and she came back to me with the cash in about two minutes, wished me 'good luck' and I gave her a kiss and said 'thank you'. Now I was in business and thought I was on my way to the big-time.

I started market trading and soon realised that this would be more eventful than racing motor bikes. Firstly, there was Dewsbury Market, where I went to sell silk flowers and vases. One day I sold out, so, feeling entrepreneurial, I ran off to Poundstretcher and purchased their entire silk flower stock, then rewrapped them to make them look fantastic and sold them all as well. Things were looking good.

I also had a bit of a party trick after the day's sales had ended. I only had one rear damper rod on the boot, so I made a wooden stick to hold it up. When I finished work, I'd kick the piece of wood out and the boot would slam shut. But I did this one day and the whole back window fell out. With shattered glass all over the place, I felt a right prat but there was more car trouble to follow.

I set off early one morning on the usual route to Dewsbury Market and could see a 45-ton lorry pulled over to one side of the road and apparently about to make a U-turn ahead of me, so I stopped and waited a few minutes. Nothing happened, so I decided to carry on. I'd built up some speed when I saw the lorry driver start to turn right across the road.

As my car locked up it started skidding faster and faster. I had remoulds on, so I skidded right under this arctic lorry, almost decapitating myself and smashing up all my stock.

Sherry's dad, Phil, who was always great to me, said: "Don't worry, just go and get another Montego – I'll pay for it," so I did. It was the same colour and even had an identical silver stripe to the one I'd wrecked. Thanks to Phil, I was now running a 1.6 blue Montego that cost £750.

It was at this point that all my mates started to take the piss by calling me 'Montego Man'. I figured if i ever got the chance, I'd run the bastards over in it.

My first business van purchase was a joke, too, because my credit rating was about as good as Ronnie Biggs's. And to be fair, my cunning plan to acquire my first van wasn't the best idea I've ever come up with.

I had zero credit rating, no cash and, to be honest, apart from nicking one, I had no hope of ever getting a van. This is where Mister Big came in – my Dad.

I arrived in his long drive, which in itself swallowed up about half-a-tank of fuel, ready to borrow some cash for my van purchase, and I wasn't looking forward to this one bit. Sitting down with Mal, I somehow plucked up the courage to ask: "Dad, any chance of £600 so I can get a van'?"

Well, he didn't have to say a word – his eyes did it for him.

"Six hundred quid, f*** off, you cheeky c***."

I was gutted. Then he said: "I tell you what, you can have an old caravan and a Kia Pride that was f*****. I want £1,500 back on the Kia and you can have the caravan for nowt.

I went outside to look at my potential trade in stock.

The caravan was worth about £100, if you were lucky, so I gave that a miss. The Kia Pride looked OK, so I took it for a spin around the moor, flat out of course, and then it cut out on me. I did re-start the engine but there was clearly something wrong with it.

I'm now out hopefully looking for a van dealer suffering senile dementia who is willing to take a Montego estate and a Kia Pride plus £400 – all the cash I had in the world – in exchange for the vehicle I needed for my market job. I looked high and low but no-one wanted to offer me anything before I stumbled across a bloke selling old post office delivery vans.

We did a deal and in no time I had to give him the four hundred quid plus two cars for the red post office van valued at £1,895. For me it was National Daylight Robbery Week.

As I came back up Dad's drive feeling like I was king of the road, my sister Tina was looking down it thinking, 'oh no, not the pikies again'. I jumped out of the van and she gave me a look of sheer disgust as she asked: "What the hell is that you're driving?" Tina had a 20 grand Mercedes at the time.

My satisfaction at doing the deal on the van also gave Big Mal his chance to use another big put-down as soon as I told him how much I'd paid for it. He nearly fell out of his chair before calling me a "dumb c***" and telling me how he could have bought the vehicle at auction for £600.

I wanted to punch him. I knew what it would have cost at auction, too, but I didn't have £600 in cash to pay for it. He could be so heartless at times.

I also found out that the Kia Pride for which I had to pay Dad back £1,500 was being advertised by him in *Auto Trader* for £1,450 or near offer. So a total stranger could buy it for 50 quid less than his only son.

I'd gone from being 'Montego Man' to 'Postman Pat' but I had some good times in that red van. Me and Dijon Compton used to cruise the streets of Huddersfield in it. He would get me pissed, then drive me home with the sliding doors wide open.

They never did lock properly, those sliding doors. I could pull hard and they would just open even when they were supposed to be locked – apart from the time I showed a local copper how crap the door locks were. "Watch this," I said to him as I went to yank the doors open, only this time it didn't work. Instead, the handle snapped off in my hand and I looked a right clown while this bobby laughed his head off.

43 DOING THE BUSINESS

How I felled Goliath . . . banned from the market . . . pound signs flash before my eyes . . . the amazing 'miracle grow'.

I EXPANDED my market trading operation and started working Huddersfield Market, where I received a far from friendly greeting on my own turf. I was allocated a stall next to an old-timer who'd been in the game about 40 years.

The market manager did what all managers do and gave me the worst position known to man. I shouldn't even have bothered and why he did this was beyond me – surely the people who ran the markets wanted newcomers like me to do well in what was a dying trade.

I turned up with a miniature stall just about big enough to accommodate a few packets of fags while matey boy next to me extended his stall to, well, about the size of Leeds, so I was virtually obscured from view.

I asked if it would be possible for him to pull his stock in a bit, so I could be seen by potential customers. He looked totally shocked at my request and told me to "go and get f*****" before adding with menace that he would be giving me a good kicking at the end of the day behind the back street of the market. Oh, and if I wasn't there at four o'clock, he'd be coming to get me and give me a good pasting.

I'd only come here to try make some money and now it looked like I was going to be visiting Huddersfield Royal Infirmary.

Anyway, I spent eight hours next to this guy as he continued to size me up. My biggest problem was how I was going to fell Goliath – he was over six feet tall while I was only two inches too big to qualify for the World Pigmy-throwing Championships. Basically, I was f*****.

Being a Carter, there was always only one option – dig my heels in hard, fight like f*** and hope for the best. This usually worked as you gained their respect. As Mal always told me, 'bang them, then talk later'.

All I wanted was to lead a normal everyday life but that would never happen.

When it came to the showdown at 4.00pm, I figured I may as well stand and fight than look a complete idiot with a six-foot giant chasing me through Huddersfield town centre. Sure enough, bang on four o'clock, there he was. I banged him with a straight right down the pipe and knocked him on his arse before screaming at the top of my voice: "Right, bastard, do you want another one?"

He shit his pants and it was all over in seconds . . . and so, too, were my Huddersfield Market trading days. I was now banned for violent conduct to a fellow trader – they didn't even want to know my side of the story.

ALAN CARTER

I did a flower show trying to sell some mirage growing gel that was crap but people really liked it and I made some good money doing this.

It was another one of Big Mal's ideas. His mate, Des McCracken, was at Dad's house one day showing him this amazing concept. Mal decided it was "a load of crap but right up our Alan's street." Cheers, Dad. He rang and said "get yer arse up here fast," so I did.

I was staring at a pan of jelly that was supposedly going to make me rich.

I took one look at it and figured, just like Dad, that this was a waste of time. But Des was insistent and said: "No, look, come to this shopping centre in Wales and have a look at it on display in all its glory – we have a guy there selling it for us."

For those of you who don't know, I'll explain how this jelly-like substance, widely known as Swellgel, works. As water is absorbed by crystals, a lattice work structure inside expands holding the water in place. If the level of water in the compost drops, then water is released from the gel into the compost. Plant roots also grow through the gel, where they can take up water directly. Plants still need watering but Swellgel reduces the amount of watering that is needed. Swellgel will continue to absorb and release for two years or more and can grow to absorb 400 times its own weight in water. It was an amazing product.

One minute I was minding my own business, the next I was at Dad's and then, in February 1995, I found myself on the way to north Wales in the hope of finding the key to my future.

On arriving at the shopping centre in Llandudno I watched this complete sales numpty take money off people faster than you could blink. I was in. This was amazing, pound signs were flashing right in front of my eyes.

I spent about two years selling the gel from a stall at shopping centres all over the north of England and had a fun time doing it. Dwayne McCracken, Des' son, came over and lived with me and we completely sold-out of the stuff on our first day of trading at the Bond Street shopping centre in Leeds.

I had never seen as much cash since the early 80s when the late Tom Wheatcroft used to give me a few grand to start at Donington.

Me and Dwayne had a great laugh in the early days as ladies queued up to buy our products – and get chatted up by us, too. One day this gorgeous lady asked: "Will the miracle grow work on my breasts?" I just winked at her and said: "You wouldn't believe how good it is!"

44 FLOWER POWER

Rondelles and a new venture ... branded a conman ... turned down by gays ... a new love at last.

WORKING the market stalls was becoming hard work for low returns. The great trading days were over. In the 70s and 80s you could wait months to get a pitch on a market but by now it was easy to find a place anywhere in Britain.

Sales of my wonder gel had just about fizzled out, so I was looking for the next great wonder to come along when I decided to do a flower show in Birmingham – the Spring Florist Event – with the main objective of clearing my remaining stock.

I was wrapping up silk flowers to sell when I ran out of flower sleeves and started to scan around the show to find some. I asked an Asian lady from a company called Suki International how much her sleeves cost. She said: "They are not sleeves, they are rondelles." I was like, 'OK, what the f***'s a rondelle?'

I introduced myself, did the usual pleasantries and we hit it off right away. The next thing, she was so intrigued by my wonder gel that she wanted to buy it all off me, before asking if I'd like to work for her company selling her products to all florists in the north of England?

I was like, 'yes, I do'.

This is how I got into the florist industry. The Asian lady I'd met at the Birmingham show turned out to be wealthy entrepreneur Mrs Nighat Awan, who was married to one of the richest men in the north of England. I found out later that her husband's Shere Khan chain of Indian restaurants was valued at £30m, although perhaps a bit less after health inspectors raided two of their curry emporiums in 2006 and they were fined thousands of pounds for insect infestations. Mrs Awan was voted Asian Businesswoman of the Year in 2002 and received an OBE two years later and I know I was impressed by her enthusiasm for business.

Born in Manchester to a Pakistani family, Mrs Awan bought up all my remaining stock of Swellgel for £750 and I started working for her on sales commission of between 10 and 15 per cent.

Arriving at the Awans' amazing house in my Montego estate, I felt like the world's number one leper. The Montego hardly had 'success' written all over it – what the f*** had happened to Alan and Kenny Carter, the 'golden boys'?

The giant electric gates opened, I reversed inside and made my way up the driveway before parking on a slight incline. I jumped out of the car and started walking towards the front door of the house when I glanced behind me and, to my horror, saw my £300 pile of shite rolling down the drive and gaining speed. 'Oh

ALAN CARTER

f***', was I about to wipe out 10 grand's worth of gates? I've never moved so fast in my life but, luckily, I'd not locked the doors and just managed to stop the car inches from the gates.

Mrs Awan's staff at Suki loaded all the samples into the Montego and I was now ready to hit the road and the florist industry.

The products were great and so, too, were the prices. Most people just laughed at me and sent me on my way but I was not a quitter. I called on a gay couple and they said: "Oh no, we've used our same suppliers for 10 years." Being a quick thinker, I responded: "It's time for a change, then lads," but they sent me packing, too.

Well, 'onwards and upwards' was my motto. I was using the 'SW-SW-SW' approach: some will, some won't, so what – who's next?

Things didn't improve when I arrived in York, where I failed to take even one order. Then I made the last call on a woman, who said: "Get out of my shop, you con man." I was stunned by her hostile reaction. I was just starting out on my latest venture but this was harder than road-racing. I told her I was that good, I'd just conned half of York, and then left.

Yes, the early days were very tough. I had no experience, was new on the block and Suki gave me no training whatsoever. I got my first break from a lady in Harrogate, who thought the cellophane looked great. "How does it come?" she asked. I said I didn't know, so she suggested I'd better ring headquarters, so I did and that's when I found out cellophane came either on a roll or in sheet form. I was about as bright as a dim bulb – the lights are on but no-one is in.

It didn't take me long to figure it all out. Basically, it came down to one thing – if they liked you, they bought from you.

The first thing I did wrong was my choice of clothing. I went out wearing an Italian suit purchased from a car boot sale that Dijon Compton had talked me into doing. Dijon's father was a sidecar racer and became mates with my Dad, and that's how I got to know him and his big brother Andre, who starred for the Sheffield Tigers speedway team. Me and Dijon, a good road-racer in his own right, became firm friends when I had the bike shop in Bradford and he'd call round and help out.

At the boot sale that day I sold one pack of gel for £2 but next to the stall me and Dijon were on was this little chap in a brand new car with all these suits. I kept thinking, they looked about my size, so I purchased a suit for £2 – long gone were the days when I went shopping in Harold Crabtree's with the Halifax elite. Talk about riches to rags, I was the number one scrote and hating every minute of it.

I got rid of the suit and started to mirror-image the customers' attire – smart but not over-the-top – and from then on my sales just got bigger and better by the week. I was now on my way and having a great time, too.

The period between splitting from Sherry in October 1997 and March 1998 must have been the most challenging ever for me in terms of trying to get a date with a woman. Here I was, Alan Carter, one of Yorkshire's finest sporting discoveries with a world-wide road-racing following – also known as Casanova the second – but I

Light in the Darkness

couldn't even pull a ligament at this time. An old lady with one eye, a false leg and grey hair would have refused a date with me and I felt so low. I felt at the time like I'd been rolled in dog shit and gave up, thinking I will never have a woman ever again.

But sales were going great and my confidence was up on the business front, so I asked one of my customers, Fiona, out for a few drinks. We were having drinks when she said: "I don't fancy you, but let's be mates." That was OK by me but I was back to square one as far as a romance was concerned.

In December 1997 Fiona said: "Why don't you put a glass vase display on in the shop – I'm having a Christmas open night?" I agreed but sold nothing, not even one piece, but Fiona's assistant felt sorry for me and said: "I will help you load up your van."

She was Carmen Mallia, who would become the mother of my next son, Joey, and stepmum to my elder boys, Louie and Jay.

We started dating the following March, soon after my first phone call. Fiona had told me Carmen was interested in photography, so I called her and said that I, too, was keen on photography. She said: "What camera do you have?" and, quick as a flash, I replied: "Canon" – it was the first name I could think of.

So my life was now settling down much better. I had a growing business, a new girlfriend and was seeing my two little bundles of joy every weekend. The next couple of years just flew by. I was making money, I felt happier than I had done for a long time and the future looked bright.

Me and my mate Dijon Compton, who helped my florist business to blossom.

Playing with Louie and Jay at home in around 1999.

Light in the Darkness

45 DEVASTATED

Expanding business . . . welcome to new arrival Joey . . . credit to Carmen . . . sadness as the loss of our baby daughter . . . but doctors save Carmen.

BY year 2000 my business was really flying. I was covering the whole north of England and was starting to work my way south, venturing as far as Leicester. When my expansion was complete I'd covered an area as far as the south-east coast of Yorkshire. I was well on my way.

When Carmen said she was expecting our first child, it came as more great news and we had a due date for our new arrival of early November 2000. My Gran Gladys was so excited. She didn't get the chance to spend too much time with Kenny's children, Kelly-Marie and Malcolm, when they were growing up but on the occasions she did get visits in the early days she was fantastic with them.

Before the baby was born we decided to take a holiday in Sorrento in southern Italy, where we met some lovely people and had a great time doing the usual things – visiting the famous Amalfi coastline and the island of Capri, where I loaned a boat and sailed around with our new friends, Steve and Lesley.

On our return to the UK, there was no sign of Carmen's dad, Joe, at the airport. He'd been admitted to hospital and was dying of leukaemia, so we were picked up by her brother Ivan. This was a very difficult time for Carmen, who was heavily pregnant and had been visiting her dad on a daily basis at the Manchester hospital. Sadly, Joe passed away on August 27, a few months before his first grandson was born.

Our Joey arrived on November 5 – Bonfire Day – and boy did he take some persuading before he finally came into the world. It felt like I'd been at the hospital about a week.

I remember this little Chinese midwife saying: "This is a waste of time, let's get the cap on the baby's head." I was thinking, 'never mind that, give me some of that gas' – every time she left the room I had a quick shot of it.

When she eventually pulled Joey out he looked like something from space. His head was so misshaped, I became a nervous wreck. I feared she was going to pull his head clean off and, I'd be left with a body with no head. It was awful to watch.

We settled in fine after taking Joey home. I now had three boys all under four-years-old and it was a very lovely period, although hard to juggle them and find places for them all to sleep in our small, two-bedroomed bungalow at 12, Badger Hill, Rastrick, Brighouse, which I'd purchased myself not long after returning from the USA.

Being a racer and having total freedom to come and go as I pleased was now a

Bath time for Louie, Joey and Jay.

thing of the past but old habits die hard. I was struggling at not being the centre of attention and, as with Louie and Jay, I found being a dad difficult. Babies were just not my thing.

Don't get me wrong, when the kids reached the age of about four, I was a great dad, taking them swimming or out playing football or travelling to the seaside, while all the time spending a fortune making sure they had a great time. But most importantly, I gave them my time.

One thing I would like to say is that Carmen looked after my kids better than their own mother. She was fantastic and would read, bake for them and play with them every weekend. She deserved much better treatment than she got from Louie and Jay, who were not easy kids to handle.

They were getting away with murder at their mother's. She was always out and palming them onto somebody else so she could do her own thing, and I could see this was becoming a serious problem.

The boys would come to mine and Carmen's place on a Friday night and it was like all hell breaking out but by Saturday night they had settled into our rules and thinking and come Sunday evening they were like different kids, fully settled down and enjoying our family way of life. I put up with this for nine years and every year that went by it got worse and worse.

I would have blazing rows with Sherry about the kids' behaviour and the way she brought them up. But all I got in return was "it's your fault." What a joke. Most days when I took the eldest two boys back to her, she couldn't even be bothered to be there when they arrived home – it was so frustrating.

Many times she'd say to me: "I'm sick of these kids, they can go and live with you." Every time this happened I'd say: "No problem, I will collect them," but then she'd change her mind.

Light in the Darkness

When Joey reached six-months-old Carmen came to me in May 2001 and said she thought she was pregnant, and the tests confirmed she was. Having been through a difficult birth with Joey, she wasn't happy about the idea of having a second child so quickly, although I tried to reassure her that everything would be fine.

She complained throughout the pregnancy that she didn't want this baby and that she had no real feelings for it. All I could say was "don't worry, it will all change when it arrives."

Our nightmare was about to begin.

I'd suffered the 1979 heartbreak of Mum killing herself, the tragedy of my little brother's death at the age of four and then Kenny taking Pam's life and his own. In addition to the deaths of close family members that devastated me at different stages of my childhood and adolescence, you can add in years of abuse at the hands of a bullying father. Then throw in the frustrations of failed racing career and the loss of some great friends who died on and off the racetrack and it all adds up to a long chain of disaster, grief and heartache.

But I was soon to suffer the biggest, most devastating blow that would ever hit me. Just thinking about what happened next still makes me feel very ill.

January 8, 2002

There was sheer panic as Carmen was rushed into Halifax's Calderdale Royal Hospital that morning. She had started to bleed badly, so we rang the hospital but by the time we set off the bleeding had slowed down. She was taken to hospital by her Auntie Cath, because I needed to drop Joey off at my half-sister Lucy's for her to look after him.

I made a quick dash into the supermarket to grab a few last minute things we needed, then went straight to the hospital. Everything seemed fine when I arrived there at about 11.00am. Carmen looked OK and the bleeding had stopped.

The unborn baby also appeared to be doing fine, the midwives were checking the baby's heartbeat every few minutes and the next five hours seemed to pass slowly with very little progress and no further cause for alarm.

Slowly but surely we started to see some movement and there were signs that the time was now here and we would soon be holding our baby in our arms. Carmen pushed and pushed and this went on for about 35 minutes as the nurses checked both her and the baby's heartbeat every few minutes.

The next thing the midwife couldn't detect the baby's heartbeat but by then the head was almost out. She tried another few times without getting a beat and then all of a sudden the baby was fully out – but not breathing.

All I can remember was people frantically running around trying to get her to breathe and shouting "get a doctor." They didn't even have one in the building, which came as a total shock to me. I kept thinking, 'where's the doctor?'

A Dr Clogger drove about six miles to reach the hospital but by the time he got there it was too late.

I just knew our baby had died and they would not be bringing her around. I don't know why I felt like this but I did. It was such a strong feeling that came over me.

By now my body had gone into total shock.

They wheeled Carmen into a side room to be with me and we both knew it was all over, that our baby daughter had died at birth. A doctor told me later that if you resuscitate a baby after 20 minutes, it would be seriously brain-damaged.

I sat in the room with Carmen and we were both speechless and exhausted – but there was another disaster looming. Nobody knew then that she was haemorrhaging on the bed and bleeding internally.

All of a sudden there was blood everywhere and I screamed for help. The whole place was pandemonium but, thankfully, the medical staff managed to save Carmen's life.

After our nightmare ordeal, the first person I rang from the hospital was Dad. Janet answered the phone and I couldn't speak. I made a noise but no words would come out of my mouth. She said: "Is that you, Alan?" I somehow managed to say "yes" just before bursting into tears and hanging up.

Janet arrived soon afterwards with my half-sisters Tina and Lindy. They tried to comfort me but Dad didn't even bother to come with them.

I was ill by now. The hospital had nowhere for me to stay, so I had to leave Carmen there and go home. It felt like my head was splitting in two. I didn't eat for three days.

I had several delivery notes saying parcels had been left with my neighbour and when I knocked at Reg and Virginia's house, they said "congratulations, Alan" and I burst into tears again before telling them the tragic news.

I called at Dad's farm, only for him to say: "Don't f****** worry, it happens all the time. I lose sheep and calves like this."

Even after all that Mal had said and done to me over the years, I was still totally shocked that he could be so heartless.

We named our baby Charlie and she was absolutely beautiful, with lovely black hair and weighing over eight pounds.

We managed to keep her in the hospital for a few days and Carmen never let her go. This was a totally heart-breaking experience. Then it was time to say goodbye to our little angel.

A few days earlier I'd been looking forward to our new baby and becoming a father for the fourth time – a lovely little daughter to join my three young boys.

Now I was standing beside a graveyard with a tiny white coffin in my hand. There was Carmen, me, her Auntie Cath and brother Ivan all saying goodbye to a life that never even started.

This very sad episode would change my life forever.

Light in the Darkness

46 DARK DAYS

Anger everywhere . . . mission of self-destruction . . . escape to the sun . . . thrill of the Subaru . . . police chase . . . Kenny's boy in trouble . . . Malky tries racing.

AFTER Charlie passed away I was angry at just about everything. First it was Carmen, who I believed had cursed us by saying she didn't want our baby. This she would have to live with for the rest of her life.

Then I turned against God. My anger towards Him went something like this: 'Why the f*** are you doing all this to me? Just f*** off and leave me alone, you bastard. If I'm that important to you, why don't you just f****** kill me and put me out of this miserable, painful life you have bestowed upon me?'

I was livid and had lost the plot. I had no regard for anyone or anything. I was on a mission of self-destruction.

I went on a bender in Halifax with our Malcolm and Welsey, who slipped some e's in my drink. I was on a roll now and met a bunch of girls from my old school who I'd not seen in over 20 years. They were about to set off to Newcastle on a girls' trip and wanted me to go with them.

And I was going, too, because I didn't give a shit about Carmen or anyone else. My head was f***** but, as it happened, Welsey and Malky wouldn't let me go. They must have figured I would probably throw myself off the Tyne Bridge or end it all some other way.

I ended that night on the bender by going up to Dad's, where I sat on the floor next to him and told him I loved him. He said in his usual affectionate manner: "I'll show you love . . ." and looked as if he was about to knock my head off. He was an evil bastard. We had a blazing row and I left. I didn't talk to him again for many years after this and as far as I was concerned he could rot in hell.

During the middle part of 2002 our Malcolm said to me: "You're always saying you're going to do this and that but basically you do nothing." After thinking about what he'd said I decided he was right and this drove me on to start looking at life a bit differently. I booked a holiday for Carmen and me on the Greek island of Corfu and we had a great time. While I was in the travel shop I also booked a holiday to Australia and this time Joey came with us.

We were finding it very difficult to come to terms with the loss of our child, blaming each other, but it was no-one's fault – it was a cruel act of nature or perhaps negligence on the part of the hospital. I really couldn't be there for Carmen – I didn't even have anything left for myself. I was a broken man.

Just before leaving for our six-week break in Australia I saw a magnificent house for sale. It was £230,000 and came with 1.5 acres of land – an absolute bargain and just what I needed to run my business from home – and we decided to buy it just before we left. I made an initial crazy offer of £170,000 which was turned down but I left it a few days and then bid £200,000. I was delighted when the estate agents, William H. Brown, informed me the house was ours and they'd be taking it off the market.

They put my place up for sale the day we left for Australia and it was sold in a week. But we were two weeks into the holiday when they emailed me saying I had been gazumped by £30,000 and 'did I still want to make an offer on the property?'

I told them they were a bunch of devious, fiddling bastards and to stick it.

The agent called me a few weeks later to say their other client had withdrawn his offer and said it was now mine at the original price of £200,000. But, again, I told them where to stick it – a mistake that would cost me more than 100k further down the line as the UK property boom was just about to happen.

The Australian holiday was a mixture of fights and some pleasure but, looking back, the writing was on the wall. Neither Carmen nor myself would ever recover from the death of our daughter.

We were sat in a restaurant near Freemantle one night when this couple came over to us and started talking. They said: "You two have got to stop fighting and start living – you're both living in the past." Although shocked by their comments, after this strange encounter we started to enjoy the holiday much more. Joey was having a great time playing in the sand on the beach and the people were so friendly. In comparison to the UK, Australia was amazingly clean and so much happier than the miserable Brits.

One day I went to the shops to purchase a chicken for dinner and the lady shop owner said: "Hi, how can I help you?" I said: "I would like a chicken, please." She said: "Great, which type would you like?" – she had about 10 different flavours available and the service was fantastic. On arriving back in the UK, I went to ASDA and asked for a chicken and this unhelpful woman said: "I'm not on the chicken counter" – and just walked off. Yes, we have a lot to learn about customer service in this country.

During our time in Western Australia we met up with a number of speedway people, including Rob Woffinden, Dave Cheshire, Nigel Boocock and Neil Machin. Rob was with his son, Tai, who was only 12 at the time but obviously already mad-keen on motorbikes. We also met up with two of our Kenny's former Halifax team-mates, Perth residents Craig Pendlebury and Mick McKeon.

The sunshine in Corfu and Perth was very welcome but the only thing that really lifted my spirits was speed – and I don't mean drugs. I purchased a new Subaru WRX in white – my favourite colour – that was good for 156mph and I seemed to clock that speed almost everywhere I went in it.

Purchasing this car didn't go down well with Carmen but, to be honest, I didn't care one bit. I was now doing things to suit myself. I had some great times in the car, which is probably reflected in the fact that the first set of tyres lasted only 900 miles – I'd ripped them to pieces drifting the thing all over the place.

One day Carmen and I were coming back from a club in Leeds. I was cruising down the M62 at about 110mph and could see a car catching up with me. I had a gut feeling it was the police, so I wound the motor up to about 145mph and pulled off near Brighouse. I was at a set of traffic lights when I noticed a Volvo T5R pull up behind me – it was the police and they were onto me big-time.

Something just popped in my head and I said to myself, 'f*** it, I'm getting a ban here anyway, so I may as well get five years in prison – let's show these dickheads how to drive a car.'

I flattened the motor and that was it, I was driving better and faster than Schumacher and I lost them no problem.

I abandoned the car in a remote place close to home and we walked back to the house across muddy fields – Carmen still in her dancing shoes and up to her ankles in mud.

As we got closer to the house I expected the police to be everywhere, waiting to arrest me, but they were nowhere to be seen, so we sneaked into the house, pulled the curtains shut and went to bed. I remember laying there thinking any minute now the door will be going 'bang bang' but nothing happened.

The next day I was so excited and impressed by how I'd shown the pigs how to drive that I wanted to ring Leeds police headquarters and ask them if they'd like me to train their lamo drivers how to do it properly.

After the latest personal tragedy to strike the Carter family I still had to pick up the pieces with my business but I'd lost all interest since the death of Charlie. My heart was just not in it. Every time I got to one of my customers, who by now I'd developed very close relationships with, they'd ask whether we'd had a boy or a girl. I'd then break down in bits and have to tell them that we'd lost our baby.

It's amazing how many people out there have lost a child in awful circumstances similar to ours, and they would all come out of the woodwork and be a tower of strength to me. There was an amazing guy called David, who owned the flower garden florist in Brighouse. He took me to one side and told me his own heart-breaking story. I'd like to thank him for being there when I needed somebody. As they say, a problem shared is a problem halved.

A local company, Helensgate Glass, became a big part of my life after I became one of their biggest customers. The managing director was a fantastic man called John Heady, who looked after me like a son. He was the kind and loving dad I never had – nothing was too much trouble for him as I tried to develop a business in very difficult trading times.

Along with John, a great guy named Julian Atkinson would help me to the hill and back. He was always there for me, while Carl the warehouse manager stayed late many times just so that I could get my stock for the next day. Carl had his own demons, having split with his wife and was trying to come to terms with bringing up his two children. We now live in times when couples break-up too easily, which in turn destroys many young children's lives. The days when people like my Gran

The lovely Uncle Bill Williams with Louie and Jay.

and Granddad stayed together forever are well gone. One of the luckiest things to happen to me was the pleasure of being around my grandparents and other salt of the earth people like my Uncle Bill and Auntie Deloris. They were so loving and kind and this is how I wanted to live my life.

Auntie Deloris was the first person the great Ron Dennis ever employed. She was the tea and sandwich maker back in the early days at McLaren.

Gran looked after our Joey many times right up to when she was in her eighties. She loved all my kids and I'm so happy that she managed to be a part of their early lives. Gladys was the best grandma in the world and we talk about her all the time, so she lives on in us.

Our Malcolm would turn 18 in May 2002, when he received his £25,000 inheritance which had been held in trust from Kenny and Pam's estate.

In the late 90s he'd had a brief go at speedway at Sheffield. He was fast and had the potential to develop into a good rider but he didn't go about it in the right way. He was fortunate to receive some good sponsorship from Brighouse multi-millionaire Jeff Bean, of Northern Municipal Spares, whose son Simon took care of Malky's bike, but they pulled the plug on him because he wasn't willing to listen and learn.

Following in his father's tyre tracks would have been a very big challenge for Malky – very few sons of successful speedway stars have measured up to their fathers' high standards – but I think Malky could have been a useful rider if Kenny had lived and been there to encourage and advise him when he was starting out at 16.

Anyway after his brief spell on the shale, Malcolm decided he wanted to try road-racing but first we had to get him a car, so he asked me if I'd go with him to purchase

Light in the Darkness

Auntie Deloris and Gran with Malky at my wedding to Sherry.

one. I told him that a Vauxhall Corsa 1.5 TD would be a great starter car – they were cheap to insure and had a nippy engine that did about 50 to the gallon.

One Saturday at about 4.00pm we managed to find a nice one which he purchased for cash. I had a drive in it and was satisfied it would be fine after having new brake pads fitted, a service plus some good tyres. Malky tried to arrange the insurance on the spot but couldn't get through to the insurers, so I said it would probably be OK to drive it home slowly and sort out the insurance on Monday morning, and this is what he did without any problems.

That night he was going to a family party and drove the car the short distance from his home at Bradshaw to his local village.

The next day – June 9 – he was invited to his auntie's in Huddersfield for Sunday dinner with his cousin Shane Moore. They rang another mate, Paul Clarke, and asked: "Do you fancy coming with us?" At first their friend declined the offer, saying he was too busy, but quickly changed his mind and about five minutes later rang back and said he would go with them after all.

It was a fatal decision.

Malky had to turn around and pick up Shane's mate. After collecting their friend, he first sat in the back seat on the left-hand side of the car and then, for some reason, after a few miles decided to change places and moved to sit behind Malky.

Being a young and still very inexperienced driver, having passed his test only a few weeks earlier, my nephew was over-excited and driving too fast. He lost control of the Corsa, which went into a spin on Brighouse and Denholme Gate Road, Coley and ended up hitting a lamppost backwards, killing the rear passenger instantly.

I received a phone call from Malky, who was hysterical. All he could say was: "Can you come to the hospital now," so I knew it was very serious.

On arriving at the back entrance of the hospital I could see a light green blanket covering a dead body. Someone had been killed in the accident and there was police keeping guard over Malky. I did my best to calm him down.

Paul Clarke, a promising 19-year-old rugby star from Queensbury, had lost his life.

Over the next few weeks there was talk of people being after Malky, so I managed to find him a safe place to live as the storm clouds gathered over yet another tragedy to affect the Carter family.

I felt awful and full of guilt towards the poor family that had just lost their young son and the thought of this, only a few months after burying my own daughter, made me even more poorly.

Malcolm didn't handle the situation very well but, then again, how do you handle something as awful as this? I've no idea.

Just before the fatal car accident we had set up a small racing team for Malky. Basically, I was going to help him get going and show him the ropes. It was only after he said a few things about me not being as good a road-racer as people said I was that I decided to also have a crack at racing again, to see if I could still do it. I suppose a bit of self-pride kicked in and I thought about Malky's comments and said to myself, 'I'll show you how good I was, kid.'

A few weeks after the accident we had our first race meeting, at Donington Park, and to be honest Malcolm was riding tremendously well and very fast. I managed to get pole position for the race and Malky was a highly respectable fifth on the grid.

But in his first race Malky crashed on the warm-up lap and was fined £50 by Jim Parker. I won the race by about five seconds and pocketed £60 for winning. After also winning the second race I said to Malky: "Try the laurel on, it feels great!"

All I really wanted was for him to have some respect for both me and my mate Derek Rhodes, because we both knew the game inside out and were there to help him.

We did another meeting at Cadwell and both Malky and me were doing well until it ended with him writing off both bikes and Derek going mad about a rider – James Rose – and his dad cheating on a bike faster than a 600cc Honda Hornet. It came close to a fight in the pits and when Derek put in a protest it was strange that they couldn't test Rose's engine due to the bike not being able to start. What a fix.

Jim Parker was absolutely no help whatsoever on this occasion but to be fair to him, in the years I had in racing he was always helpful to me.

Due to Malcolm's attitude to racing, me banging my head against a brick wall trying to teach him and Derek getting more than pissed off with the whole situation, we all decided to call it a day and let Malky do his own thing in the racing world.

47 GRAN'S GOODBYE

Malky sentenced to five years in prison ... Gran's fighting spirit ... her last days ... scattering her ashes.

RETURNING to the UK early in 2003, I basically had nowhere to live. The sale of my house was going through but I hadn't purchased another one and was in two minds whether to pull the plug on the sale – something I still regret not doing to this day. In the end we moved to a rented house in Botany Lane, Lepton, near Huddersfield, for a few years.

I had a lot hanging over my head and the other thing that was bothering me was our Malcolm, who was about to be sent to prison for killing his friend in the car crash the previous summer.

Malky had no chance of avoiding a custodial sentence. I'd read the police report and there were so many witnesses to testify that he had passed them doing crazy speeds. And when you added in the fact that he'd shown no remorse to the family of the teenage victim who died in the crash, he was going to get a stiff sentence from any judge.

On the morning of his court appearance in June 2003 I picked him up and took him for the 'last supper' because I knew I wouldn't be seeing him for a very long time.

In court, the way the judge was talking I started to think Malky might not be sent down after all but, right at the last minute, the judge slammed him with the hammer blow – five years in jail for causing death by dangerous driving and a 10-year driving ban. Everyone in the court room appeared shocked by the verdict.

What a cruel start to a young life Malky had. His dad had murdered his mum when he was just two-years-old and now, having just turned 19, he was going to prison for the next five years. I was numb to the bone, wondering 'how would he cope with this?' He'd driven recklessly on that fateful day and had to be punished but he was a smashing young kid with all his life in front of him.

He was sent to Moorlands young offenders open prison at Hatfield, near Doncaster, where he did his time and paid his dues.

I can see a lot of both Kenny and myself in Malky. He is a hard-working, lovely young man that deserved a better start in life. He is one of life's winners and I know he can put his terrible past behind him and enjoy a successful life.

Malky has never asked me anything about his parents – he was too young to know either of them or have any memory of them – but I'm here for him if he ever wants to talk about his parents and what happened to them. I will always be there for him no matter what, because he has always stood by me in my time of need.

Above: Me and Granddad Willie – he never got over Kenny's death. Below: Gran and Granddad.

I'd noticed over the course of 2003-04 that Gran's health was getting worse. Carmen had been looking after her for me because I'd been working far too hard myself running the business.

Kenny's death had finished Granddad Willie. He was devastated by it and although he lived for another three years, he became a very ill man and could hardly walk anywhere. In the end he died in his late sixties of a massive heart attack in 1989. He never got over what Kenny did.

Gladys was also heartbroken over the double tragedy of '86 and with very good reason. She saw her daughter and two grandchildren buried and it amazed me that she lived as long as she did given all the heartache she suffered.

By 2003, though, Gran was in and out of hospital far too much. It got to the stage where the hospital took me to one side and told me to prepare for the worst. But typically, Gran showed true fighting spirit and made a remarkable recovery, although she would never return to her own home because she'd become wheelchair bound and therefore unable to use the stairs.

We pulled out all the stops and managed to get a bungalow for Gran on the other side of Brighouse which both Carmen and myself worked day and night to furnish and organise. We made it look very much like the inside of her old home in Reins Road where she'd lived for the previous 50 years. I told her not to worry as all she had to do when she came out of hospital was flick the kettle on.

Gran had tears in her eyes when she first saw it. We'd made it look absolutely beautiful. I was determined to do my best for the most amazing woman in my life.

I can still see our Joey now, sat next to Gran in her sparkling new home in 2005 as she talked to him and asked him what he would like for his fifth birthday. I'm grateful that Gran did manage to see Joey one last time on his special day in that November.

Just before the end of her life Gladys was taken to a day centre where they played draughts. She told me how she'd played two men and they were rubbish and she had beaten them both. Her mind was razor-sharp and she was a winner right to the end.

Sadly, she suffered a major stroke not long after moving into the new bungalow and would never come out of hospital.

Although she never regained consciousness, she could understand everything I said to her. The nurses wanted to feed her through a tube into her stomach but when I asked Gran if that was what she wanted or would she prefer to rest and die in peace, she said: "I want to die." It was heart-breaking when I told the staff of her last wishes but I had to do it.

I'd call in to see Gran over the next seven days, sit with her, talk to her and thank her for all the wonderful things she had done for me in my life.

Gran's funeral was something very special. Her last wishes were for me to scatter her ashes in the same place where her beloved Willie was laid to rest.

I went to M&S – she loved shopping there – and purchased some beautiful, new clothes for Gran and sent her out of this world looking a million dollars. It made me feel so proud of her.

After the funeral we celebrated her life, her smile and tenderness which will live

ALAN CARTER

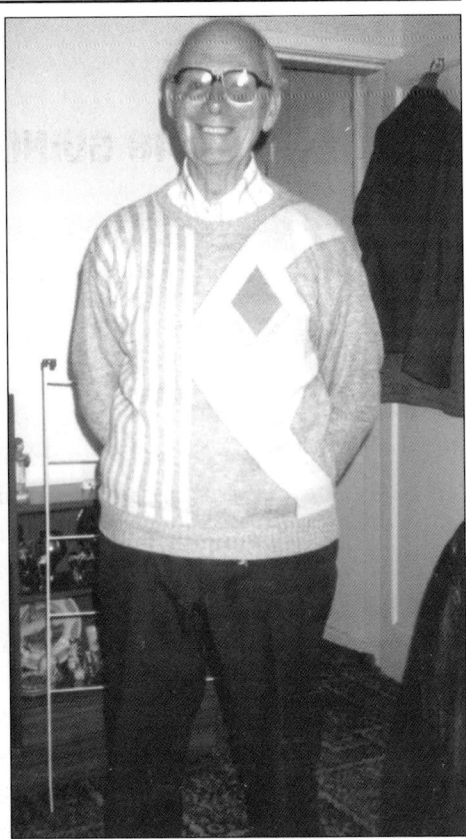

How I'll always remember Gran and Granddad, happy and smiling.

with me forever.

Gran, you were a truly amazing woman.

I love you and miss you, and I hope one day I will see you again.

Love always, Alan.

xxx.

Putting aside my deep sadness for a second, there was a moment of black comedy when I went to scatter Gran's ashes. They asked me at the funeral directors if I had a strewing urn, because the woman there said I was going to need one.

Anyway, she came out with Gran's remains in this strewing urn contraption and said: "All you have to do, Mr Carter, is pull the triggers."

Off I went and found the place in Park Wood Crematorium at Elland where Gran said Granddad's ashes had been scattered but, being a thick t**t, I never took into consideration the gale force winds blowing that day. So here I was, saying my last goodbyes to my beloved grandma, who was basically confined to a bucket, when I pulled the triggers on the urn and was instantly covered in her ashes. I looked and felt a right idiot.

Gran was cremated on the same day – November 25, 2005 – that the great George Best passed away. I'll never forget it as long as I live.

Gladys Hanner – my ever-loving Gran – will be sadly missed forever.

48 GOING DOWNHILL

Big truck leads to big problems . . . shunned by Mal . . . splitting from Carmen . . . phone call that saved my life.

THE latest truck I'd purchased for the business was from a company called Fame Commercials in Colchester, Essex. It was a Fiat and although it was in the 3.5 ton limit category, its giant bodywork enabled me to load it up with about four or five tonnes of product. The way I looked at it, the more stuff I had on board my vehicle, the more I could sell.

The problem was that the truck started to bend in half due to all the extra strain I was putting it under and it also broke down far too many times. So much for my hopes of problem-free motoring for the next few years. Instead, it cost me thousands and in the end my mate Mark Gallagher got rid of it for me – I was glad to see the back of it.

Just before we parted with the 3.5 ton truck Mark suggested I moved up to the 7.5 ton limit. I was selling a lot of gear to the flower industry, including plant pots, vases, film and paper to wrap flowers, ribbons, fancy pottery, lots of fish bowls, plus all sorts of plant food and just about everything a florist could use. I became a key contact for them because I knew a lot of people and could supply most florists with all their wedding items, so the larger truck seemed to be the next logical step as I looked to take the business forward.

We decided to rent a 7.5 ton truck from Andy Cagill for two weeks and it went so well that I decided to enquire about purchasing a new one for myself. I was told I'd need an operator's licence and a designated operating centre – and this is where I hoped Big Mal would come in useful.

I asked Dad if I could use his farm address as my operating centre and leave the van on his farm overnight, plus was there any chance of a bit of storage space? "No problem," he said, so I applied for my licence, which was duly granted, and took out an HP agreement to purchase a new van for £32,000.

I was now up and running.

Or, to put it another way, this was the beginning of me going bust.

It soon became apparent they didn't want me on the farm and basically told me to find somewhere else to park my truck. I even offered Dad £100 per month for the use of some storage space – he had various outbuildings – but he said it wasn't possible because he needed all the room he had for himself.

That's when I started to park the truck outside the house where Carmen and I lived. It was OK until one of the neighbours grassed me up, complaining that the whole of his house shook whenever I started up the truck. I received a letter from the government's Vehicle and Operator Services Agency (VOSA) saying that if I didn't

Recent pictures of my three boys – Louie, Jay and Joey.

park my vehicle at the 'operating centre' – Dad's farm – they would confiscate my licence.

I looked high and low for a cheap place to rent and eventually found one for 500 quid a month, plus the usual rates, electric and security, etc, so I moved in there. Storing stock and a truck cost money, though, so I decided to open my unit as a cash and carry with Carmen running it. At least we could break even and, if it all went well, maybe make a few quid.

I put in about £40,000's worth of stock and opened my doors to the public but in three weeks I sold just £90's worth – a total disaster. I was near melting point and to top it off, on three occasions the local pikies stole all my fuel by smashing through my fuel tank.

The thing that pissed me off about Dad was when his mate rang from America and asked if it would be OK to store a giant motorhome on the farm, Mal said: "No problem." So much for looking after your own. But that was Dad all over – he loved his hangers-on more than his own family.

With the cost of the business unit, re-payments on the van and all the running costs, I was now going backwards. Sales were dropping and the big credit crunch was just around the corner.

During my latest driving ban my mate Mark Gallagher used to drive me around and look after me. He was an ex-Halifax Dukes rider but after appearing in four matches for the team in 1983 he had to quit speedway because it was too expensive. We met in KFC in Huddersfield, got chatting and Mark said he'd been a big mate of our Kenny when they both rode at The Shay

Light in the Darkness

Joey at home with one of the few visible reminders of my racing career.

Mark had known his fair share of disaster, too. One day when he was in his early thirties he was fixing a puncture at the side of the road when he was hit by a woman motorist and left for dead. Apparently, he 'died' a few times on the way to hospital but doctors managed to save him. I believe they traced the woman who hit him and she had to cough up some compensation for Mark but the hit-and-run incident left him with permanent serious damage to both legs.

At that first meeting in KFC Mark and I hit it off right away and he and his wife Mandy became good friends of mine and have been very supportive over the past seven years or so.

My relationship with Carmen had run its course, we were living separate lives and I couldn't take it anymore, so I decided to move out of our family home for good. It was a hard decision to make because I didn't want to upset or disrupt our young son Joey.

Having known over the previous two years that my business was going downhill, I removed her name from the company details and signed the house over to her. After 12 years of trading I was heading for liquidation and possible bankruptcy and didn't want to take her down with me. I took full responsibility for our problems.

When I left, the only things I took with me were my clothes, a sofa, bed and a portable TV and the rest I left for Joey. I'd effectively lost my home, my son and my partner all in one go, plus my business was about to go bust. I was in a real mess.

Soon after I moved out of the family home and into rented accommodation some 10 miles away in Slaithwaite, I remember getting a bowl of petrol. I was going to finish it all because I just couldn't take any more. I was in a dark place.

But I didn't go through with it thanks to a phone call I received 17 days after I moved into the small cottage.

It was Sherry: "I'm sick and tired of this kid," she moaned.

She said Jay could come and live with me. "I'm on my way," I said.

I really do think that Jay saved my life.

49 FIGHTING THE DEMONS

Darkest days as depression sets in . . . psychiatric help . . . suicidal thoughts . . . my boys kept me going . . . bankruptcy . . . caring words from an old friend.

MY nine-year-old son Jay moved in with me at Wood End Cottage – surely one of the smallest cottages in the UK on a remote farm near Huddersfield – on May 17, 2007. I wasn't a well man and was suffering from serious depression. I would have to try and pick myself up but this was a truly testing time for me.

The first thing I had to do was get Jay into a school. There was a choice of three but having visited two of them I knew I'd found the right one in Clough Head Junior School after meeting Brian, the headmaster. Jay was accepted and settled in well with the other 44 kids at this little place.

Arriving at school that first morning, I heard a guy talking whose voice I recognised as that of Dave Beaumont, an old sponsor of mine from the mid-90s. We had a good, sociable chat but over the next few months Dave noticed how I'd become a completely different person. He'd noticed that I didn't look well – I knew I was ill but I told no-one – and he told me I needed to go and see a doctor.

I walked into the doctor's surgery and sat down but just couldn't speak. I tried to talk but no words would come out of my mouth and tears were rolling down my face at a rapid pace. My body was in shock after all that had happened over the years.

I'd been living on borrowed time for a very long while and now I looked to be heading towards a nervous breakdown.

My doctor, a lovely woman called Gemma Simcox, diagnosed me as suffering from Gulf War Syndrome, a form of post-traumatic stress disorder* . The illness was the delayed after-effects of my tragic past – first the loss of young Malcolm and Mum, followed by Kenny and then my baby daughter dying – and those close family tragedies, plus all the stress caused by the collapse of the business and splitting with Carmen and now bringing up a young son as a single dad, had pushed me over the top.

The doctor immediately referred me to a psychiatric nurse. She also gave me some medication and told me not to go near large groups of people.

At this stage my daily routine was to take Jay to school, call in at the butcher's for some fresh meat and call in at the greengrocer's to buy fresh vegetables so I could cook him a proper meal every night. I'd then sleep for most of the day because the depression made me exhausted.

I was living in a strange place, where no-one knew me, but this was a good thing by then. I could handle walking anonymously past strangers but every now and then I'd be spotted by someone I knew and then I'd just fall to pieces. It got to the stage where I wouldn't leave the house at all – only to take Jay to and from school.

This was the lowest point of my life.

Serious depression is a very dark place you never want to go. I mean, I'm Alan Carter, a tough nut road-racer from Halifax, what could possibly be wrong with me? Depression? You must be kidding!

But depression can strike anybody. At one point I felt like I needed to be sectioned. I was talking to a close friend, a lovely girl called Jayne, and I told her: "I'm going to get myself sectioned." She laughed at me and said: "Let me tell you a story, Alan."

Jayne said: "Firstly, you're suffering from mid-to-high-end depression, you're not mental or in need of being sectioned. I once thought the same as you do, Alan, because I was in a similar place as you are right now.

"Once I was accepted into a psychiatric unit I was stuck there for 28 days and there was nothing I could do about it apart from watch people who were mentally ill and past the point of any help. All they did was rock forwards and backwards all day long. This was when I knew I wasn't in need of full-time care and medication to sedate me 24/7."

So I took Jayne's advice and continued to see and be monitored by Colin, my psychiatric nurse, for the next year.

My visits by Colin were not a good experience, though. Both Kenny and me were very private people and would never tell anyone anything about our deepest inner-thoughts, fears and, yes, the personal demons that we kept well hidden from virtually everybody.

I don't know why, but we just didn't trust anybody. Maybe it had something to do with our terrible early years looking after Mum and seeing what she went through before she took her own life when Kenny and I were both still in our teens.

The only other person I'd really opened up to before talking to Colin was Mike Duffield, who I'd met way back in 1989 through my then personal trainer, another great guy called Gary Sparks. Gary told me I was one of the hardest trainers he'd ever seen but he couldn't understand why I kept missing sessions with him at the gym.

I explained to him that I was a big migraine sufferer, just like my dad was, and that's when he advised me to see Mike, who was a trained psychologist, nutritionist, sports injuries specialist and masseur all rolled into one – a very clever man and a bike racing nut, too.

Mike worked with me over a period of 15 years and still does to this day. He not only cured my bad headaches, he also removed the biggest obstacle of all – my fear of my father.

He would talk to me and say things like: "You're a man with your own independence. You're a great guy, I love you, you're popular. He'd give me a proper massage and say that Dad's mantra of 'second place being for losers' is bullshit, pointing out that in my racing days I was either winning races or not finishing them

Light in the Darkness

because I'd often crash trying too hard. He said I had to change my thought patterns.

He also told me Mal had no control over me whatsoever and he'd teach me things over the years about how to overcome negative thoughts about my father. It was one of the greatest challenges of my life and by the time Dad passed away in 2009, I felt in total control of my emotions as far as he was concerned.

I was a bit wary of Mike when I first met him – he had a dark beard and tash, as if he was hiding behind it, and, facially, he reminded me of the Yorkshire Ripper! But he became one of my best mates, like a father-figure to me, and I love him.

He printed out lots of information from a computer and after reading through it all it became clear that the migraines were down to my diet. Mike put me on a strict diet which basically cut out cheese, chocolate, coffee, red wine and garlic – all killers – and when I stick to it I'm fine.

I suffered headaches throughout my career. I'd often eat chocolate steam pudding the night before a meeting and wake up the next morning feeling ill. I didn't associate chocolate steam pudding as being the cause of my migraines. To get rid of the pain the next day, I'd simply take Anadin before a race but the headaches did affect my concentration at times during racing.

But migraines were the least of my worries by the time I was referred to psychiatric nurse Colin in 2007. He'd ask me all sorts of questions and many times he would ask: 'Have you ever thought of killing yourself?'

I always tried to respond by telling him that, although there were a few times when I'd had very fleeting thoughts about taking my own life, there was never any serious intent to commit suicide.

I was lying to Colin, though, because not a day went by when I didn't think of ending it all by killing myself. I've been close to doing it once or twice but always talked myself out of doing something stupid. I'd say to myself, 'you can't do that, you're the last one of your immediate family still alive – what will people think of you?' And then I'd think, 'why would I worry about what people think about me – I'd be dead!'

Suicide and death are like the Grim Reaper always knocking on my door, goading me and saying, 'come on, let's do it . . . ' but I can tell you I just couldn't do it. I could never hurt my own family and leave them in the pain I found myself in at certain times of my life.

Inevitably, thoughts always go back to Kenny. I couldn't accept that he would do this to himself and make my life a living hell. More than 25 years have passed since he killed Pam and himself but the pain remains the same. So many times I run it through my own head, asking: 'Why did he do it? What was he thinking? How could I have helped?' It's an endless loop that I can't close.

It was always the thought of my three boys that kept me from losing it altogether. My kids were all I had and when I was living at Wood End Cottage I didn't want them to take Jay away from me, so I kept these dark thoughts and my true feelings about how I felt to myself.

ALAN CARTER

Jay would come home and we'd play games and enjoy each other's company. We'd sit and eat dinner at the table – lamb chops were our favourite – and discuss many topics. He was a very smart kid.

After dinner we'd play chess. Granddad Willie taught me how to play when I was a kid and now I wanted to do the same with our Jay. I'd pour a glass of vintage sherry for myself and a miniature one for him – Gran had always given me a miniature vodka and orange when I stayed at her house as a young boy.

I loved taking Jay to the Merry England coffee shop in Huddersfield, where we'd drink milky coffee with brown sugar in it, just like Gran had done with me when I was a little boy, and I'd tell him many stories about Gran and what a great woman she was.

Jay coming to live with me in May 2007 almost certainly saved my life.

I was at Jay's school one morning when Dave Beaumont asked me why I was looking so ill and I told him I had some very serious business problems. I explained that I didn't know what to do and that I was scared and becoming nervous and paranoid and didn't know which way to turn.

He told me he'd gone through the same thing only a few years earlier and advised me to go and see an insolvency specialist friend of his called Ted. Meeting Ted was a big relief. I explained my situation and how the business had been struggling. He looked at all my paperwork and basically said: "You're f*****, you need to declare yourself bankrupt."

With the global recession looming, the banks and other lenders had been pulling the plug on thousands of small businesses and many of my own customers were also going bust.

The Yorkshire Bank would pull the plug on me, too.

My number one suppliers were also close to going under and it was only their parent company, plus a massive management reshuffle, that saved them. I'd been one of their best customers for more than 10 years but, overnight, they cut my credit limit on stock from £20,000 to £5,000 and my payment terms went from 90 days to 30 – any longer and they'd put my account on 'stop'. The new management were an arrogant bunch of arseholes who treated me like a leper. So much for loyalty to long-term customers.

Anyway, I took all Ted's advice and on January 8, 2008, in Huddersfield county court, I filed for bankruptcy. I was a nervous wreck, all I could think about was them coming to my little cottage and taking away the very few things I had left in life, and leaving me and Jay with nothing at all. It was a gut-wrenching feeling.

I'd started a business that earned me £30 per week in the beginning and within three years, with the help of some cash deals and a bit of ducking and diving, I was bringing in £40,000 a year and everything was brilliant. But after my daughter died the business and my life just collapsed and I lost everything – my house, my missus and my business.

And before long I couldn't even speak.

Light in the Darkness

But living in the cottage on a remote derelict farm was just what I needed. I only had a handful of visitors in the first few years I was there, so no-one really knew how poorly I was.

One day my old friend Chris Knight rang me and I couldn't speak. This voice problem would remain with me for a few years and it was only when I had to tell somebody about my condition that my body would go into denial and shock mode.

Chris now knew how poorly I really was and immediately set off up the M1 from his home at Loughborough in Leicestershire to see me. I was very grateful that someone cared for me enough to drive 100 miles to be with me and as we talked he reassured me that I would be OK. Chris promised to keep an eye on me, which he did. Thank you, mate.

I stayed under Colin, the psychiatric nurse, for about a year and then one day he said to me: "There is nothing I can do for you, Alan. The only thing you need is time." I thanked him for all his support and that was the end of my supervision.

Before and during the period I declared myself bankrupt, I was frightened to death of the phone ringing and the mail I'd receive. I had letters saying they would be collecting my works van, which I'd almost finished paying for. I was bitter about this and the fact they would be taking away my Renault Clio Sport. Despite having worked 15 hours a day for the last 12 years, I'd be left with nothing.

Living the high life was just a fading memory for me, because I was now living with shame and guilt that I'd failed in life, too. Well, that's how I saw things.

Dad said I was a disgrace to the family and was no support to me whatsoever after I became ill. This just made me feel even worse, so I continued to live a secluded life, afraid of people and what they would think of me. I'd gone from a road-racing superstar to the rubbish dump in 20 years. How cruel life can be.

One day I was outside chopping up some wood so I could keep Jay and me warm at night - we certainly couldn't afford coal, two big men came walking towards me in long trench coats. I started to panic, thinking this was it, maybe they had a shotgun and I was going to be getting it.

I went towards them and shouted: "What do you want?" I was thinking, 'you mad bastard, Alan, why don't you just start running, it's all over.' By now my mind was running wild.

Then the men said they were Jehovah's Witnesses and it was just a friendly call. I couldn't believe my luck. I made them tea and biscuits and enjoyed their company. I felt relieved that I would live to fight another day.

I do feel guilty at times that my three beautiful boys have not really seen their dad at his best. I've had to put myself before them, which has been heart-breaking for me at times, but when you are ill your hands are tied. There was nothing I could do.

I know I'm not the man I once was and never will be again. I'm still fighting the demons of both my dad and brother and this tragic life I've had to live.

I'm sure many people who have taken their own life have regretted what they did. My only advice to those who are deeply troubled and struggling to cope is go to bed and try to rest. You will probably feel a little better in the morning. We live in difficult times and many people are suffering in one way or another.

I think of life as a revolving wheel in which your health, wealth and happiness are constantly changing. You get some time at the top of the wheel when you're feeling so fantastic and 'juiced' that you believe you can do almost anything. Then you have days when you are at the bottom. These are the days you just have to ride out and get through and wait for the second wave to come in and get you going again. It always happens. And then you have days when you feel fine, not on top of the world exactly, but things are just moving along nice and steady.

When I'm feeling low and sorry for myself, I always remember a great saying in one of the books I read. It goes like this:

I felt really bad because I had no shoes until I met the man who had no feet.

I've felt like a trout swimming upstream and fighting against the current, only to die at the end of the journey totally worn out by the struggle of life. It was only when I finally broke and suffered serious mental illness, and had almost nothing left to live for, that I could start all over again.

I do live in hope that things will work out well for me in the end.

It's great to be among true friends ... Chris Knight, Tariq Yassin, Derek Rhodes and me in 2011.

*Gulf War Syndrome (GWS) is a collection of symptoms reported by veterans of the first Gulf war since August 1990. Veterans from every country that made up the coalition forces have been affected; in the US alone more than 110,000 cases had been reported by 1999, according to official government sources.
The symptoms reported by veterans include:
Fatigue.
Persistent headaches.
Muscle aches/pains.
Neurological symptoms – e.g. tingling and numbness in limbs.
Cognitive dysfunction – short-term memory loss, poor concentration, inability to take in information.
Mood and sleep disturbances – depression, anxiety, insomnia.
Dermatological symptoms – skin rashes, unusual hair loss.
Respiratory symptoms – persistent coughing, bronchitis, asthma.
Chemical sensitivities.Gastrointestinal Symptoms – diarrhea, constipation, nausea, bloating.
Cardiovascular symptoms.

50 MEETING MY MATCH AND SAVIOUR

Cathy enters my life ... dressing to impress ... misunderstanding over Kenny turns sour ... a dig from Collins ... our new 'baby' ... swallowing my pride.

I'VE always supported my kids no matter what. If I could be there for them, I was and it wasn't often I missed any of their football matches or sporting events.

Over the last few years I'd been on a few blind dates, too, but nothing was looking at all promising until a very interesting woman called Cathy Shillabeer walked into my life.

I unexpectedly met her one day late in November 2008 during a boys' under-13s football match in which my eldest son Louie and her boy Chad were playing on opposite teams.

My son was a striker and I was one of those irritating dads shouting inspirational and insightful things from the sidelines such as: "Get stuck in, you lazy little bugger." I drove our Louie mad.

During the game Cathy walked across to my side of the pitch with her sister and other family members, and I was thinking, 'she looks pretty good.'

That's when I shouted to Louie to "chip that f****** midget goalkeeper."

Cathy shouted back at me: "Oi, that's my son you're talking about!"

What an ice-breaker.

We started chatting and I made a fuss of her Jack Russell dog named, er ... 'Jack'. 'That's a nice original name,' I thought. Anyway, I turned on the Carter charm and soon left the playing field with her phone number.

We chatted on the phone every night for about a week before finally arranging a date – I said I'd come over to her house and take her out for drinks. At first I pretended I was an international businessman, which was a laugh because I didn't actually have any income at the time.

I turned up in my maroon Vauxhall Zafira with cowskin covered seats – courtesy of PM Gordon Brown – which I'd managed to purchase the day before I went bust on my credit card, just like my friendly insolvency adviser Ted had told me to do.

Knocking on Cathy's door for the first time, I felt very nervous to say the least. I'd put on my best gear – black moleskin pants – and I was dressed to impress.

The date was a great success – at least I figured it was – and the hours just flew by. It was only later that she told me she'd hoped I wouldn't ever ring again, as my car was crap and I had about as much dress sense as Albert Steptoe. Cheers, Cathy. Well, I wasn't going to give up that easily. Winners never quit and I needed a girlfriend. And this girl was drop-dead gorgeous in my eyes.

ALAN CARTER

Match of the Day. Cathy and me at home in May 2011.

Light in the Darkness

Cath and me hadn't been seeing each other long when I took her to a bar near Halifax called The Casa, where I'd become friendly with the owner, an Irishman named Jack. We got on great but I could never understand why his wife, who came across as rude and a bit ignorant, seemed to hate me.

All became clear when I took my new girlfriend, Cathy, to The Casa soon after we got together in 2008 – in fact, it was our first real date. We were sitting at the bar when I invited Jack and his wife to come and join us. She was reluctant, though, saying: "No, we're all right," but eventually they did both come and sit next to us.

After a drink or two, I said I was just popping to the toilet. Once I'd disappeared from sight, Jack's wife said to Cathy: "What are you doing with him, a murderer?" and then went on to tell Cathy how I'd supposedly shot my wife.

On my return from the loo, Cathy didn't react to me – I guess she must have been in shock because, as we'd only been together a very short while at that point, I hadn't explained to her about Kenny and Pam. All she said was: "Come on, let's go."

It was only after driving a mile or so that Cathy opened up and told me what the obnoxious woman in the bar had said to her.

I rang Jack from my mobile and went ballistic, telling him what his wife had said to Cathy. He phoned me back a few hours later to say 'sorry', followed by a text message from his wife also apologising for this massive misunderstanding. Unfortunately, the damage was done, though, and the landlady's words ended a nice, new friendship with her husband. I couldn't ever go back to his bar for fear I may lose control of my actions.

The only other time I've received any hostility towards me as a result of what Kenny did to Pam came on a visit to Hull Speedway some years back. Way back in the mid-80s my brother had clashed with Sheffield's Neil Collins at Halifax and I'm told Kenny knocked Collins' teeth out. Apparently, after the race finished and the riders were slowing down before making their way back to the pits, Neil – the younger brother of Peter and Les Collins – tried to kick Kenny's broken leg. This sent Kenny into a rage and when they returned to the pits and took off their helmets, he punched Collins in the face.

But I didn't know anything about this at the time. It was only many years later, when I went to watch my mate Garry Stead ride at Hull Speedway and I was introduced to Neil Collins in a VIP lounge, that I became aware of the fight he had with Kenny.

Neil and I were chatting and I said how our Kenny could "sure blow them away on the track in his day."

Collins then turned and said to me: "Yes, and then he blew himself away."

I was totally taken aback by his comment and he walked away before I even had a chance to respond, which was probably a good thing for both of us.

Before the misunderstanding with the landlady in the bar, that comment from Collins was the first time anyone had said a negative word to me about what Kenny did to Pam and himself, although I also felt very nervous and uneasy on the few times I bumped into Pam's brother, Adrian. Knowing my brother had shot dead his

ALAN CARTER

Our Kenny (centre) and Neil Collins riding for England against the USA's Dennis Sigalos at Sheffield in 1983.

sister, I thought that maybe he would want to take out some form of revenge on me but he never said a word to me about what had happened.

As Cath and I got to know each other over the next few months, it soon became apparent that we were made for each other – she was even madder than me and more than capable of putting me in my place.

She was from a no-nonsense, straight-talking family, too, and if you didn't like it, then hard luck. I liked this about her even if it was a bit over-the-top at times. Cathy was just like me, she'd been through the mill and back in life and wasn't about to be putting up with any crap from me.

She told me: "If you even think about cheating on me I will probably poison you or do something else bad to you, I'm not to be messed about with." I took this very seriously.

We probably met at the wrong time, because we were both struggling with our own lives but we've managed to pull together and be a tower of strength for each other.

There have been many times when I've driven her mad and she could've left me, so there must be something special she sees in me. Thank God that at last I've found someone who can understand me and is willing to spend her life with me. Thank you, Cathy.

She took me into her home at New Sharlstone, near Wakefield, and made me feel like the king of the house, and that's when we decided to have a 'baby' together. We talked about our imminent new arrival and then made the biggest decision of our life. I was 45 and Cathy was 38, so we agreed that we would purchase a puppy – a baby Bassett Hound and we named him 'Mylo'.

Well, she slept with it for the first six weeks and I didn't get a look in. It grew bigger and bigger and now protects her while at the same time hating me, like I'm the house imposter. Yes, I'm now well down the pecking order.

I was going to propose to Cathy on the London Eye but she was so tired after working six or seven days a week – she's a real hard grafter – so I had another plan.

Cath, me and our 'baby' Mylo.

We had a delicious Chinese meal and lots of drinks before I said I'd get a big fire going outside in my chimenea.

After Cathy accepted my marriage proposal and we'd enjoyed a great night, we decided to continue the celebrations in bed. I was first in and then she came up the stairs behind me and asked: "What's burning?"

Me being a bit thick, I'd placed the red-hot chimenea on our wooden decking in the back garden – and now all the decking was on fire. I was still naked as I frantically tried to put out the flames.

Apart from spending all my time with Cathy, the year of 2009 would turn out to be a sad and difficult one, too, at times Jay moved back in with his Mum after Sherry decided the three of them would all like to be a family unit again. That was great for her, Louie and Jay but what about me? I'd be left high and dry again.

Jay had been fantastic in the two years he lived with me but now he was going to the big school with the older boys, he needed to be hanging out with others his age and I could understand that. The cottage where we were living at the time was in the middle of nowhere and he had no real friends close by.

So I said farewell to my middle son. I'd done my best and it was heart-wrenching to watch him pack his bags but, as I say, I fully understood his needs. He was growing up fast.

Sherry said she didn't need any financial support from me and that she was fine to bring the two boys up on her own. I told her that when I got myself back into a better financial position I would support my boys like any good father would want to do. I'd given her a large amount of money every month for the first nine years of their lives and had them over to stay every weekend, so I'd done my bit, too.

Me and the boys had also enjoyed holidays in Italy but It wasn't long before she had the Child Support Agency on my back even though I was very ill at the time. Thanks, Sherry.

Dad's life was coming to a close in the latter part of 2009. I hadn't seen him for some time – by now I was far too wise to his old tricks of making me feel like dog poo every time he saw me. I had enough on my plate without being crucified by him again.

All I'd wanted to do was spend some time with Mal and enjoy his company but he was just so hit and miss with his moods that I couldn't take the chance. I was living on the edge myself.

But, yet again, I swallowed my pride and decided to go and see him. Our Malky told me: "You might not get another chance," so I decided to visit him once more.

I told Cathy I could be gone a long time, gave her a kiss and left for Dad's house.

51 MAL'S LAST WORDS

Anxious wait for our final farewell ... the four-letter word he could never say ... last respects for the self-made showman who always spoke his mind.

I SPENT more than 20 years trying to gain my father's love but, in all honesty, I had more chance of sprouting a rocket from my arse and firing myself to the moon.

I was looking for something I figured all kids wanted – just to be loved by your Dad, be encouraged and nudged along in life. Even a sign, a wink or a nod – anything – would have done.

But it would never happen. Mal Carter was just not capable of doing the thing I craved for most, the thing that cost nothing only a little compassionate spirit.

He could eff and blind better than any of us but 'love' is the four-letter word I never heard him say or express.

Dad gave me all he could, or should I say all that he felt was necessary – his time, his money, but still I wanted more. Just an occasional hug or phone call, anything, but still it never came.

He'd throw money – 50 or 100 quid a time – at my kids at Christmas but he never wanted to spend even two minutes with them. He never did the simple things in life, like sit down with my boys and drink coffee or share a fish and chip supper with them. He simply wasn't interested in kids or their needs.

Many people say what a great guy my dad was in the road-racing world and I wouldn't disagree that he was the ultimate showman. He was a popular man in the racing world when he could flash the cash like it was water and treating most of his friends or hangers-on, but where were they when he was dying? I can tell you, they were nowhere to be seen because they had long gone by this point.

Mal lived by the sword and died by it, too.

When I arrived for what was my final meeting with Dad he was in the toilet, connected to an oxygen supply that he had to wheel around with him on a trolley. I sat down feeling very uneasy – I always was a nervous wreck in his presence.

I waited anxiously in his lounge for about five minutes wondering what he was going to say when he did eventually come into the room.

He had a home with Janet that was worth a couple of million quid but I didn't give two f***s about that. All I wanted was for him to be pleased to see me again and to say "take care of yourself."

But when he came into view, there was no hint of warmth or a welcome from him. He took one look at me and said: "What the f*** do you want?"

I couldn't believe what I was hearing. There he was, a dying man who had buried

ALAN CARTER

Mal pictured in later life, including one of him with his second wife Janet.

his other two sons, talking to me, his one surviving son, as if I was the scum of the earth.

I listened to his usual bullshit for about 10 minutes and then said: "I've got to go now." I didn't even bother wasting my time to shake the man's hand. By now I had no respect left for him. That was our final farewell and he didn't even say "take care, son" or anything.

So we weren't able to put aside our differences and now I never will. I was broken-hearted and had to leave.

That was the last time I saw my father.

He threw a 70th birthday party in March 2009 at a place in Huddersfield called Orlando's, which is run by my mate and located about a mile from my home. Although close friends and family were apparently invited, I never received an invitation and neither did my half-sister Lynn, Dad's eldest daughter.

In fact, I only found out the party had taken place when I saw pictures taken on the evening posted on another of my half-sister's Facebook pages.

I was also told by Malky that he wasn't on the guest list either. In his typically heartless way, Dad said to Malky: "It's for close family only, not orphans like you."

What a shocking thing to say to the lad.

During a rest period Mal was having at the local hospice, he suddenly suffered a massive heart attack and died there on September 13, 2009, aged 70-years-old.

His funeral was a massive occasion. He was larger than life, one of the great characters of this world, and for all that I've written about him here he is still missed by many.

Despite the 70th birthday party snub, I changed my mind and decided to attend his funeral even though it cost me about £750 for flowers, a wreath and new clothes for me and Cathy. I felt I had to go and pay my last respects regardless of all the abuse I'd taken from him over many years.

I never really got to know my father as well as I would've liked to have done. He was just too hard-faced to get close to and he showed neither Kenny nor me any love or affection whatsoever. It's a great shame but that's how it was.

Even so, I will always treasure the great times me and Dad spent going to race meetings all over the world. We gave it everything we had as a father-and-son team and if I could pick anyone in the world to be my coach and start my racing career all over again, it would be my dad.

I also respect what he achieved and how he became a self-made man. Mal came into the world with nothing and didn't have a great upbringing himself, but more than made up for that with typical Yorkshire grit and determination. There's no doubt about it, he got where he did in life through sheer hard work.

When Dad passed away he left me nothing, not even a note. I told him a few years before he became ill to blow the lot, go and explore and enjoy as many holidays as he could, but this didn't interest him. He'd been everywhere he wanted to go, and he was at his happiest wheeling and dealing and making money.

It's obviously too late now but I still crave his love and will do 'till the day I die.

ALAN CARTER

The last picture I have of Dad, together here with his wife Janet.

52 UNDER ARREST

Selling again . . . drugged up man goes berserk . . . police raid at the cottage . . . another ban and a suspended prison sentence.

SPENDING close to two years as a recluse was doing me no good, so Cathy told me I needed to get back out there in the real world and start selling again. Her pep talks went on for weeks but she never gave in and eventually wore me down.

I had a chat to a mate, David Halliday, about a van. He and his brother had quit moto-cross and were selling their Iveco van for £4,000. I didn't have that kind of money but they agreed to take my Zafira, valued at £2k, in part-exchange and let me pay the £2k balance in instalments.

I was lucky that so many people were always willing to help me and that I had a good group of proper mates around me. Although others clearly believed in me, I still lacked my old self-confidence and felt very nervous going out selling in the van for the first time.

I decided to call on my core customers in Huddersfield, including the Yorkshire Rose Florist owned by Mark Earnshaw, a fantastic guy who I always looked forward to seeing. After Mark purchased a few things from me, it was late in the day and I was now going home.

But as you well know by now, my life has rarely run without a hitch of some kind or another. A problem, if not potential disaster, seems to lurk around almost every corner and this time it turned out to be a big one.

I jumped in the van, started the engine and just put a bit of lock on the wheels, so I could see behind me. That's when this man on a bicycle came out of nowhere and swerved violently in order to miss me. I couldn't believe what I was seeing, it almost made me laugh.

But he clearly saw nothing to laugh about and started to punch the van and shout abuse at me. I told him to piss off but he stopped and came back to get me. I got out of the van and we had a big confrontation.

He said he was going to kill me and I told him to "go get f*****" before it all seemed to calm down.

He then got back on his bike and mounted the pavement about 20 yards in front of me. He was now staring me out – he was definitely drugged up – and I should've just driven off and ignored this intimidation.

Instead, I pulled up alongside him and stared back. That's when he went berserk and snapped my wing mirror off the van. I reacted instantly by turning into him and knocking him off the bike. 'I'll teach you a lesson, you cheeky bastard,' I thought, before driving off.

I heard nothing more about the incident for three months, until this giant of a copper came to my cottage and told me I was under arrest for assault. I said: "You must be kidding, I've never done that."

All hell broke loose. I resisted arrest. The police were all over my place like vermin and aimed CS gas at me. I felt like John Rambo.

In court I pleaded not guilty, as I maintained that not only had the crazed black man assaulted me, he'd also broken my 100 quid mirror off the van. It was a joke and the police were definitely on his side.

Anyway, after several visits to court my barrister decided we were not going to win the case, so he advised me to change my plea to guilty, which is what I did.

My barrister had done a deal before we entered court. If I pleaded guilty they'd drop the charge against me of assaulting the police officer at my home and I would definitely not be going to jail for 19 months, as looked likely if I'd stuck to my original not guilty plea.

The judge agreed it was 'tit for tat' but, as I was in a van, I was given a 12-month driving ban for knocking the man off his bike.

It was all a sham, to be honest, but the case had dragged on for around two years and made me even more ill in the process. My already fragile confidence had suffered another big blow.

I was also given an 18-months suspended sentence and put on probation for a year – until I charmed my probation officer and she got it all squashed. Cheers, Bernie.

So much for trying to get back on track in the floral industry.

53 REFLECTIONS

Always wanting more . . . the man who hated me . . . men who inspired me . . . advice for beginners . . . dangers of alcohol and drugs . . . the importance of friends . . . back on the road.

I CAN look back with pride knowing I lived the dream and rode in one of the golden periods of road-racing. Being watched by crowds of more than 100,000 at some of the world championship rounds made the hair on the back of my neck stand up.

Even after I'd won the Daytona single cylinder race on my comeback at Daytona in 1994, I still wasn't happy because I wanted to beat the world's best, not a bunch of club racers that meant nothing to me. But then I was always too hard on myself, always wanting more.

Sometimes there are great sporting talents who, for one reason or another, don't make it to the very top and I regard myself as one of them. Not a day goes by that I don't think if I'd done this or that differently, maybe I could've been world champion.

There was only one guy who seemed to really hate me during my racing days and that was Didier De Radigues, the then golden boy of GP racing who rode one of the fastest bikes in the Elf Chevallier.

He didn't take too well to me being the new kid on the block and numerous times I caught him staring at me, as if to say 'I'm going to have you'. I did find this a bit intimidating, so I tried to keep out of his way – he was a big lad, a real lady killer, and looked more like a male model than a bike racer.

Looking back, one racer who really inspired me as a young kid in the mid-70s was watching the late Dave Potter. What a great racer and a real gent he was in and around the British race paddocks. I just loved the livery of the Ted Broad BP Yamaha that Dave rode. His OW31 Yamahas were immaculately turned out at every meeting.

Another hero of mine was Barry Sheene, the fans' idol. I can still see his amazing, smiling face that could melt any lady's heart. A great chap, Barry just oozed charisma and charm and what a brilliant racer, too.

I loved the idea of becoming the next Barry Sheene after I started to make a name for myself in the early 80s. I was billed as England's next world champion and asked to perform many personal appearances. I judged beauty competitions and never missed an opportunity to drop my phone number into the winner's cup along with a nice, cheeky wink, while thinking, 'I'll show that Barry Sheene how to do it.'

Kenny with Kelly Moran of Sheffield at the start of the 1986 season.

Light in the Darkness

Life was great.

Would I do it all again? You bet, I would.

What would I change about myself? Nothing.

You are who you are, and that's it. You can't please everyone in life. I had the best brother in the world in our Kenny and the best coach in the great Mal Carter. What a winning team – I was lucky.

Kenny and me were born winners and we sacrificed everything to try and become world champions. Sadly, we just fell short on the home straight.

The one thing above all I'd like to say to any kid starting out in racing today is: everything I knew when I was at the top I learned at the bottom. The early period is the most enjoyable part, so go club racing first and enjoy the fun of this great sport. The pressure to succeed will soon come, my friends, far faster than you ever dreamed and it will all be over at the blink of an eye.

Whatever work you put in now or however hard you are training to get to the top, double it. Never look back and think, 'if only I'd done this or done that'.

I gave every ounce of passion, desire and willpower a man could possess to get to the top. I wanted it badly but still never fulfilled my dream of becoming the 250cc world champion. Realise that you are on a very hard road and only a few will ever make it to the very top. Be bold and mighty forces will come to your aid.

Dad taking me to all the racing meetings as a kid and being the team's dogsbody was just the right schooling I needed. After all those practice days and Dad telling me I was going to be the champ, I had little respect for any racer. In my mind, I was going to be having them all, and I was very blasé about the whole thing. But little did I know when I started out racing competitively in 1980 that I would soon be racing against multi-GP winners and world champions.

You can if you think you can.

Looking back, I moved up the ranks way too fast. Dad pushed and pushed and I performed. I had desire plus determination and a massive will to win. Mal was very ambitious for me but the truth is I wanted it even more than him.

I did try and help some kids in the beginning of their careers. The first was Jamie Robinson, the cutest 16-year-old you could ever wish to meet and a local kid to me as a native of Huddersfield. He started racing in the 125 class and had the full backing of his parents, who were lovely people.

Basically, what Jamie did in 1992 was crash his brains out, he couldn't stay on the bike. He would ring me after every practice and be close to tears, whinging about all sorts. I'd tell him to get a grip, remind him that the race was tomorrow and tell him it's not over yet. I'd say: "Come on, kid, pull yourself together, you can do it. I believe in you."

Jamie was brilliant. In the beginning he listened to everything as I tried to teach him all I knew and had learnt over the previous 20 years.

But it wasn't long before he figured he knew more than me and got involved with

A rare shot of Kenny and his big rival Bruce Penhall both smiling together in 1982.

Light in the Darkness

the wrong crowd in London – the rave or dance scene, or whatever they call it – and I was old school.

If only he could've focused more on his racing, with a bit of luck he could have been world champion. Unfortunately, he would become just another great racer that fell by the wayside.

Two things I would recommend is to avoid alcohol and drugs like the plague. Racing is a far greater buzz than this rubbish. When your racing days are over, you can drink and do whatever you desire.

Take the former great stunt rider Eddie Kidd. It's well documented that the night before the 1996 crash that nearly killed him he was off his head on cocaine. He sure paid an awful price for a night's fun by having to spend the rest of his days in a wheelchair.

I was tested for drugs and drink at race tracks many times and although I was known as the rebel of the paddock, I always passed the tests with flying colours. Booze and drugs weren't my thing at the time. Racing, and being around some of the most beautiful girls in the world, was more than enough for me.

I was a real party animal but I knew my limits and when to drink and when not to. Racing was everything to me. To watch people like Alex Higgins, George Best and many others self-destruct was so sad.

I remember the popular American speedway star Kelly Moran turning up at Halifax like it was yesterday. He was such a happy, bubbly teenager with the world at his feet but he got consumed by the fast-paced world of racing and ended up partying and drinking himself to an early grave in 2010. It was awful seeing the pictures of him in his final days, they hit me hard. Alcohol and drugs are a killer.

There were Kelly and his brother Shawn hitting the bottle hard and our Kenny with his own mental demons, apparently having convinced himself that Pam was up to no good. He should have taken a long, hard look in the mirror.

I have it on good authority that most of the Yanks who rode speedway in Britain in the late 70s and 80s were doing drugs of some kind or another. Maybe Kenny should've tried some, too, it might have calmed him down and allowed him to open up a bit. Can you imagine Kenny and Bruce Penhall getting stoned together – now that would've been funny.

As with all talented sporting stars, the key to their success is hard work, plus a little rub of the green along the way to keep the cogs running smoothly. That's all you need – oh, and some great friends to pick you up again when you've fallen down.

Don't believe everything people tell you. Many times I've got my hopes up based on the whim of somebody's bullshit. Try to surround yourself with the right people. As they say, you become the people you associate with.

One great guy that supported me was my second wife's dad, Phil Masters. What a fantastic man he was, I'll never forget the support and companionship he showed me. Phil sponsored me all over the world and taking him to Daytona that time I won

ALAN CARTER

I couldn't wait to be racing again when we began building the TZ350 Yamaha for my use in the classic series at the start of 2011.

Left: We even revived my old Mighty Mouse logo that originally appeared on the back of my 1981 race bike.

Light in the Darkness

the single cylinder race was brilliant. He had a grin from here to Timbuktu.

Trying to get sponsorship in England was like going down to Bradford looking for Elvis Presley. One lady who gave me a break owned the local pizza shop, JJ's Pizza in Elland. Linda said she'd love to sponsor me but all she could offer was £10's worth of free pizzas a week. I was still grateful – at least I knew I could eat twice a week.

Another sponsor who supported me was Bob and his business partner David Caldwell, who co-own Spectrum Screen Print, the people behind Jamie Whitham's band, The Po Boys, who paid for all my posters and graphics.

Another backer was John of Ogam Textiles said he'd give me £100 per month for the season, which was a nice little deal. John was the best paying sponsor I ever had, coughing up on the dot every month without fail. Other sponsors who helped me include Arai, Alpinestars (boots), Kushitani Leathers (made by Alan in the Isle of Man) and Steve King of Abingdon Motorcycles.

I officially retired from competitive racing in 1994 but, apart from that comeback inspired by nephew Malky's taunts early on in the last decade, I'd stayed away from the race track until the start of 2011, when I returned to the saddle for a classic bike racing series. Riding around Cadwell Park, Pembrey and the rest of the UK tracks on a 350cc Yamaha again has taken me back to my youth.

My great friend Chris Knight has worked hard with me to get the show back on the road and our team are looking forward to having a great year in 2012. Giles Waite and Ian Coles have also been fantastic – their company, Watches of Distinction, have backed me all the way – and, along with some other great guys, they all want to see the smiling, happy-go-lucky Alan Carter back on track and enjoying myself again doing what I've always loved best.

Although I made another track comeback in the spring of 2011, getting back on the road after my 12-month driving ban expired on February 18 has not been such plain sailing. Believe it or, I even had to pass a test before I was legally allowed to ride a 50cc scooter!

I couldn't even afford to take driving lessons or put in for my test because first I had to sit a re-test exam to regain my road licence. I managed to purchase a scooter from my old sparring partner Kev Mitchell whose brother Gary owns Fastline Superbikes in Preston.

We did a deal for a few hundred quid and I was now the proud owner of a 50cc scooter, a Peugeot Jetforce that couldn't pull the skin off a rice pudding. My mate Eddie told me it did 60mph, so I was feeling happier with it until I got a big shock just before I was about to take the scooter for a spin. My neighbour John said: "You can't ride that."

I didn't have a clue what he was on about but then he asked if I'd passed my CBT. I was like, 'what the f*** is that?'

That's when he explained that I had to pass a test even before I was permitted to ride a 50cc motorcycle.

They can't take this one away from me – my trophy for winning the French GP.

Light in the Darkness

Above: Friends Eddie Bedford, Chris Knight and Ivor Dickinson at the Pembrey meeting in April 2011.
Below: With Giles Waite whose company Watches of Distinction kindly sponsored my latest comeback.
Bottom: With my fellow former 250cc GP winner Jeremy McWilliams at Thruxton.

I rang a company called Anchor Motorcycle Training and booked in for my CBT (Compulsory Basic Training). It turned out to be an enjoyable five-hour course at which I met some fantastic people, including Adrian, the friendly owner of the company, and one of his best buddies Hughie, who was a real gent. They really looked after me and I passed.

They then helped me to book my theory and hazard perception parts of the course in Huddersfield, which I also passed with flying colours. What a ball-ache it had all been trying to get back on the road at my age, having done over 50,000 miles a year, every year, for the last 20 years.

Adrian rang the Driving Standards Agency on my behalf to organise my next test on a bike. The DSA said if I passed an extended test I could have both my car and bike licences back at the same time, which sounded great to me.

I was trained by Adrian's top man, a former army sergeant called Bill, who

Back on track, me in action at Pembrey in 2011.

drove me mad telling what I should and shouldn't do.

I failed the first part of the bike test when the lady examiner said I didn't use the rear brake on the emergency stop. I told her I won a grand prix without a rear brake but she wasn't impressed and told me I'd failed.

I passed the test second time around, though, and, at the time of writing this at the end of May 2011, I'm now close to getting back on the road. I just have the modular 2 to do and then the Carter bandwagon will be rolling again.

Getting back into road-racing in the classic series this year at the age of 46 has also helped rebuild my confidence. Slowly my life is falling back into place. We all live in hope because that's all we have to cling to sometimes, so hang in there my friends and remember, when you're on your last legs and have no hope, just think of me and stay strong. There is always another day. Sometimes we have to lose the battle to win the war.

I moved in with Cathy in the winter of 2010-11 and we started a new life together. We're just little people living in a little house with little money, but do you know what? We've found the one thing in life that many people never find – happiness.

Thank you for reading.

Light in the Darkness

ALAN CARTER

Index

Aksland, Bud 130, 139
Agostini, Giacomo 197
Appleyard, Colin 223
Appleyard, Peggy 223
Appleyard, Robin 223
Atkinson, Chris 39
Atkinson, Julian 277
Awan, Nighat 267, 268

Bailey, Ray 152
Baldé, Jean-François 105
Ballington, Kork 198, 200, 201, 203, 204
Barros, Alex 93
Beacham, Ian 25, 61
Beaumont, Mr 40
Beaumont, Dave 289, 292
Beck, Simon 229
Beck, Stan 229
Bedford, Eddie 313, 315
Beedon, Carol 20
Beedon, Mrs 20
Beedon, Susan 20
Beedon, Tony 20, 40
Bell, Bobby 83
Biagi, Carlo Dr. 161
Bins, Carol 259
Binns, Nigel 230
Bland, Christine 40
Blagbougher, Jayne 40
Bolle, Jacques 105, 111
Bolle, Pierre 105
Boocock, Eric 69
Boocock, Nigel 276
Boothroyd, Bonnie 50
Boothroryd, Eric 47, 50
Bosworth, Nigel 236, 239, 245, 250, 251, 254
Briggs, Barry 183
Briggs, Elaine 29
Briggs, Mick 29
Broad, Ted 66
Broadbelt, Eric 47, 50
Brown, Paul 245, 251
Buckmaster, Simon 229
Burnett, Roger 241
Butler, Paul 130

Cagill, Andy 285
Caldwell, David 313
Campbell, Malcom (Wally) 162, 163
Cardús, Carlos 105
Carruthers, Kel 130
Carter, Alan (uncle) 28, 43, 123
Carter, Christine (mother) 15, 17, 19-21, 29-33, 39, 43, 45, 50, 55-58, 124, 131, 164, 181, 182, 202, 219, 289, 290
Carter, Charlie (daughter) 274, 277
Carter, David (uncle) 28, 123
Carter, Gail (cousin) 28
Carter, Janet (stepmother) 19, 28, 29, 54, 57, 58, 60, 77, 95, 263, 274, 301, 302
Carter, Jay (son) 262, 269, 270, 272, 278, 286, 288, 289, 29 292, 299
Carter, Joey (son) 269, 271-273, 275, 276, 283, 286, 287
Carter, Katie (Lionel's second wife) 28, 54
Carter, Kelly-Marie (niece) 126, 162, 163, 164, 157, 189, 255, 256, 271
Carter, Kenny (brother) 15, 19-22, 31, 33-41, 43, 45, 47-51, 53, 55-57, 59, 60, 67-76, 81-94, 96-98, 100-102, 114-119, 122-129, 131-135, 143-147, 149, 156-176, 178-190, 193, 202, 207, 213, 216, 225, 237, 241, 253, 256, 276, 278, 286, 289, 290, 297, 298, 303, 308-310
Carter, Lee (cousin) 28
Carter, Lewis (nephew) 29
Carter, Lindy (half-sister) 29, 262
Carter, Lucy (halfs-ister) 29, 107, 273
Carter, Lionel (grandfather) 28
Carter, Louie (son) 262, 269, 270, 272, 278, 295, 299
Carter, Mal (father) 15, 17, 19-21, 23, 28, 29, 31, 41, 43, 45, 47, 50, 52, 55, 57, 59-62, 65, 68, 69, 71-73, 75, 77-80, 85, 87, 95-97, 103, 104, 107-111, 116, 119, 122, 123, 125, 136, 140, 143-145, 149, 153, 155, 156, 162, 170, 171, 173, 176, 178, 182-184, 190, 201, 202, 207, 210, 213, 216, 219, 223, 231, 237, 239, 243, 246, 253, 256, 263, 264-266, 274, 285, 286, 293, 300-304, 309
Carter, Malcolm (brother) 15, 17, 19, 43, 289
Carter, Malcolm 'Malky' (nephew) 162-164, 187, 189, 255, 258, 271, 275, 278-281, 303, 313
Carter, Mary (grandmother) 28
Carter, Pam (Kenny's wife) 73, 96, 154, 160, 162-164, 166, 170-173, 175, 176, 178-187, 189, 255, 256, 278, 297
Carter, Pat (aunt) 28
Carter, Paul (cousin) 28
Carter, Samantha (cousin) 28
Carter, Wayne (cousin) 28
Cartwright, Ian 50
Challinor, Iain 245
Chatterton, Derek 69
Cheshire, Dave 166, 276
Chili, Pier-Francesco 252
Clark, Paul 279, 280
Clarke, Fred 87, 240, 242
Clogger, Dr. 273
Cobas, Antonio 169, 177
Coburn, Vaughan 162
Coles, Ian 313
Collins, Les 91, 93, 94, 133, 297
Collins, Neil 297, 298
Collins, Peter 49, 50, 91, 98, 114, 115, 131, 133, 171, 172, 297
Compton, Andre 268
Compton, Dijon 264, 268, 269
Coppock, Harold 66
Cornu, Jacques 104, 105, 154
Coulter, Woolsey 245
Costa, Claudio Dr. 109, 235
Crafar, Simon 248
Crouch, Beverly 40, 73, 259
Crouch, Graham 40, 41
Crump, Phil 91

Davis, John 160
Davis, Linda 136
De Radiguès, Didier 105, 307
Dennis, Ron 122
Denton, Wilf 43
Dickinson, Nicola (first wife) 154, 155, 164, 165, 175, 210, 229
Doherty, Gary 125
Duffield, Mike 246, 290, 291
Duhamel, Miguel 220
Duhamel, Yvon 220
Dunlop, Joey 72, 109
Dunn, Graham 125
Dunn, Richard 28
Earnshaw, Mark 305

Eckl, Harald 105
Eddie (neighbour) 35
Eliot, Robert 15
Ervine, Mathew 39
Espié, Thierry 105
Estrosi, Christian 96, 105
Evitts, Neil 94

Farlow, George 72
Fern, Dave 240
Fernandez, Patrick 103, 105
Ferrari, Virginio 252
Ferretti, Paolo 105
Filice, Jimmy 211
Flannery, Tracey 33
Flatman, Nigel 166
Flaws, Lynn (half-sister) 28, 303
Flaws, Peter 28
Fogarty, Carl 252

Gallagher, Mark 285-287
Gardner, Wayne 79
Garside, Peter 116, 167
Gavros, Dennis 50
George, Alex 79
Grant, Mick 43, 62, 72
Gregory, Howard 62, 113, 139, 147, 148, 161, 175
Grimshaw, Mr 40
Guilleux, Herve 113
Gundersen, Erik 83
Guy, Chris 79, 80

Hailwood, Mike 194
Hart, Barry 97
Haslam, Ann 67, 175
Haslam, Phil 61, 69
Haslam, Ron 62, 63, 65-67, 83, 162, 175, 176, 235
Haigh, Paul ('Eggis') 30, 39, 47, 49, 69, 72, 84, 95, 100, 130, 139, 175, 176, 247
Halliday, David 305
Hanner, Gladys (grandmother) 17, 19, 29, 30, 31, 41, 179, 181, 182, 272, 277-279, 282, 283, 284
Hanner, Willie (grandfather) 17, 19, 29-31, 179, 181, 278, 282-284, 292
Hartle, John 43
Head, Tony 105
Heady, John 277
Henshaw, Steve 66
Herweh, Manfred 142, 154
Hislop, Steve 235, 236, 239-242, 244-246
Hitchin, Mark 40
Holesworth, Dale 40
Hollingworth, Phil 125
Holt, Bob 108, 313
Holtom, Doug 84, 95-97, 217, 218, 220, 229, 243, 251, 252
Holtom, Owen 229
Hudson, Paul 260
Huewen, Keith 259
Hughes, Ray 246-248
Hurst, Edward 29
Hurst, Luke 29
Hurst, Scott 29

Iddon, Paul 84
Ismail, Raymond 39

Jackson, Tina (step-sister) 29, 264
Jeffries, Kate 244
Jeffries, Nick 244

Jupp, Martin 236, 245

Kempster, Julie 222, 223, 225
Kidd, Eddie 103
King, Steve 313
Knight, Chris 205, 213, 214, 215, 293, 294, 315
Kocinski, John 200-202, 204, 207, 208, 210, 211, 213, 214, 216, 223, 236
Knudsen, Tommy 83, 158

Lawson, Eddie 127, 136
Larner, Bryan 49, 125
Lassak, John 198, 208, 209, 217, 220, 227
Lavado, Carlos 103, 113, 148, 154
Leisner, Andy 205, 10, 213, 220
Leisner, Jayne 205
Leisner, John 205, 210
Leisner, Sue 205
Lee, Michael 49, 71, 89, 98, 173
Lynda, (Kenny's fan club) 49
Lohmann, Klaus 50
Lohmann, Mike 50
Lund, Adrian 73, 187, 297
Lund, Bob 75, 187, 256
Lund, Diane 187, 256
Lund, Heather 187
Lund, Veronica 75, 187
Lund, Wendy 187

Machin, Neil 276
Machin, Steve 61, 69
Mackenzie, Niall 155, 162, 163, 250, 251
MacLean, Bob 196-201, 206, 209, 217, 222
Mallia, Carmen (ex-partner) 269, 271-277, 283, 285-289
Mallia, Ivan 271, 274
Mallia, Joe 271
Mamola, Randy 65, 95
Mang, Toni 149, 150, 153, 154
Marshall, Michelle 259
Marshall, Roger 62
Masters, Phil 252, 363, 311
Masters, Sherry (ex-wife) 244, 245, 252, 257, 260, 262, 268, 272, 287, 299, 300
Mattioli, Jean-Michel 105
Mauger, Ivan 49, 71, 89, 91, 172, 183
McCallem, Phillip 245
McConnachie, Ian 236, 238, 240, 245
McCracken, Des 266
McCracken, Dwayne 266
McDowell, Mr 40
McElnea, Rob 84, 250
McKeon, Mick 50, 166, 276
McKeon, Graham 114
McLeod, Donny 155
McMillan, Bob 237, 251
McNaughton, Geoff 162
McQueen, Alistair 169
Mitchell, Gary 313
Mitchell, Kevin 242, 245, 313
Moore, Glyn 40
Moore, Shane 279
Monaghan, Brian 75
Moran, Kelly 83, 93, 115, 116
Moran, Shawn 83, 93, 115, 116, 157, 158
Morton, Chris 131
Moss, Emilia (great-grandmother) 17, 30
Müller, Egon 114, 117
Myers, Craig 237

Neal, Dennis 162-164
Newbold, John 66
Newton, Ian 245
Nielsen, Hans 97, 98

Oguma, Yoichi 233
O'Leary, Neil 39
Oldham, Richard 172
Oldham, Ron 167, 172, 182
Oliver, Rich 210, 216
Olsen, Ole 49, 118
Orton, Dave 66
Overend, Kevin 95
Owen, Tom 49

Pace, Sacha 214
Padgett, Gary 184
Palazzese, Ivan 105, 113
Parker, Jim 280
Pave, Bjorn 214
Pave, Bob 210, 214, 220, 221, 228
Pearce, Andrew 29
Pearce, Bernard 28, 29
Pearce, Elaine 29
Pearce, Mary (Mal's twin sister) 28, 29
Pearce, Steven 29
Pendlebury, Craig 276
Penhall, Bruce 71, 83, 89, 91, 93, 94, 98, 115-117, 125, 136, 310
Peterson, Robbie 224
Pickering, Richard 71, 125, 173
Pons, Sito 104, 105, 140
Potter, Dave 62, 66, 307
Prime, Chris 49
Puckas, Mrs 235
Pusey, Chris 47, 50, 83, 125

Rainey, Wayne 62, 120-122, 127, 130, 136, 139-142, 199, 252, 253
Rapicault, Thierry 105, 192
Rayborn, Cal (Jnr) 207
Read, Phil 194
Reggiani, Loris 154
Renfrew, Randy 200
Rhodes, Derek 230-235, 237, 239, 241, 242, 247, 250, 280, 294
Ricci, Fausto 154
Roberts, Kenny 62, 95, 111, 113, 118, 120-122, 127, 130, 134, 136-141, 153, 194, 201, 204, 207, 208, 217, 219, 253
Robertshaw, Mr 40
Robertson, Mr 40
Robinson, Donny 65, 79, 103, 104, 105, 109, 110, 136, 254
Robinson, Jamie 309
Rose, James 280
Ross, Jimmy 101
Rossi, Valentino 105
Roth, Reinhold 105, 154

Sanderson, Tessa 170
Sarron, Christian 103, 108, 113, 142, 150
Sarron, Dominique 150, 154, 192
Sawford, Steve 245
Schloegl, Sepp 153
Schwartz, Bobby 115, 158
Schwartz, Kevin 199
Senna, Ayrton 252
Siedel, John 68
Sigalos, Dennis 115, 298
Silcox, John 116

Simcox, Gemma Dr 289
Sheene, Barry 37, 62, 95, 96, 106, 111, 136, 137, 149, 209, 234, 307
Sheene, Franco 136
Sheene, Iris 136
Sheene, Stephanie 111, 136, 137
Shillabeer, Cathy (fiancée) 295-300, 303, 305, 316
Shillabeer, Chad 295
Spencer, Freddie 79, 111, 113, 116, 147-149, 153, 154, 233
Slater, Mandy 67
Smart, Malcolm 260
Smith, Andy 160
Smith, Bill 111
Smith, Peter 40
Smythe, Daryl (Baz) 40
Spalding, Mr 37
Spalding, Simon 37
Starbuck, Phil 261
Sparks, Gary 290
Stead, Garry 29, 297
Stevens, Tom 216
Stewart, Dave 35, 40
Stewart, John 35
Stewart, Linda 35
Sulley, Eric 66
Sunderland, Eric 43
Suter, Eskil 248
Swallow, Vicky 73
Swift, Guy 247
Swift, Peter 247
Symons, Barry 66, 149

Tatum, Kelvin 157-159, 173
Tobias, Oliver 77
Toffolo, Jean Marc 105
Toney, James 222
Thomas, Ian 49, 69
Tournadre, Jean-Louis 96, 104
Tuxworth, Neil 229, 231-234, 236, 237, 239, 241-246, 248, 250, 251, 259

Vitali, Maurizio 188, 189

Waite, Giles 313, 315
Walker, Tom 246
Watton, Dave (Yank) 206, 220-223, 225-227
Webster, Steve 141, 142
Wells, David ('Welsey') 30, 39, 47, 69, 101, 147, 275
Wells, Mark 39
Williams, Bill (uncle) 278
Williams, Deloris (aunt) 278, 279
Williams, John 79
Wimmer, Martin 149, 154, 197
Wheatcroft, Tom 95, 144, 145, 154, 156
White, Norrie 104
Whitham, James 236
Whitworth, John 167
Woffinden, Rob 276
Woffinden, Tai 276
Wolfenden, Clyde 162, 163
Womanlea, Mrs 39
Wood, Alan 57
Wood, Dave (stepfather) 21, 22, 33, 39, 55-57, 181, 202
Wood, Debbie 57
Wroot, Matt 98, 230

Yassin, Tariq 294